AI in ELT

A practical exploration of responsible, research-based Artificial Intelligence use

Vicky Saumell and Belén Albarracín

Series editors: Carol Lethaby and Patricia Harries

ACTION ON ISSUES

Pavilion elt

AI in ELT:
A practical exploration of responsible, research-based Artificial Intelligence use

Published by:
Pavilion Publishing and Media Ltd
Blue Sky Offices, 25 Cecil Pashley Way, Shoreham by Sea, West Sussex, BN43 5FF

Tel: +44 (0)1273 434943
Email: info@pavpub.com
Web: www.pavpub.com

Published 2026

A catalogue record for this book is available from the British Library.

ISBN: 978-1-80388-500-1

Pavilion Publishing and Media is a leading publisher of books, training materials and digital content in mental health, social care and allied fields. Pavilion and its imprints offer must-have knowledge and innovative learning solutions underpinned by sound research and professional values.

Authors: Vicky Saumell and Belén Albarracín
Series editors: Carol Lethaby and Patricia Harries
Cover design: Tony Pitt
Page layout and typesetting: Emma Dawe
Printing: Independent Publishers Group (IPG)

Contents

Foreword

The term 'AI' or 'Artificial Intelligence' is everywhere and the field of ELT is no different. One look at conference programmes from 2025 and 2026 tells you that it is very much on the minds of teachers and materials writers alike. But as many of us will freely admit, it's easy to feel confused, overwhelmed, and even exasperated by the hype, the rapid new developments and the explosion of information that we face. In 2024, Vicky Saumell delivered a plenary presentation at the IATEFL International Conference entitled "The AI Factor: have we figured it out yet?". In it she clearly laid out the definition of AI and what the issues and concerns were for ELT. As series editors for the *Action on Issues* series, Vicky was our immediate choice to write about AI in ELT. The *Action on Issues* series aims to bring to the fore the important issues of the time in our field, to look in-depth and critically at these issues, as well as to equip our profession with practical tools and information to take ethical action in the classroom, and in the industry as a whole. Vicky Saumell and Belén Albarracín have met these objectives impressively in this volume, particularly as the technology continues to evolve and maintains its grip on public imagination.

In the first part of the book, the authors explain the concept of AI and what it is and what it can refer to. They give us a clear and balanced view of the serious moral and ethical considerations in the use of AI, as well as an overview of the implications of and potential for AI in the ELT classroom. In part two, they give examples of real and practical uses for AI in English teaching and learning, placing the emphasis on establishing ethical guidelines, codes of conduct and having principled reasons for the incorporation of AI into our teaching. We're sure you'll find the book both informative and eye-opening, and an indispensable addition to the literature on Artificial Intelligence use in our field.

Carol Lethaby and Patricia Harries

Acknowledgements

AI in ELT has been both a joy and a challenge to write, particularly as it is a rapidly evolving topic. We have had to read, research both technical and pedagogical aspects of AI and try out the many ideas in the book. We were determined to find positive strategies to address the many concerning issues around AI and we are content with the result.

We would like to thank:

Carol Lethaby and Patti Harries, our series editors, for trusting us to write this book and giving us freedom to express our views.

Ellie Thackway and Darren Reed at Pavilion ELT for being open to our suggestions while also guiding us to make this book what it is.

Mike Benge, our editor, who was a pleasure to work with and ensured a smooth process throughout.

The schools where we work, Colegio Bayard and Buenos Aires English High School, as they were fertile territory for our exploration of AI related innovative practices.

Our close friends and colleagues who supported us during the writing process. Cecilia Lemos Harmer, Tyson Seburn and Divya Madhavan, who were always ready to bounce off ideas and offer honest analysis and criticism. Viviana Miglino, and Paula Miniño for their unyielding support and critical eye during the process.

The innovative ELT professionals who have been experimenting with AI and have kindly shared their experiences with us, especially Shaun Wilden, Joe Dale, Kateryna Protsenko, Paola Danesi and Sam Gravell.

Belén's children, Nacho and Santi, who were a source of inspiration and willingly tried out many of the tasks in the book.

Vicky's children, Jazmin and Manu, who were staunch supporters and witty critics throughout the whole process.

Introduction

The current state of **artificial intelligence** (AI) in education is characterised by rapid advancement and widespread integration, offering both significant opportunities and complex challenges. The discourse has shifted from initial attempts to limit the overuse of AI or to ban it altogether, to a more cautious integration within educational environments.

An AI taxonomy

It is important to clarify what AI refers to in this book. AI is an overarching term for applications that mimic human intelligence, encompassing areas like problem solving, perception, decision-making and learning. AI includes concepts like **machine learning** (ML), **Deep Learning** (DL) and **generative AI** (GenAI).

Figure i: AI taxonomy

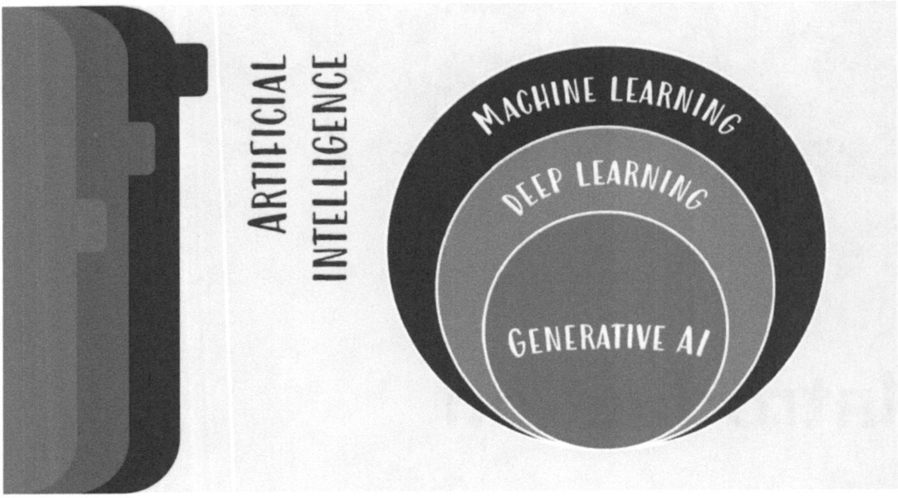

Machine Learning and Deep Learning, categorised as reactive, predictive or limited memory, have been around since the 1960s, but they flourished in the 1990s. Reactive AI systems respond to different kinds of stimuli, but they cannot 'remember' or 'learn' from previous experience, and therefore can't use previous experience to inform their reactions in the present. Reactive machines are best at responding to inputs and will not change or improve their reactions over time.

Machine Learning is a data-driven approach that involves 'training' algorithms using large data sets, which are labelled, so that they can learn and adapt. Predictive AI uses data to forecast or infer a highly likely prediction of what could happen in the future. It uses statistical models and analysis to identify patterns, anticipate future events and make predictions. Some examples are product recommendations either on social media or streaming services, spam email filtering and algorithmic trading.

Deep Learning can 'process "unstructured data", which means that the data sets don't need pre-defined formats or manually created labels' (Stodd *et al.*, 2023). Any AI system that uses DL is trained on large volumes of human data. Limited memory AI systems can do everything that reactive systems can do, but they can also learn from previous experience to make decisions and adapt its reactions in the future. In healthcare, DL is used to develop predictive models for disease diagnosis, prognosis and treatment. Other examples are facial recognition, speech recognition, self-driving cars, virtual assistants and automatic machine translation.

A newer concept within limited memory AI, generative AI, is currently receiving the most attention due to its content-creation capabilities and that is what we will be focusing on in this book. Although not the same, technically, the term AI and GenAI will be used interchangeably in the book.

Generative AI refers to 'a set of Deep Learning techniques used to generate new, previously unseen artefacts, such as images, videos, or text by uncovering and remixing patterns from old, human-created (for now) things… [It] makes enough sense of those creations to uncover their underlying grammar; then it mimics the languages with which they were created to wholly generate new – if technically derivative – artefacts' (Stodd *et al.*, 2023).

So, GenAI analyses data and uncovers the underlying grammar within the data sets by recognising objective patterns and working out frequencies within them. It then mimics that language to create something new, though derived from the existing data. GenAI uses neural networks and machine learning to mimic human production. It is not designed to be factual, but rather to be a processor that mimics what humans do in the areas of communication, language and art. Limited memory systems can use their experience with this training data as a reference to respond to future prompts. Its accuracy should increase over time as it 'learns' and adapts. Currently, these AI systems can only perform specific tasks based on the prompts it receives. They cannot do more than what they are programmed to do, and the quality of the response depends on the quality of the prompt given by a human.

Familiar types of GenAI tools include chatbots, agents text, image, audio, video and code generation, among others. Although tools like ChatGPT are commonly called chatbots, they are agents. The difference between a chatbot and an agent lies in the complexity of the responses. A traditional AI chatbot is a computer program that uses pre-defined rules, decision trees and scripted responses to interact with users. It is commonly found in customer support and is primarily used for information retrieval, and to handle basic interactions. An AI agent is an advanced AI assistant designed to augment human capabilities across a wide range of tasks. It can understand and generate natural language, process and analyse large amounts of information, and assist with complex activities such as writing, coding, problem solving and creative tasks.

When we talk about **GenAI agents** like OpenAI ChatGPT, Google Gemini, Microsoft Copilot, Claude, etc., and other GenAI tools, we are talking about tools that are based on **large language models** (LLMs), which use **natural language processing** (NLP). NLP is 'a powerful computational approach to allow machines to meaningfully understand human spoken and written languages' (Schwartz *et al.*, 2022), particularly the structure, grammar and meaning of words. NLP technologies are used in many applications that include algorithmic search, speech translation, scanning texts to turn them into editable text, speech to text, voice-based computer help systems, grammatical correction, summarising texts, and even conversational text generation.

These LLMs have been fed huge amounts of data, have analysed it and have come up with statistical correlations to articulate these interactions and predict the next word (token) given some initial text (prompt). So, basically, GenAI does not 'really' know or understand things, it is doing advanced mathematical calculations.

Since the advent of GenAI agents in 2022, multiple benefits and opportunities have been identified, as well as challenges.

AI in education

AI is a promising tool for use in education as it may provide students with personalised guidance, support or feedback. The possibility of providing personalised learning options through AI-powered platforms, such as adaptive learning technologies and intelligent tutoring systems, has become a reality. These technologies allow us to tailor educational experiences to an individual student's needs, enhancing learning outcomes and academic performance. These systems can provide instant, personalised feedback, guide students through content and adapt to diverse learning styles and proficiency levels. AI may also 'enable greater customisability of curricular resources to meet local needs' (Cardona *et al.*, 2023).

Regarding teacher support and workload reduction, AI tools can streamline administrative tasks, like automated lesson planning, resource creation and efficient record-keeping, thus reducing the burden on educators and freeing up time for teaching and mentoring.

AI can improve feedback and assessment quality by providing automated grading, immediate feedback, and tracking learning progress, which allows teachers to focus on more complex aspects of student work.

AI can help with increased accessibility and inclusion by supporting learners with disabilities, multilingual learners, and those in remote areas through tailored support like voice assistants, translation tools and adaptive content.

If we consider preparation for the future – an essential goal of education – integrating AI into the curriculum helps equip students with essential AI literacy, computational thinking skills and understanding of AI's societal impact, preparing them for future academic and career pursuits.

AI in English language teaching (ELT)

English is the world's most widely spoken and studied language, so AI tools are a great opportunity to overcome obstacles such as insufficient exposure, limited practice opportunities and lack of quality teaching.

In addition to the general education considerations mentioned above, there are some specific AI applications that benefit ELT.

Regarding speaking skills, AI can be used for pronunciation practice, providing automatic speech analysis and voice assistance. AI can also serve as a conversational partner, offering practice outside class and helping alleviate students' anxiety about speaking.

In terms of writing skills, AI tools like grammar checkers, writing assistants and translation tools can help with vocabulary improvement, grammatical accuracy and lexical variation. AI-powered systems can provide automatic feedback on writing, focusing on aspects like grammar, spelling and mechanical errors.

Reading skills can also be improved with AI. AI can support vocabulary learning within reading contexts, often through game-based learning environments.

An added benefit is students' self-regulation, as AI can support students to develop self-regulation skills, such as goal setting and learning independence.

Challenges and limitations

Reflective task

Have you faced any challenges or concerns while using AI?
If so, what were they?

Despite all these benefits and opportunities, there is an urgent need to address the potential risks of this technology. Several challenges and limitations have also been identified.

AI models are trained on vast datasets that often reflect existing human **biases** and assumptions. This can cause AI to reproduce and amplify these biases, leading to unfair or inaccurate outcomes, especially against underrepresented populations. Many complex AI models operate as 'black boxes', making it difficult to understand how they arrive at decisions. This hinders the detection and correction of biases, leading to trust issues and potentially harmful outputs.

GenAI is data-driven, which means it is only as good as the data with which it has been fed. Many teachers perceive AI as currently unreliable for certain tasks. AI struggles with complex content, nuanced understanding and creativity, occasionally producing illogical or imprecise outputs to such an extent that the term **hallucination** has been coined to explain it. Some uses of AI may be 'infrastructural and invisible, which creates concerns about transparency and trust' (Cardona *et al.*, 2023).

The extensive environmental impact of AI cannot be ignored. GenAI training and use have resulted in a spike in energy consumption, water consumption, carbon dioxide emissions and e-waste.

Uneven varieties of English and multilingual representation is another issue related to the data sets used for training the models. Standardisation of English in particular may endorse specific ideologies or groups while overlooking or marginalising others, particularly linguistic nuances and diverse varieties of English. GenAI output may lack cultural insight, potentially leading to inappropriate or taboo content in certain contexts. This issue also leads to pitfalls in plagiarism detection.

The rapid pace of AI advancement has outstripped the development of comprehensive regulations and policies. This regulatory void allows for issues like intellectual property problems and the proliferation of **deepfakes** and misinformation. Addressing the ethical considerations related to GenAI management of data privacy and copyright issues is essential.

The development and deployment of advanced AI tools require significant financial resources, computing power and data, primarily available to large technology companies and developed economies. This unequal access creates a 'data poverty' for many countries and disadvantaged communities, widening existing digital and educational divides.

Of course, there is also the further risk of possible unintended or unexpected consequences that have not yet been identified.

In conclusion, AI is revolutionising education, including ELT, by promising personalised learning and significant support for teachers. However, its implementation must be carefully managed to mitigate biases, ensure equitable access and uphold human agency and critical thinking, ensuring that AI genuinely enhances, rather than undermines, the quality and inclusivity of education.

Why this book?

Since the early discussions about the use of GenAI in ELT, there have been multiple perspectives shared by professionals, ranging from the deniers and resisters to the enthusiasts and preachers, but also including the indifferents and the cautious optimists.

We have taken time to analyse these developments and, although we believe GenAI will be applied in multiple fields and can be useful in education, we need to be aware of the issues around it and work out strategies and action plans to address them in such a way that we can use it responsibly. We have not seen this perspective laid out openly and in a comprehensive way. So, this was the starting point for this book.

Who is this book for?

This book is for curious and open-minded teachers and administrators who are interested in integrating AI into their lessons and institutions. As with any tech tool, we envision two possible scenarios for AI integration: one where educators use AI to reduce their workload, create lesson plans and materials, and another where teachers create digital learning experiences with AI, which might be completely facilitated by the teacher, in the case of younger learners, or where AI is in the hands of the students themselves. This book is especially useful for educators who have explored AI tools but are now looking for practical examples and real-life classroom experiments. Whether you are tech-savvy or not, this book offers step-by-step plans to help you confidently bring AI into your teaching practice, with no advanced technical knowledge required.

Reflective task 2

How do you envision AI impacting education in the next five years?

How is this book organised?

The book is thoughtfully structured to guide readers from awareness to action, moving from a critical exploration of AI's complex challenges, to providing practical solutions for its responsible use in the classroom. Part 1 therefore takes a clear-eyed look at the complex issues surrounding AI in education, helping educators navigate concerns that are often overlooked, while Part 2 shifts the focus to empowering teachers with frameworks, tools and classroom practices for engaging with AI critically and creatively. This book acknowledges the range of attitudes teachers may have, from curiosity and caution to resistance or excitement, and it provides a thoughtful exploration of the key concerns and ethical dilemmas surrounding AI.

What makes this book different? What will you gain from it?

This book offers a comprehensive, critical and practical guide for teachers navigating the complex world of generative AI in education, especially in the context of English language teaching.

Each chapter addresses a core issue or opportunity related to AI in education, reflecting both the promises and the pitfalls of this rapidly evolving technology. Reflective tasks throughout the book are meant to provide thinking time at key moments to reflect on specific content and personal contexts.

It aims to empower educators with practical strategies, ethical guidelines and ready-to-use classroom ideas. You will gain a solid foundation in AI literacy, a critical lens to evaluate tools and outputs, and a set of actionable resources to use AI meaningfully and responsibly.

Whether you are new to AI or looking to deepen your practice, this book equips you to make informed decisions that centre pedagogy, equity and the learner's agency, ensuring AI becomes a thoughtful addition to your teaching.

How have we used AI in this book?

Although all the content in this book is our original work, informed by the sources we have consulted, we have used AI in certain ways, which we consider ethical and responsible.

We have used NotebookLM, a Google AI tool that enables the uploading of documents of all sorts and links so that you can later summarise them or interrogate them, among other things. We have uploaded all our sources, categorised by chapter or topic, and we have used them to locate certain information more easily and to speed up our referencing process.

We have used NapkinAI to generate figures based on information we have provided.

We have also used ChatGPT to create charts and generate example tasks mentioned in the relevant chapters.

Specific tools, such as ChatGPT, Claude, Copilot, ImageFX, OpenArt and Reve, have been used to generate examples that highlight the issues described in the book.

Part 1:
Identifying and understanding the challenges

Chapter 1:

Inherent biases and assumptions in AI algorithms

In this chapter, we describe the inner workings of AI that can explain the inherent biases and assumptions present in its output.

> **Reflective task 1**
>
> What biases and assumptions have you encountered when using GenAI? In an educational context, how can these biases and assumptions be harmful? Where do you think they stem from?

One of the most evident issues with Gen AI output is its inherent biases and assumptions. These stem primarily from the ways AI systems are designed, trained and operate, particularly their reliance on data and complex algorithmic processes.

GenAI models training and operation

We cannot possibly understand this issue without looking into how **GenAI models** are built and used. As we mentioned in the introduction, GenAI models are based on LLMs, which work with natural language processing. According to Hovy and Prabhumoye (2021), 'the NLP field has grown faster than anticipated without fully understanding its unintended consequences and harmful usages like bias, which might lead to unintentional outcomes of the developed NLP systems'. Predictive models in NLP do not generalise well, as they are sensitive to a variety of biases introduced during the development process. Shah *et al.* (2020) define bias as 'the mismatch of ideal and actual distributions of **labels** and user attributes in training and application of a system'. As a result, NLP models produce 'performance and reliability losses on unseen data' (Shah *et al.*, 2020). There are multiple variations of human-generated language, both written and spoken, that 'reflect the diverse demographics, backgrounds, and personalities of the people who use' them (Shah *et al.*, 2020).

Swinton (1981) explains predictive bias as 'a situation in which a [predictive model] is used to predict a specific criterion for a particular population and is found to give systematically different predictions for subgroups of this population who are in fact identical on that specific criterion'. In other words, 'the label distribution of a predictive model reflects a human attribute in a way that diverges from a theoretically defined "ideal distribution"' (Shah *et al.*, 2020). For example, models based on data and labels from a particular demographic, being it a profession, age, race or gender, diverge from the population as a whole. An example of this could be a loan application AI tool or model trained on historically male-dominated professions. It might implicitly learn that certain career paths are stronger indicators of repayment ability, even if those indicators are not universally applicable. The results for women in historically female-dominated or emerging professions, or for younger applicants with a strong but unconventional career path, might not align with the patterns the AI was trained to recognise as 'low risk' because those patterns were predominantly derived from male-dominated professions.

Another example is the 'Wall Street Journal effect', which is explained in more detail in the on selection bias below. A model should only be applied to a specific context as related to the data it has been trained on. AI models are excellent at interpolation (making predictions within the range of data they have seen) but struggle significantly with extrapolation (making predictions outside that range). If you apply a model to data that is fundamentally different from what it was trained on, it's essentially guessing, leading to unreliable and often nonsensical results. Applying a general-purpose model to a highly specialised domain, such as ELT, without specific training will miss critical nuances and make errors. Predictive bias is not an intrinsic property of the model, but a property of a model given a specific application which is different from the one intended originally.

Reflective task 2

'A model should only be applied to a specific context as related to the data it has been trained on.'

Why do you think this might be important? How would you extrapolate this general statement for an ELT context? What examples can you think of?

The origin of biases

The origin of biases has been researched extensively. Hovy and Prabhumoye (2021) and Shah *et al.* (2020), for example, categorise and name these origins differently but almost agree conceptually. These origins can be traced to:

- the data, i.e. the samples used for training (selection bias)
- the **annotation** process, i.e. the labels manually created by a human during the training process (label bias)
- the input representations, i.e. the representation of data (semantic bias)
- the models (bias overamplification)

Figure 1.1: The origin of biases in AI systems

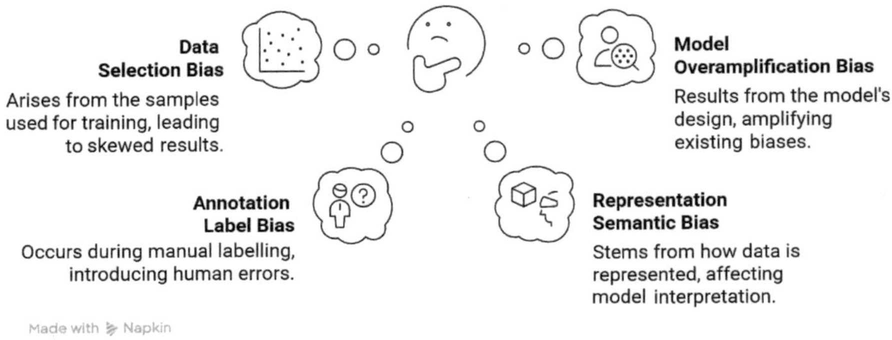

Selection bias

Selection bias (or sample bias) appears when the data used to train the model is non-representative, i.e. 'when the users generating the training (source) observations differ from the user distribution of the target where the model will be applied' (Shah *et al.*, 2020). A well-documented case of selection bias is the 'Wall Street Journal effect', where labels are most accurate over language written by 'the predominant authors' demographics of the WSJ articles' from the 1980s and 1990s (typically white, middle-aged, educated, upper-middle-class men), 'which are traditionally used to train syntactic models' (Garimella *et al.*, 2019). So, these modern syntactic tools 'expect everyone to speak like journalists from the 1980s' (Hovy & Prabhumoye, 2021). But language evolves, and most people today do not speak this way. NLP is ill-prepared to cope with this demographic variation. The model output is dissimilar to the ideal distribution and leads to lower accuracy for any demographic that is different from the one represented by the training data. Hovy and Prabhumoye (2021) state that 'given that a large part of the world's population is currently under 30, such models will degrade even more over time and ultimately not meet their users' needs'.

Along similar lines, Heinrich *et al.* (2010) introduced the acronym **WEIRD** (western, educated, industrialised, rich and democratic) to describe the specific demographic of research participants in a behavioural science study and then questioned 'whether researchers can reasonably generalise from WEIRD samples to humanity at large'. Stodd *et al.* (2023) reclaimed this acronym to refer to the demographic behind the data used to train LLMs used by GenAI.

When choosing a text data set to work with, decisions are made about the demographic groups represented in the data. Some demographic attributes that are important to consider are age, gender and race, but also socioeconomic class, profession, religion, etc.

Reflective task 3

Why is selection bias important, and why is it difficult to tackle for ELT purposes?

Label bias

Text or data annotation, which is often invisible to the end user, is a key process in the development of artificial intelligence models, especially those specialised in natural language processing (NLP). It transforms unstructured text into structured, labeled data. Manual annotation, where humans label or tag specific parts of text to ensure accuracy, is often used in this context. 'Annotators' or 'Data Labelers' label, categorise and tag data to provide algorithms with the information they need to understand, interpret and process textual data effectively.

A typical text annotation process involves several steps:

1. Data selection, where raw text data is gathered from various sources.
2. Pre-processing, which removes 'noise' (unnecessary characters, formatting or irrelevant information) from raw data to ensure clean input for annotation.
3. Labelling, where annotators assign meaningful labels or tags to specific parts of the text. These labels might include names (e.g., people, places, dates), parts of speech, key

phrases, coreference resolution (words or phrases that refer to the same entity in a text), dependency analysis annotation (grammatical relationships between words in a sentence, for example, dependencies between a main word and its complements or modifiers), sentiments (positive, negative, neutral), the underlying intent of a sentence or text (a request for information, a service request, a complaint), text segmentation (dividing text into logical units such as sentences, paragraphs or thematic sections), document classification, translation annotation or alignment or other relevant categories. Clear annotation guidelines are essential as a reference manual for annotators as they define labels and provide examples. Collaborative annotation, supported by regular communication, helps ensure consistency and quality when multiple annotators are involved.

4. Quality control, where the data undergoes a review and validation phase to ensure that the annotations are consistent, accurate and aligned with objectives. Any discrepancies or errors are corrected.
5. Compilation of Final Annotated Dataset, where a high-quality, labeled dataset is compiled and can be used to train and test machine learning models.

The consistency of this process ultimately contributes to the improved efficiency and accuracy of AI models.

Label bias emerges when the labels themselves are erroneous. This can happen for a variety of reasons such as a non-representative group of annotators (Joseph *et al.*, 2017), a lack of domain expertise (Plank *et al.*, 2014), or the preconceived notions and stereotypes held by the annotators (Sap *et al.*, 2019). For example, some words carry negative connotations in one language but are widely accepted in other languages and cultures. The word 'negrito' in Spanish is widely used affectionately in Argentina and Uruguay to talk to friends, but its English translation is overall rejected as racist. A while ago, a South American football player, who was playing in the Premier League in England, was fined for posting an

Instagram story where he referred to a friend of his as 'negrito'. It seems obvious, but linguistic complexity is also at play and the fact that languages are constantly evolving requires regular updates of annotated data sets.

Reflective task 4

Think of some examples of label bias relevant to English and another language of your choice?

Semantic bias

To understand semantic bias, we need to address **word embeddings**. LLMs' training objective is to predict the most likely next term, given the previous context, or **n-grams**. N-grams are contiguous sequences of n items (words, characters, or symbols) from a given text or speech sequence. While this objective of LLMs captures distributional semantic properties, it may itself not contribute to building unbiased embeddings.

Word embedding is a technique in NLP to map words into **vector space representations** in order to capture the semantic meaning of words, i.e. contextual information by considering the words that co-occur in a given context. This helps models understand the meaning of a word based on its surrounding words, and leads to better representation of phrases and sentences. Words with similar meanings are closer together in the embedding space, which makes it easier for the model to classify documents based on their content.

There are different word-embedding methods. The two earliest models are distributional semantic models (DSMs) and **neural word-embedding models**. DSMs support the idea that words with similar meanings tend to occur in similar contexts. Neural word embeddings, which started in the 2000s, build upon this concept by using neural networks to learn dense, low-dimensional vector representations of words, which capture semantic and syntactic relationships. Progress has been made. For example, the Word2Vec model, introduced by Tomas Mikolov and his colleagues at Google in 2013, marked a significant breakthrough as it can efficiently learn word embeddings from large corpora in a simple and effective way.

Embeddings are flexible representations that feed both traditional and deep learning models. But these representations 'often contain unintended or undesirable associations and societal stereotypes (e.g., connecting medical doctors more frequently to male pronouns than female pronouns)' (Shah *et al.*, 2020). This phenomenon is called semantic bias.

This particular bias is not only associated with people, but with words in contexts that produce non-ideal associations. For example, although it is true that more of the training data for word embeddings is authored by a particular gender, this is made worse by the fact that 'gendered pronouns are mentioned alongside occupations according to a non-ideal distribution (e.g., texts talk more about male doctors and female nurses than vice versa)' (Shah *et al.*, 2020). Hovy and Prabhumoye (2021) mention that 'word embeddings have been shown to pick up on racial and gender biases in the training data (Bolukbasi *et al.*, 2016; Manzini *et al.*, 2019). For example, "woman" is associated with "homemaker" in the same way "man" is associated with "programmer".'

These biases also hold for the contextual representations of LLMs. The fact that they are 'pre-trained on almost the entire available internet, makes them even more prone to societal biases' (Hovy & Prabhumoye, 2021). Silva and Amarathunga (2019) state that 'none of the existing neural models is capable of capturing different types of contexts at once in their models'.

Although there are efforts to improve methods and debias word embeddings, their impact and applicability are still unclear.

Reflective task 5

What might be a problem associated with relying only on predicting the most likely next term? What can be a consequence of word embeddings that work for certain contexts but not others?

Bias overamplification

So, a solution might be to use/find better training data. But languages evolve continuously, so even a representative sample can only capture a snapshot.

According to Shah *et al.* (2020), 'in [bias] overamplification, a model relies on a small difference between human attributes with respect to the objective but amplifies this difference to be much more pronounced in the predicted outcomes. The model learns to pick up on imperfect evidence for the outcome, which brings out the bias.'

Further studies have used other examples:

- According to Hovy and Prabhumoye (2021), 'Zhao *et al.* (2017) demonstrated that systems trained on biased data exacerbate that bias even further when applied to new data, and Kiritchenko and Mohammad (2018) have shown that **sentiment analysis** tools pick up on societal prejudices, leading to different outcomes for different demographic groups. For example, by merely changing the gender of a pronoun, the systems classified the sentence differently.'
- Hovy *et al.* (2020) found that **machine translation** systems changed the perceived user demographics to make samples sound older and more male in translation.
- Shat *et al.* (2020) mention that 'Yatskar *et al.* (2016) found that in the imSitu image captioning data set, 58% of captions involving a person in a kitchen mention "women". However, standard models trained on such data end up predicting people depicted in kitchens as women 63% of the time (Zhao *et al.*, 2017).'

Bias overamplification is rooted in the models themselves.

Reflective task 6

'Sentiment analysis tools pick up on societal prejudices, leading to different outcomes for different demographic groups. For example, by merely changing the gender of a pronoun, the systems classified the sentence differently.'

What might be an example of this?

Other sources of biases

Another problem is that models pick up **spurious correlations**. 'A spurious correlation occurs when two variables are statistically related but not directly causally related. These two variables falsely appear to be related to each other, normally due to an unseen, third factor' (Bock, 2025). Although these correlations are statistically present in training data, they don't reflect genuine causal relationships. The result is poor model generalisation and performance on unseen data.

Yet another issue with the design of machine learning models is that they always make a prediction, even when they are unsure or when they cannot know the answer. A common mistake is when a machine translation tool translates a gender-neutral language occurrence into a gendered translation for a gendered language. Instead of reporting to the user that it could not translate it, it produces the wrong translation. This will be addressed further in Chapter 4.

We have addressed model training so far, but another source of bias introduction is data-collection processes. GenAI models collect data for further training their models in two ways: direct user inputs, and passive and behavioural data collection.

When users provide inputs, such as prompts (text, data, images), these inputs can be used for further training AI models. This means that anything shared with a public model, even in prompt form, may be added to the model for future reference and potentially shared with other users. There is a risk of sensitive or confidential data being inadvertently used for training if entered into unauthorised AI tools that lack proper data-privacy agreements.

AI **algorithms** silently collect data on user profiles and online activities, such as content views, ads watched, links clicked, time spent, time of day, and location. This data is used to create individual and group profiles to predict what online information people will like or believe. The more personal information collected, the more likely a personally identifiable profile can be created. The continuous collection and utilisation of user data raise significant concerns regarding privacy, intellectual property rights and the perpetuation or amplification of existing biases. We will address data privacy in Chapter 5.

A further issue is that many advanced AI systems, especially **artificial neural networks** (ANNs) and LLMs, are considered 'black boxes'. Their inner workings are opaque and not open to inspection, making it difficult, if not impossible, to understand why particular content has been created or how specific decisions are made. This contributes to a lack of transparency and trust, leading users to blindly trust AI recommendations without critical engagement or accountability.

Reflective task 7

What is your attitude towards using a GenAI agent? What kinds of tasks do you use it for? How much do you trust the output?

Why is this relevant for ELT?

All the information so far is quite technical, but necessary in order to move forward. You may be wondering why this is relevant for ELT. The answer is because language is deeply contextual, culturally nuanced, and varies significantly across different learner demographics, proficiency levels and learning goals.

A general AI model or a model for ELT that is not specifically trained on data relevant to its intended use can lead to inaccurate feedback and irrelevant content, leading to demotivation. For example, pronunciation feedback from an AI model trained on Standard American English (SAE) used with users of other varieties of English or English learners will give inaccurate or unfair feedback. In the case of grammar checkers or correctors, an AI model trained primarily on formal academic essays written by native English speakers at university level will give inaccurate or unfair feedback if used to correct learners of different ages or language levels. An AI tool that recommends useful vocabulary to master that has been trained on news articles and business reports, but applied to general English learners, young learners or learners looking for a conversational use of the language, will most definitely produce irrelevant and unhelpful suggestions. The same is true for a GenAI agent created for speaking practice and trained on general conversational data from native speakers with no specific pedagogical design. It will fail to guide learners looking for more specific uses, grammar points or scenarios.

Figure 1.2: AI in ELT: The tip of the Iceberg

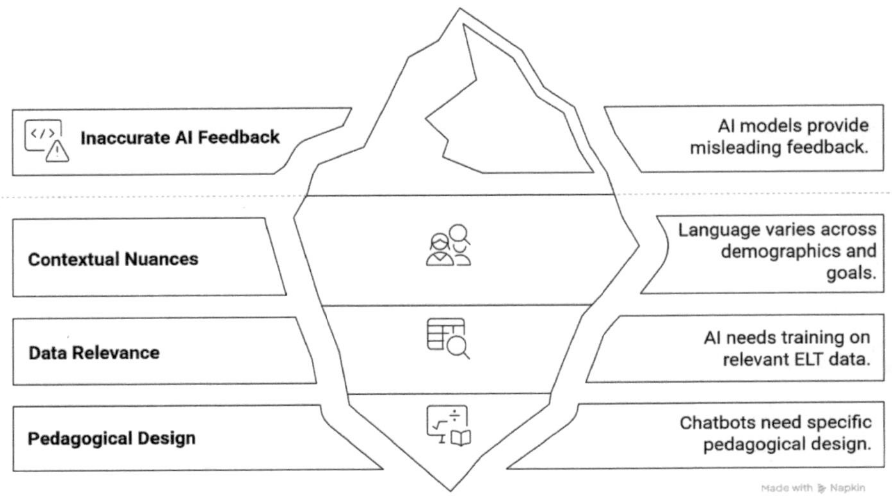

If we look at the different sources of biases one by one, we can start to understand the relevance to ELT more fully.

Selection bias is particularly difficult to tackle for ELT because of the vast diversity of languages, learners and learning contexts. A representative sample would need to guarantee linguistic diversity by including a wide variety of accents and dialects, a distinction of different registers and styles, and understand the L1 influence in the English learning process. It should also be able to reflect the diverse demographics and contexts of learners by differentiating between learners of different ages, proficiency levels, learning goals and socioeconomic and cultural backgrounds. For example, an automated essay scoring system trained on data that lacks sufficient representation of essays written by non-native English speakers from diverse L1 backgrounds, different educational systems, examples of common 'interlanguage' errors, or varying proficiency levels, will penalise ELT learners for syntactic structures that are common in their L1 but less so in native English, vocabulary choices that are technically correct but not idiomatic for a native speaker, errors specific to their L1, or cultural references.

Regarding AI speech recognition and pronunciation tutors, if their training data lacks recordings from non-native English speakers, especially those with diverse L1 accents, they might struggle to recognise and accurately transcribe the speech of learners with strong L1 accents, they might incorrectly mark valid yet non-native pronunciations as 'wrong' because they don't match the native speaker patterns they were trained on, or they might fail to detect critical pronunciation errors. If we look at content generation of language learning materials, an AI model trained on data heavily skewed towards topics, cultural references and social norms prevalent in Western, English-speaking countries, including gender or racial stereotypes, the generated content might be culturally irrelevant or insensitive to learners from different backgrounds, it might use idioms or slang that are common in a specific native-speaker context but less universally understood or appropriate for some learners, and characters in stories might reinforce stereotypes impacting learners' perceptions and feelings.

Figure 1.3: Selection bias in ELT

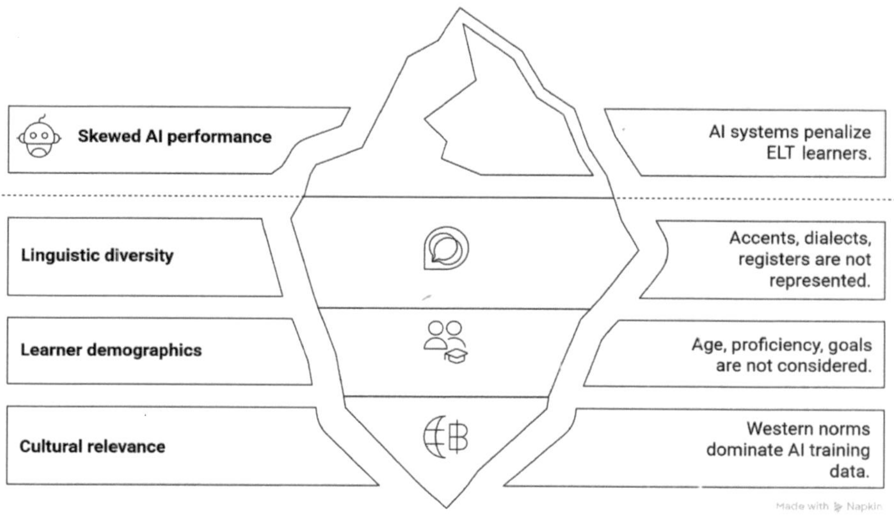

Label bias can be traced to several factors, some related to the training data and others to the human annotators' interpretations, lack of expertise or preconceived notions. One of the most prominent and well-documented examples of label bias, particularly when translating between languages with different grammatical gender systems, is gender bias caused by machine translation, as English language learners often default to their own L1 when using GenAI tools. Gender bias is commonly found for professions which are gender-neutral in English (also Turkish, Basque, Armenian, Finnish and Japanese, for example) but gendered in other languages (Spanish, French, Italian, Portuguese and Arabic, for example). In the sentence 'The doctor is speaking to the patient', either the doctor or the patient can be male or female in Spanish and other languages. AI translation models will pick on certain professions which are stereotypically associated with a particular gender and can mistranslate the phrase in a gendered language. Gender bias is also common for gender-neutral adjectives, which have a gendered version in another language. In 'The CEO is strong and decisive', the CEO can be male or female in Spanish, but the adjective 'decisive' has a female version and a male version. AI translation models will probably render the CEO as male and therefore use the male version of 'decisive'. This gender bias is very noticeable in GenAI image generators.

We used three image generators to test this: Google's ImageFX, Open AI's OpenArt, and Reve. For 'The doctor is speaking to the patient', we generated eight images. OpenArt and Reve produced doctors talking to doctors, where five were male and three were female. ImageFX produced four images, where two doctors were male, white and of different ages, and the other two were female, white and both middle-aged. The patients were all women.

Figure 1.4: "The doctor is speaking to the patient" images

Made using: Openart

Made using: Openart

Made using: Reve

Made using: Reve

Made using: ImageFX

Made using: ImageFX

Made using: ImageFX

Made using: ImageFX

For 'The CEO is strong and decisive', we generated seven images. Six of them were male and only one was female (generated by ImageFX). All except one were white. One of them even added unintelligible text, which was not asked for in the prompt.

Figure 1.5: "The CEO is strong and decisive" images

Made using: Openart

Made using: Openart

Made using: Reve

Made using: Reve

Made using: ImageFX

Made using: ImageFX

Made using: ImageFX

Another example that makes this relevant for ELT is label bias stemming from sentiment analysis, which can appear if human annotators, influenced by their own biases, label similar statements differently based on the demographic characteristics implied by the text, i.e. the combination of gendered language and behaviour or emotion. In the sentence 'He complained loudly about the service', 'complained' could be analysed as a reasonable complaint and labelled 'negative', whereas in 'She complained loudly about the service', 'complained' could be labelled as 'strongly negative' or 'aggressive'.

A third problem is toxicity and hate speech detection. Label bias can occur when annotators, intentionally or unintentionally apply different thresholds for what constitutes 'toxic' or 'hate speech' based on the identity of the speaker or the group being referenced, without attention to cultural differences. Certain words, which might be deemed racist in one language, can be harmless in another. Code switching and dialectal variations can also be mis-labelled. A further problem is label bias stemming from speech recognition. If the training data for a speech recognition model is labelled primarily by native speakers who are less accustomed to non-native accents, their transcriptions might be less accurate for non-native speech, or even other regional accents. This will be addressed in Chapter 4.

Figure 1.6: Label bias in ELT

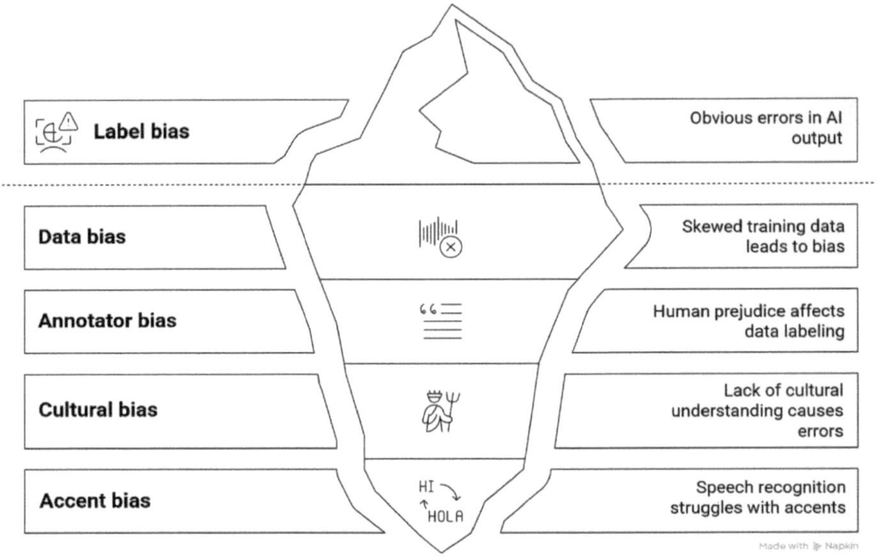

Semantic bias is closely related to the inner workings of LLMs and therefore word embeddings. Issues related to word embeddings are significant for ELT. The biggest problem with static embeddings is their inability to capture the different meanings of a word based on context. The word 'bank', for example, has different meanings (bank of earth/soil, bank of a stream, financial institution). A static embedding for 'bank' would be a single vector, averaging all its meanings. The embedding for 'bank' might be closer to 'earth, soil or stream' than 'money' if these occurrences were more prevalent in the training data, leading to incorrect interpretations in NLP tasks. Although contextual word embeddings address the polysemy issue by generating context-dependent embeddings, problems still arise if the context itself or the domain of training is limited. A model trained on a specific domain (e.g. medical texts) will create word embeddings optimised for that domain. That is why we stress the fact that a GenAI model should only be applied to contexts relevant to the data it has been trained on. A further issue is AI's inability to reflect cultural and societal contexts. Certain slang words or idiomatic expressions might have a specific meaning and sentiment in one cultural context but be nonsensical or even offensive in another, which might have serious implications in GenAI agent generated output. And, of course, there is the inability to capture temporal context or 'semantic drift', where the meaning of words changes over time. For example, the word 'sick' used to mean 'ill', but now it can also mean 'cool' or 'impressive' in slang.

Figure 1.7: Semantic bias in ELT

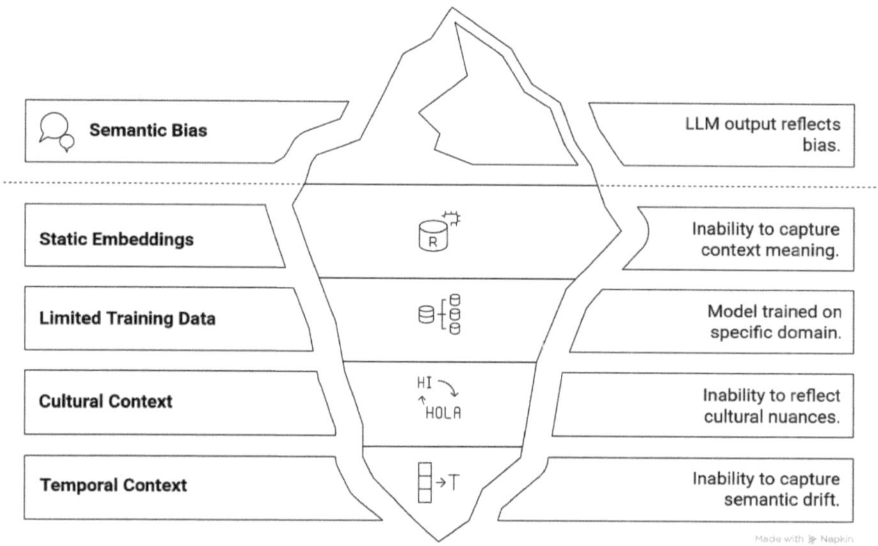

Overamplification, where an AI's output is either too generic, overly confident in potentially incorrect information, or struggles to adapt to nuances beyond its training data, can have very real consequences for English language learners. An AI grammar checker, trained on a vast corpus of formal English, can correct a student's perfectly natural and idiomatic spoken English phrase to a more formal, but less authentic, written equivalent. An AI writing assistant can provide feedback on a student's essay, repeatedly using the same pre-programmed phrases like 'This sentence is well-structured' or 'Consider expanding on this point', without considering the specific strengths or weaknesses of the text as a whole. A GenAI agent designed for conversation practice can struggle to understand or respond appropriately to slang, idioms or emerging linguistic trends that were not heavily represented in its training data. An AI tutor, overprogrammed for positive reinforcement, can consistently provide effusive praise even for a student's rudimentary or error-filled sentences, in an attempt to be encouraging. An AI-generated quiz can focus too heavily on surface-level recognition of 'correct' answers, where a student can guess based on patterns or common phrases, rather than truly understanding the underlying language concept.

Figure 1.8: Bias overamplification

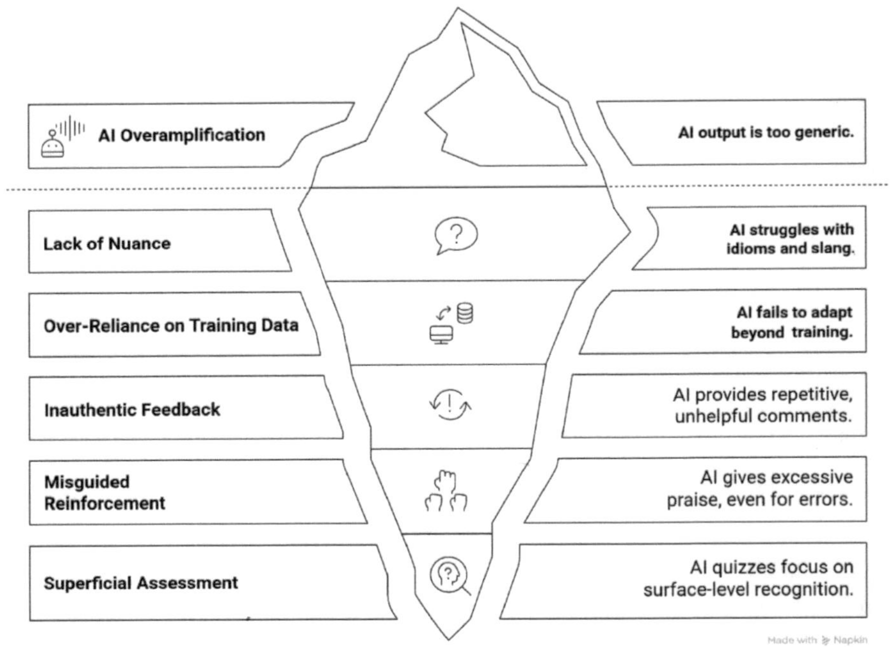

Chapter 1 Key Points

1. **Bias is systemic, not accidental.** Biases and assumptions in Generative AI are not glitches but inherent features stemming from how systems are designed, trained, and operated.

---

2. **The problem of extrapolation.** AI models excel at *interpolation* (predicting within the range of known data) but struggle with *extrapolation* (predicting outside that range).

Using a general-purpose model for a specialised domain like ELT is essentially "guessing".

---

3. **Selection bias and the "WEIRD" demographic.** Training data often suffers from selection bias, representing specific demographics, often "WEIRD" (Western, Educated, Industrialized, Rich, and Democratic), rather than humanity at large.

---

4. **Label bias and human error.** Bias is introduced during the manual annotation process where humans label data. This can result from annotator stereotypes, lack of cultural knowledge, or errors.

---

5. **Semantic bias in word embeddings.** Large Language Models use word embeddings that map words into vector spaces. These embeddings capture and freeze societal stereotypes found in training data.

---

6. **Bias overamplification.** Models do not just reflect existing biases; they exacerbate them. A model might take a small statistical difference in training data and amplify it into a "rule" in its output.

---

7. **The "black box" issue.** Advanced AI systems are opaque "black boxes," making it impossible to inspect how specific decisions are made.

---

8. **Penalising linguistic diversity.** In ELT, selection bias means AI might penalise valid non-native English usage.

---

9. **Gender translation errors.** Label bias frequently manifests in translation tasks relevant to learners. Because English has many gender-neutral professions , AI models translating into gendered languages often default to stereotypes or incorrectly gendered adjectives, reinforcing social biases rather than linguistic accuracy.

---

10. **Generic or misguided feedback.** Due to bias overamplification, AI tutors may provide overly generic feedback or excessive praise (positive reinforcement) even for error-filled work. Conversely, they may correct natural, idiomatic speech into formal written English because the model over-relies on formal training texts.

Further reading

Lee, S. (2023). AI Toolkit for Educators. *EIT InnoEnergy Master School Teachers Conference 2023*. Retrieved from www.paradoxlearning.com

Stodd, J., Schatz, S., and Stead, G. (2023). *Engines of Engagement: A curious book about generative AI*. Bournemouth, UK: Sea Salt Publishing. https://seasaltlearning.com/engines-of-engagement-generative-ai-book/

Chapter 2:

(Im)Precise output

In this chapter, we explore the various factors that influence the precision of AI-generated content, including limitations and hallucinations.

Reflective task 1

What imprecise output have you encountered when using GenAI, if any? How have you been able to notice it? How serious was it? What factors and skills are at play to be able to spot imprecisions?

Another evident problem with GenAI is the accuracy of their output. Back in 2023, when I started becoming familiar with ChatGPT, I thought I needed to test it with something I was an expert on, so I could evaluate its performance. I therefore prompted GPT-3.5 to write about me. This is what I got.

Prompt: *Write an article about Vicky Saumell's contributions to ELT. Include references.*

Title: Vicky Saumell: Pioneering Contributions to English Language Teaching (ELT)

Introduction:

English language teaching (ELT) is a dynamic field that constantly evolves to meet the changing needs of learners worldwide. Within this realm, Vicky Saumell stands as an influential figure, renowned for her innovative contributions and dedication to the advancement of ELT. Through her expertise, passion and commitment to professional development, Saumell has made a lasting impact on teachers and learners alike. This article explores the remarkable contributions of Vicky Saumell, highlighting her groundbreaking work and significant influence on ELT.

1. Revolutionary Role in Technology Integration:

Vicky Saumell has been at the forefront of integrating technology into ELT practices, equipping teachers with tools to enhance their teaching methodologies and engage learners effectively. As an advocate for digital literacies, she has promoted the use of various digital platforms and tools to create interactive and engaging learning experiences. Her insights into blended learning, online resources, and educational apps have revolutionised ELT classrooms globally. *Saumell's book, Digital Play: Computer games and language aims,* <u>published in 2012, remains a cornerstone resource for teachers seeking to incorporate gamification and technology-based activities in language learning</u>.

2. Pivotal Contributions to Professional Development:

Recognising the importance of ongoing professional development, Vicky Saumell has made substantial contributions to empowering English language teachers. Through her engaging presentations, webinars and workshops, she has shared practical strategies, innovative ideas, and inspiring approaches to enhance classroom instruction. <u>Saumell's</u>

commitment to collaboration and networking has also resulted in the creation of vibrant online communities, such as the Electronic Village Online (EVO), where teachers can connect, exchange ideas and learn from one another.

3. Leadership in Content Creation and Curriculum Design:

As an accomplished author and curriculum designer, Vicky Saumell has played a significant role in shaping ELT materials and resources. Her contributions to renowned ELT publishers, including her work on coursebook series such as *Think* and *Treetops*, have provided teachers with comprehensive and engaging materials that align with current pedagogical approaches. Furthermore, Saumell's involvement in curriculum design projects, such as the Cambridge English Syllabus for Argentina, has contributed to the development of learner-centred curricula that cater to the specific needs and contexts of English language learners.

4. Advancement of Critical Thinking and Creativity in ELT:

Vicky Saumell is a staunch advocate for fostering critical thinking and creativity in language classrooms. She believes that these skills are crucial for students to thrive in the 21st century. Through her workshops and publications, Saumell has offered practical strategies to promote critical thinking, problem solving and creativity in language learning. Her book *Creativity in the English Language Classroom*, published in 2015, has become a valuable resource for teachers seeking to incorporate innovative activities and projects into their lessons.

Conclusion:

Vicky Saumell's contributions to the field of ELT have left an indelible mark, inspiring and empowering teachers worldwide. Through her pioneering work in technology integration, professional development, curriculum design and the promotion of critical thinking and creativity, Saumell has enriched ELT practice and positively influenced language learning outcomes.

Her commitment to innovation, collaboration and lifelong learning continues to shape the future of English language teaching, ensuring that educators are equipped with the necessary tools and strategies to meet the evolving needs of learners in the digital age.

References:

1. Saumell, V. (2012). Digital Play: Computer Games and Language Aims. Delta Publishing.
2. Saumell, V. (2015). Creativity in the English Language Classroom. British Council.
3. Cambridge English Syllabus for Argentina

This is my analysis of the output. At first look it seemed reasonable but... First of all, it made me sound far more important and influential than I really am. Second, it got many things wrong! All the underlined parts are inaccurate. I haven't written those books, or created EVO or helped writing the Cambridge English Syllabus for Argentina (which doesn't exist, by the way). All the references at the end were made up. And the writing style is simply overdone.

So I tried another, Bing (now Copilot), to see if it was better.

Figure 2.1: Example of Bing generated text

Vicky Saumell is an EFL teacher and teacher trainer from Buenos Aires, Argentina. She is also an educational technology consultant who has been involved in several projects to promote the use of digital tools in language teaching and learning. She has written articles and books on topics such as coursebooks, homework, assessment, and digital literacy. She is also a frequent speaker at national and international conferences, where she shares her insights and experiences with other ELT professionals.

Some of her contributions to ELT include:
- Co-authoring the coursebook series "Spotlight on English" for primary and secondary students, which aims to develop language skills as well as critical thinking, creativity, and intercultural awareness.
- Developing the online platform "Digital Learning Hub", which offers a variety of resources and activities for teachers and learners to enhance their digital skills and competencies.
- Creating the blog "Educational Technology in ELT", where she posts reviews, tips, and tutorials on how to use different web tools and apps for language teaching and learning.
- Leading the "Digital Literacy SIG" of IATEFL, which is a special interest group that focuses on exploring and promoting digital literacy in ELT contexts.

Vicky Saumell is a passionate and innovative educator who has made a significant impact on the field of ELT. She is an inspiration for many teachers who want to integrate technology into their practice and enrich their professional development.

References:
- Vicky Saumell - Facebook. https://www.facebook.com/vickysaumellELT/
- Vicky Saumell - Coursebooks as guides - TeachingEnglish. https://www.teachingenglish.org.uk/professional-development/teachers/managing-resources/articles/vicky-saumell-coursebooks-guides
- Vicky Saumell - Turning homework into an effective learning opportunity - TeachingEnglish. https://www.teachingenglish.org.uk/professional-development/teachers/understanding-learners/magazine/vicky-saumell-turning-homework

Well, it wasn't... It did get the references right, but its selection was really arbitrary. As for its accuracy, again it made up my contributions as a co-author of a coursebook, a developer of an online platform, the coordinator of the Digital Literacy SIG at IATEFL, which doesn't exist. Even if my blog exists, I haven´t posted in it since 2018.

Since 2022 (the launch of ChatGPT) seems a long time ago from an AI development perspective, I asked ChatGPT and Copilot again, and this time the result was much better. No inaccuracies now, although the writing style is still pompous. These improvements can be attributed to improved models and the use of 'RAGs' (Retrieval Augmented Generation), which I will address later.

My question, though, was whether the fact that it got it right this time means there are no more inaccuracies in its output. Sadly not. Although inaccuracies went down in this particular case, they still happen. We will try to untangle the origin of these errors, commonly called hallucinations. This term has been made popular since the limitations shown by GenAI models became evident. However, the term can be traced back to 1985 in a thesis discussing 'hallucinations' in output by an AI fingerprint recogniser based on neural nets. The rhetorical discourse around the term is very interesting as it 'frames [these undesirable] outcomes as an exception to AI's general ability to recognise and report real information about the world' (Pearson, 2024). Bergstrom and Brandon Ogbunu (2023) add that it implies that AI 'accidentally' reported something unreal as if it were real. The data from different GenAI models show that hallucinations are not an exception, and some reports (Moore-Coyler, 2025) state that this isn't getting better in newer, more advanced models:

> 'Research conducted by OpenAI (2025) found that its latest and most powerful **reasoning models**, o3 and o4-mini, hallucinated 33% and 48% of the time, respectively, when tested by OpenAI's PersonQA benchmark. That's more than double the rate of the older o1 model. While o3 delivers more accurate information than its predecessor, it appears to come at the cost of more inaccurate hallucinations.'

Eleanor Watson, an Institute of Electrical and Electronics Engineers (IEEE) member and AI ethics engineer at Singularity University states in an interview that, 'this raises a concern over the accuracy and reliability of large language models (LLMs) such as AI agents... When a system outputs fabricated information – such as invented facts, citations or events – with the same fluency and coherence it uses for accurate content, it risks misleading users in subtle and consequential ways.'

Models with relatively lower hallucination rates (generally below 10%) include:

- Google Gemini-2.0-Flash-Exp: 1.3%
- OpenAI-o1-mini: 1.4%
- GPT-4o: 1.5%
- GPT-4o-mini: 1.7%
- Claude 2 (Anthropic): 5-12%
- GPT-4: Around 3% on a specific leaderboard, but potentially higher in other contexts (e.g., 28.6% in legal queries)
- Google Gemini (Bard): 8-15%

Models with relatively higher hallucination rates (generally above 10%) include:

- Llama 2 (Meta): 10-15%
- Mistral 7B: 10-20%
- Cohere: 29.1%
- GPT-3.5: 39.6%
- Google Gemini (Bard): 64.5%
- Older OpenAI models (e.g., o3 and o4-mini): can exceed 30% and even reach 48% in specific tests

Figure 2.2: Ranked of AI Models With the Lowest Hallucination Rates https://github.com/vectara/hallucination-leaderboard

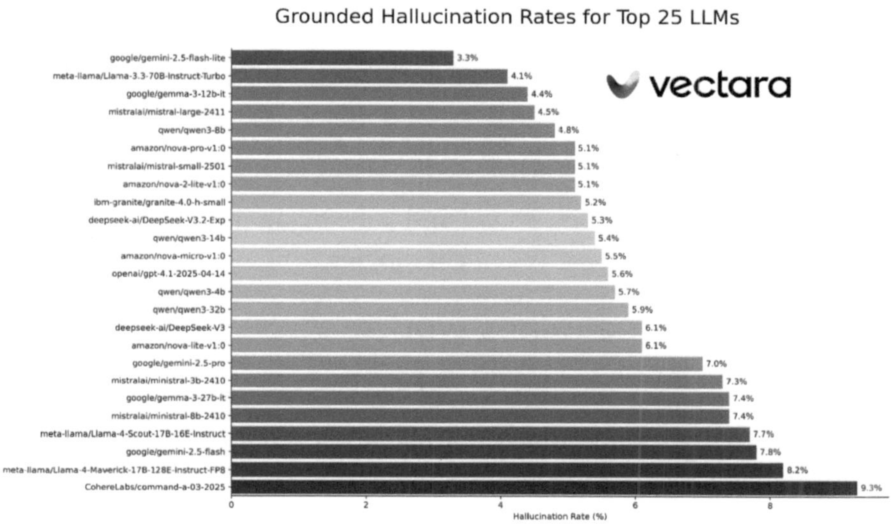

User trust is a coveted metric. There have been a few recent reports about users losing trust in AI systems. A METR report (Model Evaluation & Threat Research, 2025) found that AI coding tools actually slow developers down. The reason is that GenAI models, even the very latest ones, often get things wrong and 'hallucinate', which requires considerable human oversight to correct. According to IT consultancy Gartner (Claburn, 2025), AI agents fail to complete office tasks around 70% of the time. The amount of human oversight necessary, even for simple tasks, almost always undermines whatever productivity gains are made. So, in many cases, it is more productive not to use AI than to use it.

Reflective task 2

What is your personal stance regarding hallucinations? How do you think they should be dealt with in educational contexts in general, and your specific context in particular?

GenAI agents vs search engines

> **Reflective task 3**
> What do you think the difference is between GenAI agents and search engines, if any?

A common misconception when using GenAI agents is equating them to a web search tool, so we will start by analysing the differences between these two technologies.

How do search engines work?

Search engines follow these four steps:

Step 1: Crawling. *They crawl the web with a robot to find pages and save the new HTML code found.*

Step 2: Rendering. They process the fetched HTML code and add the page to a render queue. If the page is rendered correctly, they have a complete view of the page.

Step 3: Indexing. The rendered HTML is passed over to indexing systems, which analyse the page's content to assess whether it meets quality standards. If it does, the page is added to the index.

Step 4: Ranking. When a user conducts a search query, the search engine accesses the index to find the most relevant pages for the query and their algorithms decide in what order to rank the relevant websites, as well as adding ads and sponsored links, which are evaluated in significantly different ways. Although these algorithms also rely on AI, their function is not to create new content but to return a list of what already exists. In a traditional search, your results are based on exact matches to specific keywords.

How is GenAI different?

We have already described how GenAI works in Chapter 1, but there are some new developments that are relevant here. We have stated that GenAI tools are mostly based on LLMs, which provide a statistical model that mimics language and understanding. Going back to semantic bias and LLMs core mechanism of predicting the most likely next term, we can state that the first problem is lack of true understanding and reasoning. This stems from the way they prioritise statistical probability over logical coherence, which can be seen on generated text that sounds plausible but is factually incorrect, contradictory or nonsensical when examined closely. They don't 'know' what is true, only what sequences of words are probable. They don't have an overarching goal or long-term plan for the entire generated output. They build the text piece by piece, which can lead to rambling, repetitive or off-topic responses, especially for longer generations or complex tasks. The second problem is repetitiveness and lack of creativity as it picks the absolute most likely next **token**. While in some models you can choose to generate a more creative output, this can be more diverse, but probably less coherent and accurate. It is important to note that LLMs are not a database. They do not use words directly, but vector representations to capture meaning, relationships and context through word-embedding techniques. They do not try to organise the training documents or retain key facts.

Table 2.1: Search engines vs. Generative AI workflows (created with Claude, based on our input)

🔍 Search engine workflow	🤖 Generative AI workflow
1. **Crawling:** Web crawlers discover and scan web pages across the internet 2. **Indexing:** Content is processed, analysed and stored in massive databases 3. **Query processing:** User search terms are parsed and interpreted	1. **Input processing:** User prompt is tokenised and encoded into numerical representations 2. **Context understanding:** Model analyses input using attention mechanisms 3. **Pattern matching:** Neural networks identify relevant patterns from training data

4. **Retrieval:** Relevant documents are identified from the index	4. **Token prediction:** Model predicts next most likely tokens/words
5. **Ranking:** Results are scored using algorithms (PageRank, relevance, etc.)	5. **Generation:** Response is built iteratively, one token at a time
6. **Presentation:** Ranked results are displayed with snippets and metadata	6. **Output formatting:** Generated content is formatted and presented to user

Retrieval Augmented Generation (RAGs)

What's new is the introduction of **Retrieval Augmented Generation (RAGs)** to improve the initial limitations. RAGs supplement LLMs by retrieving information (documents, concepts) related to the user's prompt from an external knowledge base. The results are compared with the LLM's vectors and any matches are passed back to the LLM, which then combines the retrieved data, its training data and the prompt to generate a response. The introduction of RAGs, which are not used by every GenAI, can partially make up for limitations in its training data, mostly due to their knowledge cut-off date. In vector searches, the tool does not look at the phrases, instead it maps words in the prompt into a vector. This optimises the search because queries match content based on intent, not just specific words. ChatGPT Search was introduced in October 2024 to make up for being unaware of information or events after their training data cut-off date. According to Kerner (2025), ChatGPT search RAGs bring back information from additional sources, such as third-party providers and media partnerships (The Associated Press, Reuters, *Financial Times*). There are a few other GenAI agents with search functionality: JBT, Gemini, Text Cortex. However, they still have limited real-time capabilities, as opposed to Google, for example, which continuously crawls and indexes the web. There is another set of tools, generative AI search tools, like Perplexity, Bing and Brave, which are capable of understanding context, intent, and sometimes even creativity, and generate custom answers and summaries based on queries.

Different goals

We need to be clear, however, about the fact that these two technologies have different goals. A search engine's goal is to return a list of pages relevant to a search query, based on keywords. GenAI may help to find information, but their goal is to create new, unique responses related to a prompt. According to Yann LeCun, LLMs do not have 'some sort of objective other than just satisfying statistical consistency with the prompt' (Edgar, 2025). There are still several limitations when compared to a traditional web search, as mentioned by Kerner (2025): narrower information access and data scope, limited access to real-time information, lack of visual search capabilities, accuracy concerns and verification challenges. So, we can conclude that GenAI is still not a full replacement for traditional web searching.

Table 2.2: Search engines vs. Generative AI

Search engines vs generative AI 🔍		
Aspect	**Search engine**	**Generative AI**
Primary purpose	**Information retrieval** Find and rank existing content across the web based on relevance to user queries	**Content generation** Create new, original content by understanding patterns and generating responses
Core technology	**Indexing & ranking algorithms** ▪ Web crawling and indexing ▪ PageRank and relevance scoring ▪ Keyword matching and semantic search	**Neural networks & transformers** ▪ Large language models (LLMs) ▪ Deep learning architectures ▪ Attention mechanisms and pattern recognition

<table>
<tr><th>Aspect</th><th>Search engine</th><th>Generative AI</th></tr>
<tr><td>Data source</td><td>Real-time web content
Continuously crawled and indexed web pages, documents and multimedia content</td><td>Training data
Large datasets used during training phase, with knowledge cut-off dates

RAGs (available in some models) supplement LLMs by retrieving information (documents, concepts) related to the user's prompt from an external knowledge base</td></tr>
<tr><td>Query matching</td><td>Parse search query
■ Match against indexed content
■ Rank results by relevance
■ Return list of links</td><td>Pattern generation
■ Process input context
■ Apply learned patterns
■ Generate probabilistic responses
■ Produce coherent text</td></tr>
<tr><td>Output format</td><td>Ranked list of results
■ Links to external content
■ Snippets and previews
■ Related searches
■ Knowledge panels</td><td>Generated content
■ Direct answers and explanations
■ Creative content
■ Conversational responses
■ Code and structured data</td></tr>
</table>

Aspect	Search engine	Generative AI
⏱ **Information currency**	**Real-time/near real-time** Can surface the latest information as it's published online ✔ Always up to date ✔ Breaking news coverage	**Training cut-off limited** Knowledge limited to training data with specific cut-off dates ✘ Knowledge cut-off dates ✘ May lack recent information
🎨 **Creativity & synthesis**	**Limited** Primarily retrieves existing content; minimal synthesis capabilities ✘ No content creation ✘ Limited analysis	**High** Can create original content, synthesise information, and provide creative solutions ✔ Original content generation ✔ Cross-domain synthesis
🎯 **Accuracy & verification**	**Source-referenced** Provides links to original sources for verification ✔ Traceable sources ✔ Multiple perspectives	**Generated response** May hallucinate or provide confident-sounding but incorrect information ✘ Potential hallucinations ✘ Hard to verify claims

Aspect	Search engine	Generative AI
Interaction style	**Query-based** ▪ Keyword searches ▪ One-shot queries ▪ Results browsing ▪ Limited follow-up	**Conversational** ▪ Natural language dialogue ▪ Context awareness ▪ Follow-up questions ▪ Iterative refinement

(created with Claude, based on our input)

Imprecision in image generators

GenAI image generators are not immune to imprecisions. These can be aesthetic or related to representation. In Chapter 1, we showed some images in which representation from the training data makes its way to the image. The training data comes from human creations, so the model brings along all the social baggage that those humans had. As discussed, common biases are related to gender and professions, race stereotypes and diverse people with real-world bodies. Doctors are mostly men, for example. So biased images are, unfortunately, very common. Detailed prompting might improve results, but many people do not know how, or do not take the time to learn, the skill needed to generate diverse images, and they default to using the images they get. According to Koidan (2023), this default often results in a limited representation of people and can perpetuate stereotypes and biases, which 'creates a feedback loop where the resulting AI-generated content reinforces existing biases, further exacerbating the problem'.

Aesthetic imprecisions stem from GenAI image generators' lack of real-world understanding, leading to issues like:

- incorrect anatomical features (too many fingers, for example)
- incoherent compositions, including relative size of objects

- complex compositions with multiple ideas in one image, such as large crowds, dynamic poses, battle scenes
- unnatural textures or lighting
- blurred or merged elements
- misrepresentation of text (letters, words, symbols) resulting in gibberish or distorted text that is difficult to read or completely unintelligible

These limitations arise from the models' design and workings. According to Marcus (2024), image 'hallucinations come from systems exploding data into tiny bits and then reconstructing them without having a mechanism like a fact-checker to assess the coherence of those reconstructed bits'. Marcus also mentions near-plagiarism, where too many images look similar: 'Near-plagiarism comes from reconstructing those bits in statistically probable ways, without having a mechanism like an originality-assessor to investigate the novelty of the reconstruction'.

Figure 2.3: AI image generation issues

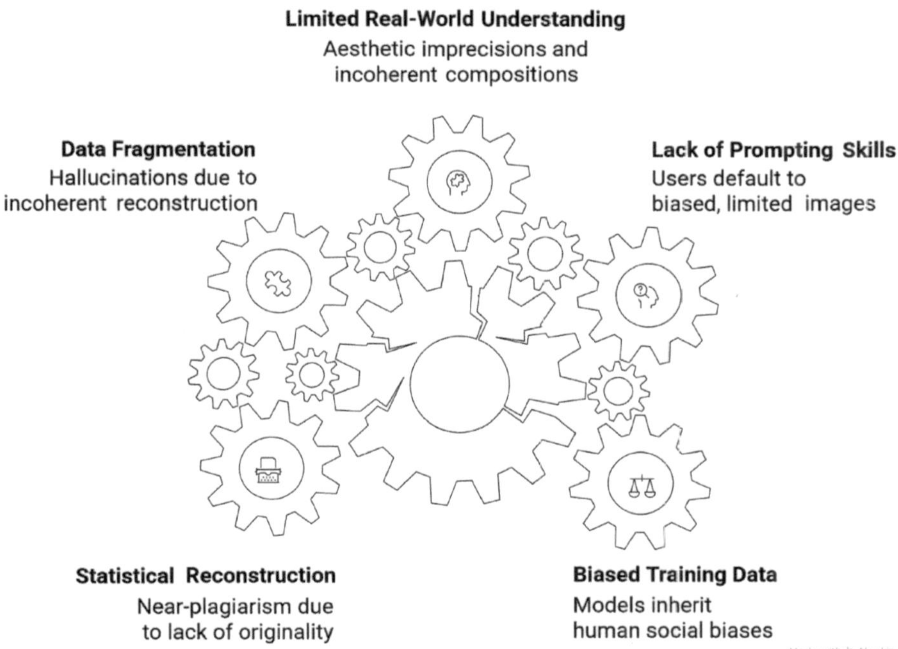

In the following examples, you can see our first experiment with AI image creators in July 2023 in the left column. These images were generated with different tools using the same basic prompt: *a dirty beach scene which shows the following: pollution, fish, turtle, birds, plastic bag, plastic bottle, litter, a reduce reuse recycle sign, with a clean spot*. We then tried the same prompt (for the sake of true comparison) in October 2025, with two of the same tools and two new ones, in the right column. You can see the stylistic differences and variations, which are common in GenAI image generators.

Figure 2.4: AI image generation examples

July 2023

1 *Picsart*

The first pair of images (1 and 2) were created with the same tool. In the earlier version, if you look closely at the people in the background, you can see they have missing body parts and the sign is also absent.

October 2025

2 *Picsart*

In the newer version, the sign was added and it is spelt correctly. The clean spot is there, but the composition looks a bit off.

3 *Gencraft*

The second pair of images (3 and 4) were also created with the same tool. In the earlier version, the fish and the turtle have been merged into a 'mutant' creature, maybe due to the pollution at the beach?

4 *Gencraft*

In the newer version, the sign has been added though the text is rendered incorrectly. And the turtle seems to be missing parts.

5 *Hotpotai*

In image 5, you can see the issue of relative size when you compare the woman, the bottle and the turtle.

6 *Craiyon AI*

In image 6, you can see some improvements, but the sign is still unreadable.

7 *Fotor*	**8 *Nano Banana (Google Gemini 2.5*)**
In image 7, the colours in the original (colour) version are almost too bright. The sign is also missing.	In image 8, with the latest model launched by Google, the sign appears and it reads correctly. But the plastic bottles look like they are merged into each other.

Reflective task 4

Why would imprecise outputs and hallucinations be relevant to ELT? Think of at least one example where this issue might influence the learning process negatively.

Why is this relevant for ELT?

One of the main issues within ELT concerns human-AI interaction challenges. One such challenge has been identified recently as **cognitive offloading**. Cognitive offloading occurs when individuals 'delegate cognitive tasks to external aids' (Loga, 2025), such as AI tools, search engines, or even notes and calculators, 'to reduce the cognitive load on [their] working memory' (Risko & Gilbert, 2016). While this can initially free up human cognitive resources, when individuals become overly dependent on AI tools for tasks like memory, decision-making and information retrieval, this can diminish critical thinking abilities, independent problem solving and 'their engagement in deep reflective thinking' (Gerlich,2025), and can lead to a decline in cognitive resilience over time. Users might blindly trust AI recommendations without questioning or evaluating them. Although this can be true for anybody, it is even more important in the case of learners, who have yet to acquire the necessary knowledge base and experience to analyse AI output critically and spot imprecisions.

Critical thinking

Regarding the impact on critical thinking, studies (Gerlich, 2025; Kosmyna *et al.*, 2025) show a significant negative correlation between frequent use of AI tools and critical thinking abilities.

Gerlich's study (2025) investigated the relationship between AI tool usage and critical thinking skills, focusing on cognitive offloading as a mediating factor. He categorised 666 participants from 17 to +55 years old into three age groups: young (17-25), middle-aged (26-45) and older (46 and more) in order to facilitate the examination of age-related differences. He provided a structured questionnaire to measure AI tool usage, cognitive offloading and critical thinking skills, and then complemented it with semi-structured interviews. The results were that, 'Younger participants (17–25) exhibited higher AI tool usage and cognitive offloading, but lower critical thinking scores. In contrast, older participants (46 and above) showed lower AI tool usage and cognitive offloading, with higher critical thinking scores.'

The MIT study by Kosmyna *et al.* (2025) provided the first neurological evidence. They sought out to find the cognitive cost of using an LLM in the educational context of writing an essay. Fifty-four participants, all college students, were assigned to one of three groups of 18 participants: an LLM group, a Search Engine group, and a Brain-only group, where, in each of the first three sessions, each participant used a designated tool (or no tool in the case of the latter group) to complete the same group assignment, an essay. In the fourth session, they asked LLM group participants to use no tools (LLM-to-Brain), and the Brain-only group participants were asked to use LLM (Brain-to-LLM). They used electroencephalography (EEG) to record their 'brain activity in order to assess their cognitive engagement and cognitive load, and to gain a deeper understanding of neural activations during the essay writing task':

> 'EEG analysis presented robust evidence that LLM, Search Engine and Brain-only groups had significantly different neural connectivity patterns, reflecting divergent cognitive strategies. Brain connectivity systematically scaled down with the amount of external support: the Brain-only group exhibited the strongest, widest-ranging networks, Search Engine group showed intermediate engagement, and LLM assistance elicited the weakest overall coupling. In session 4, LLM-to-Brain participants showed weaker neural connectivity and under-engagement of alpha and beta networks; and the Brain-to-LLM participants demonstrated higher memory recall, and re-engagement of widespread occipito-parietal and prefrontal nodes, likely supporting the visual processing, similar to the one frequently perceived in the Search Engine group. The reported ownership of LLM group's essays in the interviews was low. The Search Engine group had strong ownership, but lesser than the Brain-only group. The LLM group also fell behind in their ability to quote from the essays they wrote just minutes prior.'

Relying heavily on AI for analysis can undermine the development of human analytical skills, leading to a superficial understanding of information and reduced capacity for critical analysis. By offering quick solutions and ready-made information, AI tools can discourage users from engaging in the active cognitive processes essential for critical thinking, such as analysing, evaluating and synthesising information to make reasoned decisions. AI tools can also inadvertently reinforce biases by recommending content that aligns with existing beliefs, creating **echo chambers**. This algorithmic bias hinders critical evaluation by limiting exposure to diverse perspectives and reducing critical scrutiny of information. The opaqueness of AI processes ('black box' problem) often leads users to accept AI-generated conclusions without scrutiny, diminishing critical engagement and accountability. Learners may blindly trust AI recommendations without questioning or evaluating them.

Memory and retention

The availability of information at one's fingertips through tools like search engines and AI can reduce the need for internal memory retention. This is called the Google effect (Sparrow *et al.*, 2011). This is not a new phenomenon or unique to AI, but is due to the 24/7 availability of information on the internet. Individuals are more likely to remember where to find information rather than the information itself, diminishing the brain's tendency to internally store and connect knowledge. Although this might be useful for some things and facts, it should not be relied on for everything. This offloading can lead to shallow encoding of information, where content is not deeply integrated into episodic memory networks, impairing the ability to recall or correctly quote or use previously accessed material, which is the basis of meaningful learning. The LLM group in Kosmyna's study (2025) showed significantly reduced low-frequency neural connectivity, associated with memory consolidation and semantic encoding, compared to those who didn't use AI.

Problem solving and creativity

As for the impact on problem solving and creativity, over-reliance on AI for problem solving can lead people to become less proficient in developing and applying their own problem-solving strategies, thus reducing cognitive flexibility and creativity. Generative AI can promote **cognitive laziness,** where students offload cognitive and metacognitive responsibilities to the AI, hindering their ability to self-regulate and engage deeply. This can lead to an accumulation of **cognitive debt**, where avoiding short-term mental effort results in long-term costs like diminished critical inquiry and decreased creativity. As learners increasingly depend on GenAI, their work may become impersonal, lacking individual authenticity or a personal touch.

Overusing AI in creative domains can lead to formulaic writing and limit imagination, creativity and alternative perspectives. The use of GenAI can be characterised as 'writing without thinking', potentially affecting skill acquisition. We teachers know that writing is thinking. Lo (2025) describes it as the soulless revolution. Referring to the MIT study by Kosmyna *et al.* (2025), he states that 'while unassisted writers produced essays with wild variability in approach and perspective, the ChatGPT group generated statistically homogeneous content', which was described by the evaluators as 'soulless, grammatically perfect but lacking genuine insight'.

Figure 2.5: Impact of AI on cognitive skills

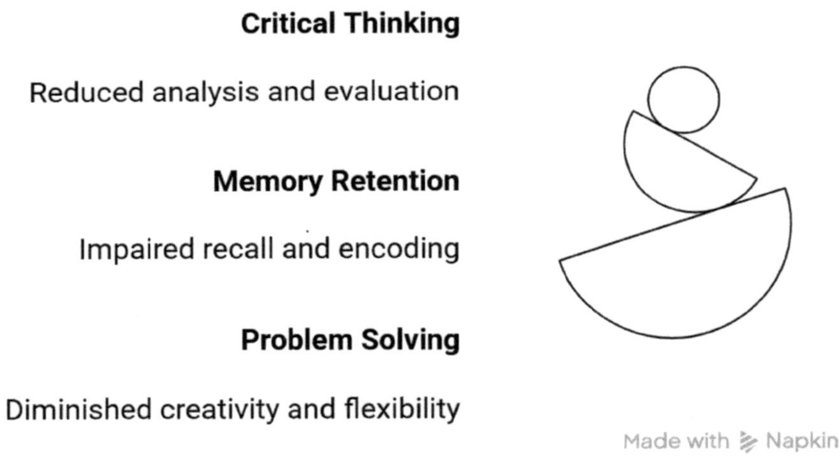

Educational implications

There is neural evidence to support concerns about cognitive offloading. The Brain-only group in Kosmyna's study (2025) exhibited significantly stronger neural connectivity across all frequency bands, indicating greater engagement in internal brainstorming, semantic retrieval, executive functions and motor planning, compared to AI-assisted groups. AI-assisted writing (LLM group) elicited generally lower connectivity, suggesting that some human thinking and planning was offloaded. We need to address this trade-off and evaluate its worth. While AI tools can personalise learning, enhance engagement and improve basic skill acquisition, they may not foster the deep analytical thinking required for applying skills in novel or complex situations.

Educators must balance AI usage with activities that promote critical thinking and cognitive engagement. Strategies should encourage students to engage deeply with content rather than passively relying on AI-provided solutions. Repeated unassisted practice strengthens brain networks associated with planning, language and attentional control. Outsourcing most of our brain capacity might have unwanted consequences later on. Early age AI use, as demonstrated in Gerlich's study (2025), can modulate this trajectory, potentially limiting this integration and leading to a less coordinated neural effort when the AI is removed. Delaying AI integration until learners have engaged in sufficient self-driven cognitive effort may therefore promote both immediate tool efficacy and lasting cognitive autonomy. Hybrid strategies, where AI handles routine aspects of a task but core cognitive processes remain user-driven, are advisable. But this needs to be carefully planned in the curricula.

It seems clear that over-reliance on AI models has a direct impact on learning. Biased materials generated by GenAI are increasingly spreading across the internet, 'polluting' a useful source of knowledge for learners. This poses significant risks, especially for young learners without solid prior knowledge, and creates a recursive risk for future AI models trained on previously generated, flawed content, which might eventually lead to **model collapse**, the decline in performance of generative models as they become increasingly biased, homogeneous and inaccurate. Model collapse can lead to less useful AI systems, potentially impacting the reliability and creativity of AI-generated content.

While GenAI is superficially easy to use, getting precise, desired outputs can take multiple iterations of careful **prompt engineering**. Inexperienced users, especially young learners, might unknowingly accept superficial or inaccurate outputs.

So cognitive offloading, particularly to AI, is highly relevant for learning because, over time, it fundamentally alters how individuals engage with information, potentially leading to a decline in their capacity for independent thought, critical analysis and deep knowledge internalisation.

Figure 2.6: Educational implications

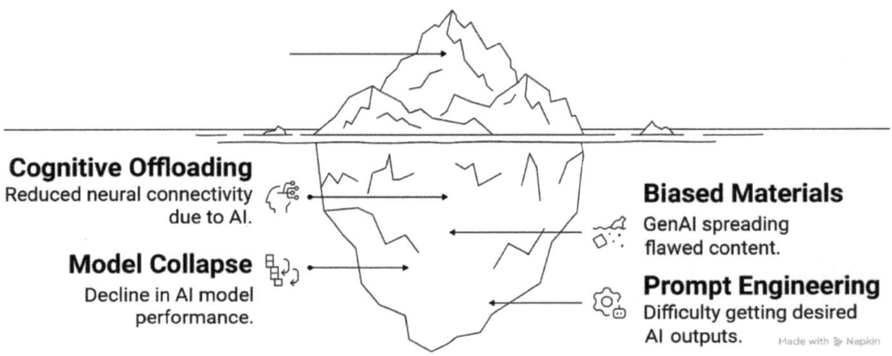

Reflective task 5

How can imprecisions and cognitive offloading be dealt with in your specific context? Make a list of three to five ideas or strategies.

Chapter 2 Key Points

1. **Hallucinations are persistent features, not bugs.** AI "hallucinations" occur when models fabricate information, such as invented facts, citations, or biographies, while maintaining a fluent and coherent tone. This happens because models prioritise statistical probability over logical coherence or truth.

---

2. **Newer models may be less accurate.** Contrary to the assumption that technology always improves accuracy, newer reasoning models may actually hallucinate *more*.

---

3. **Fundamental difference from search engines.** A common misconception is equating GenAI with search engines. Search engines work by crawling, indexing, and ranking existing web pages to retrieve relevant links. In contrast, GenAI uses neural networks to generate new, unique content based on pattern matching and token prediction. It does not "know" what is true, only what is probable.

---

4. **Retrieval Augmented Generation (RAG) improves, but does not cure.** To combat inaccuracy, some systems use RAG, which allows the LLM to fetch external data (like a search engine) to supplement its response. While this reduces hallucinations and helps with current events (overcoming training data cut-offs), it does not eliminate errors entirely.

---

5. **Imprecision in image generation.** AI image generators suffer from both aesthetic and representational imprecisions.

---

6. **Cognitive offloading and cognitive debt.** "Cognitive offloading", where learners delegate mental tasks (like memory or decision-making) to AI, is highlighted as a major risk. While this frees up immediate resources, habitual reliance creates "cognitive debt," where avoiding short-term mental effort leads to long-term deficits in critical inquiry, creativity, and the ability to think deeply.

---

7. **The "Google Effect" on memory.** The availability of instant information leads to the "Google effect," where individuals remember *where* to find information rather than the information itself. In education, this offloading leads to shallow encoding, meaning content is not integrated into long-term memory, which impairs the ability to recall or synthesise knowledge later.

8. **Neurological evidence of reduced engagement.** Some studies provided neurological evidence that using LLMs reduces brain activity.

9. **The threat of homogenised, "soulless" output.** While AI-generated essays may be grammatically perfect, they tend to be statistically homogeneous and lack genuine insight or variability in perspective.

Further reading

Gerlich, M. (2025). AI tools in society: Impacts on cognitive offloading and the future of critical thinking. *Societies*, *15*(1). https://doi.org/10.3390/soc15010006

Kosmyna, N., Hauptmann, E., Yuan, Y. T., Situ, J., Liao, X.-H., Beresnitzky, A. V., Braunstein, I., and Maes, P. (2025). *Your Brain on ChatGPT: Accumulation of cognitive debt when using an AI assistant for essay writing task*. Retrieved from http://arxiv.org/abs/2506.08872

Chapter 3: Environmental impact

In this chapter, we analyse the extensive environmental impact of AI, including energy consumption, water consumption, carbon dioxide emissions, e-waste and resource extraction.

Reflective task 1

Is information about the environmental impact of AI at the forefront of AI-related news? Is it readily and transparently available when you look for it? Why might that be?

While GenAI can be considered an agent of change for sustainable education, it also presents a number of significant environmental challenges that need to be considered. It therefore requires a balanced approach that harnesses the benefits and possibilities that come with GenAI, while also trying to minimise environmental and ethical downsides.

The facts and figures related to GenAI's environmental impact cannot be ignored. The carbon footprint of GenAI training and prompting is considerable, both in terms of the electricity and water resources needed to run and cool down the servers used for their operation. In addition to water and energy consumption, **data centres** also produce large carbon emissions and generate e-waste at a worrying rate. A further concern is centred around the issues associated with resource extraction of rare metals and rare earth elements. These aspects of GenAI are definitely at odds with efforts to achieve a more sustainable and carbon-neutral society. However, when we speak about data centres, it is worth noting that they handle the vast transfer of all data through the internet, and are involved in everything we do digitally. Common online activities like streaming high-quality video, making Zoom calls, uploading files to the cloud, browsing social media, using GPS navigation or streaming music are also putting a strain on the data centres' energy and water use (Masley, 2025). It is not in the remit of this book to explore all of this in depth, but we should be aware of the impact of all our online activities and hopefully make lifestyle changes accordingly. Masley states 'what matters when considering what to reduce is the energy used compared to the amount of value produced'. What is alarming about GenAI is the scale of use and rate of growth compared to these other activities.

Figure 3.1: Environmental impact of AI

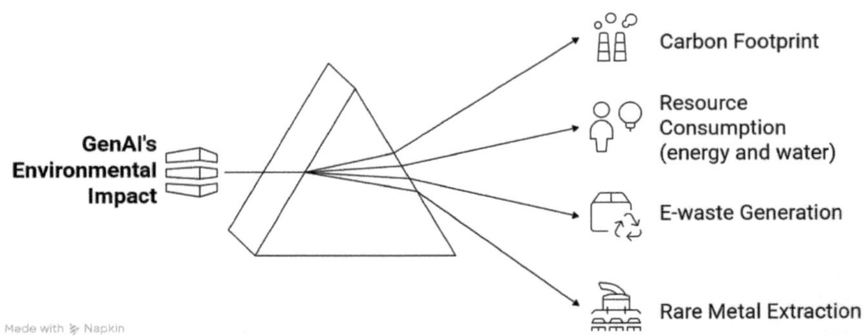

Energy consumption

Generative AI operations involve two energy-intensive phases: the **training phase** (where the model learns from data), and the **inference phase** (where it generates new content based on training and user input). Training and running large GenAI models require massive computational power. While the training phase is energy intensive, the usage (inference) phase also contributes significantly. According to Luccioni *et al.* (2024), inference is estimated to account for 80-90% of total machine learning (ML) cloud computing demand. Google reported that 60% of its ML energy use was for inference, compared to 40% for training. Similarly, Meta attributed about one-third of its end-to-end ML carbon footprint to inference. The majority of energy used by GenAI is attributed to the data centres needed to run these complex models. Data centres already consume approximately 1-1.5% of global electricity use (AI for Education, 2023), and the rapid growth of AI is expected to significantly increase this percentage. Ligozat *et al.* (2024) are slightly more conservative, estimating that the 1.5% figure may not be reached until 2029, but whichever figures are correct, it is clear that this demand is significant: for comparison, this is around ten times more than traditional search queries. The International Energy Agency predicts that AI data centre energy consumption could double by 2026, and quadruple by 2030 (IEA, 2025). The worldwide surge in AI technology is expected to consume nearly as much energy by the end of this decade as Japan, but only around half of that demand is likely to be fulfilled by renewable energy sources (IEA, 2025).

High-performance **Graphic Processing Units** (GPUs), often used for AI processing, are particularly energy intensive, contributing significantly to the overall power consumption. Historically, data centres relied mainly on **Central Processing Units** (CPUs), which ran at roughly 150 watts to 200 watts per chip. GPUs for AI ran at 400 watts until 2022, but in 2023, state-of-the-art GPUs for GenAI ran at 700 watts, and 2024 next-generation chips are expected to run at 1,200 watts (Ramachandran *et al.*, 2024).

Studies (Calvert, 2024) indicate that training a model like ChatGPT could consume around 1,300 megawatt hours of electricity, equivalent to the annual power consumption of 130 average US homes. According to Périssère (2025), 'the electricity consumption from training GPT-4 may be approximately 40 to 48 times higher than that required to train GPT-3'. Predictions suggest that by 2027, NVIDIA could release 1.5 million AI server units annually, potentially using over 85.4 terawatt-hours (TWh) of electricity each year (AI for Education, 2023). This amount is greater than the annual electricity consumption of many small countries. If Google's nine billion searches per day were AI agent queries, they would require as much power as it is needed to run an entire country like Ireland (AI for Education, 2023). The number of data centres has spiked from 500,000 in 2012 to eight million in 2024 (UNEP, 2024). It is reported that concern about the pressure data centres exert on electricity grids, in addition to the impact on national climate targets, have brought a complete halt to the building of new ones in some countries (Périssère, 2025). For example, Ireland's state-owned electric power transmission operator EirGrid has confirmed that it will not connect new data centres in Dublin for 'the foreseeable future' and possibly until 2028, as the greater Dublin area is under grid pressure and any new data centre applications will only be considered for other parts of the country on a 'case-by-case basis'. They estimate that 'data centres will account for 28% of the country's power use by 2031' (Périssère, 2025).

Generating an image is even more energy intensive as it can use as much power as fully charging your smartphone. Luccioni *et al.* (2024) report that charging an average smartphone requires about 0.022 kWh of energy. The most efficient text generation model for 1,000 inferences uses about 9% of a smartphone's charge, while the least efficient image generation model uses energy equivalent to 522 smartphone charges (11.49 kWh) for 1,000 inferences, or roughly half a charge per image generation.

Factors influencing energy consumption:

- Model size: Larger and more complex GenAI models generally require more energy to train and operate.
- Usage frequency: The number of times a model is used directly impacts its energy consumption.
- Hardware efficiency: Advances in chip design can improve energy efficiency of AI models.

Potential mitigation strategies:

- Optimising models: Researchers are working on developing more efficient AI architectures to reduce energy consumption.
- Renewable energy sources: Powering data centres with renewable energy can help offset the environmental impact of AI.
- Responsible usage: Promoting a mindful use of GenAI models can help reduce unnecessary energy usage.

Carbon dioxide emissions

Carbon emissions are closely linked to energy consumption. According to research, training a single large GenAI model like GPT-3 is estimated to have consumed around 1,287 Megawatt hours (MWh) of electricity, resulting in approximately 552 tonnes of carbon dioxide emissions, roughly equivalent to the emissions from 110 petrol-powered cars over a year, or the lifetime emissions of five average passenger cars (Saenko *et al.*, 2023). Google, on the other hand, estimated that GPT-3's carbon footprint is about 8.4 tonnes of CO2 per year (Net Zero Business, 2024). The environmental impact of newer and bigger models is even more substantial. The carbon intensity of AI training can vary depending on the electricity grid where the data centre is located. According to Périssère (2025), 'the initial training phase of GPT-4 would have emitted between 1,200 and 15,000 tonnes of CO_2, depending on whether the model was trained in a data centre in Canada East (the lowest carbon Azure region thanks to its predominantly hydroelectric grid) or on grid electricity in California, where natural gas still makes up a significant portion of the energy mix'.

The energy consumed by the world's data centres accounts for 2.5% to 3.7% of global greenhouse gas (GHG) emissions, more than the aviation industry, which accounts for around 2.5% of global carbon dioxide emissions (Lavi, 2023). This percentage has remained relatively stable since 1992. By 2030, data centres are predicted to emit triple the amount of CO2 annually. The amount of GHG emissions predicted – 2.5 billion tonnes – equates to roughly 40% of the US's current annual emissions (Franklin, 2024). However, according to an analysis from *The Guardian*, real emissions from the data centres of companies that are pioneering AI, like Meta, could be 7.62 times higher (or 662%) than reported due to creative accounting (O'Brien, 2024).

The carbon footprint of a GenAI prompt is four to five times higher than a search engine query. The equivalent of each query was estimated at 4.32g of CO2. A Google search is 0.2g per query (Net Zero Business, 2024). According to this calculator, 16 queries equals the emissions generated by boiling a kettle. If each unique visit results in an average of ten queries, that's 15 trillion queries per month. However, Google has recently implemented AI overviews powered by their GenAI model Gemini, which cannot be turned off. Google states in their help pages that 'AI Overviews are part of Google Search like other features, such as knowledge panels, and can't be turned off'. A single Google search with AI integrated in it will consume ten times more energy (3 KWh) than the traditional Google search (Kerr, 2024). There's a complex way of managing to not see it, but the operation is still carried on in the background, so you would not be avoiding the impact. A second workaround is to use another web browser other than Chrome, like Safari or Firefox. But this only works on your computer, not on mobile.

Image generation is again the most damaging task. Producing 1,000 images with Stable Diffusion XL is responsible for as much CO2 as driving 4.1 miles in a car (AI for Education, 2023). According to the study by Luccioni *et al.* (2024), the most carbon-intensive image generation model (stable-diffusion-xl-base-1.0) generates 1,594g of CO2 for 1,000 inferences. In contrast, the least carbon-intensive text generation model (distilbert-base-uncased) generates carbon equivalent to 0.0006 miles driven, or 6,833 times less.

It is important to point out that model size matters. Larger AI models with more parameters generally have a larger carbon footprint.

Factors contributing to high emissions:

- Hardware production: The manufacturing process of specialised chips needed for AI training can be energy intensive and generate significant emissions.
- Data centre cooling: Maintaining optimal temperatures in data centres requires significant energy consumption.
- Power grid reliance on fossil fuels: If the electricity powering the data centres comes from fossil fuels, it contributes to higher carbon emissions.

Potential mitigation strategies:

- Improving energy efficiency: Developing more efficient AI algorithms and hardware.
- Renewable energy sources: Using renewable energy sources to power data centres.
- Model optimisation: Reducing the size of AI models while maintaining performance.
- Carbon offsetting: Investing in carbon credits to offset emissions from AI operations.

Water consumption

According to recent studies, GenAI, particularly LLMs like ChatGPT, consume a significant amount of water due to the energy needed to power the data centres that are used to train and run them, with estimates suggesting that AI could be using between 4.2 and 6.6 billion cubic metres of water annually by 2027, equivalent to the water consumption of a country like Denmark (Ren, 2023).

This water is primarily used for cooling, with up to nine litres of water potentially being used per kWh of energy consumed (Ren, 2023). Data centres' server rooms must be kept cool, typically between 10-27°C, to prevent equipment malfunctioning. Data centres must use clean freshwater sources to manage the heat generated by processing large amounts of data. and to avoid the corrosion and bacteria growth associated with seawater. Freshwater is necessary to avoid the corrosion and bacteria growth associated with seawater, and for humidity control.

O'Brien and Fingerhut (2023) report that Microsoft's global water consumption spiked by 34% from 2021 to 2022 to nearly 1.7 billion gallons, or more than 2,500 Olympic-sized swimming pools. This sharp increase seems to be tied to Microsoft's AI research, including its heavy investment in generative AI and partnership with OpenAI. Google reported a 20% growth in water use during the same period (2021-2022), also largely attributed to its AI work.

ChatGPT-3 training can use as much water as producing 370 BMWs or 320 Teslas (McLean, 2023). ChatGPT prompting gulps up 500 millilitres of water (a 16-ounce water bottle) for a series of between five to 50 prompts or questions (McLean, 2023). In July 2022, Microsoft pumped about 11.5 million gallons of water to its Iowa data centres for training GPT-4, which accounted for approximately 6% of all water used in that district (O'Brien & Fingerhut, 2023). Generating a simple meme or image via ChatGPT could consume between two to five litres of water (Périssère, 2025).

Data centres located in regions with limited water resources can put additional strain on local water supplies. Google's data centres in The Dalles, Oregon, consume more than a quarter of all the water used in the city (Rogoway, 2023). According to O'Brien and Fingerhut (2023), some districts are taking measures to limit future data centre projects until the implementation of technology that significantly reduces peak water usage to preserve the water supply for residential and other commercial needs. In addition, the environmental impact of wastewater produced by these cooling processes, which often contains chemicals or pollutants, adds another layer of concern (Périssère, 2025).

As AI usage increases, so does its water footprint, raising concerns about the sustainability of this technology in the face of global water scarcity.

Potential mitigation strategies:

- Data centre location: Choosing locations with abundant water resources can mitigate the impact on local water supplies.
- Water efficiency technologies: Implementing advanced cooling technologies and water recycling systems in data centres can help reduce water consumption.
- Transparency and reporting: Tech companies are increasingly being called upon to be transparent about their water usage and take steps to minimise their environmental impact.

E-waste and resource extraction

GenAI operation requires more hardware than many other types of computing, in particular, high-performance hardware such as GPUs, which were mentioned earlier, and other specialised processors. And GenAI cycles through that hardware faster, meaning the replacement cycle is also more intensive than in other types of computing. So more e-waste, which often contains hazardous substances, like mercury and lead, is also a byproduct of GenAI. An added concern is the fact that some of the materials used in GPUs, or elsewhere in data centres, are non-recyclable, which exacerbates environmental pollution and waste-management challenges. Although this isn't an issue unique to AI, the advancement and scale of AI technologies and services are likely to intensify the problem.

According to a study published in Nature Computational Science (Wang *et al.*, 2024), Gen AI, particularly LLMs, could potentially generate between 1.2 and 5 million metric tonnes of e-waste by 2030

(Ren, 2024), representing a significant increase in e-waste due to the growing demand for powerful computing hardware needed to run these AI models. This could equate to up to 2.5 million tonnes of e-waste annually if no waste-reduction measures are implemented.

Going back to the GPUs and other specialised processors, these chips rely on a variety of rare metals, like tantalum and cobalt, as well as critical raw materials for their manufacture, including rare earth elements (REE) like neodymium, dysprosium, terbium and others. The global REE supply chain includes production and processing. The extraction and processing of REE also have significant environmental costs. Mining operations are often concentrated in a few regions, particularly in China (60%), but also Vietnam, Brazil and Russia. According to Périssère (2025), the extraction process typically involves open-pit mining, chemical separation and radioactive waste generation, leading to soil and water contamination, deforestation and greenhouse gas emissions. The extraction process is also associated with exploitative forms of labour.

Potential mitigation strategies:

- Extending the lifespan of hardware.
- Improved recycling practices.
- Designing more energy-efficient AI chips to reduce e-waste generation.

Reflective task 2

What are the long-term consequences for resource availability if AI usage continues to grow at its current rate?

Despite ambitious long-term climate pledges, the carbon emissions of major firms, which have adopted AI fully, have increased drastically. Amazon's emissions surged by 6% in 2024 vs. 2023 due to the embedding of AI into its operations, including data centre expansion (Amazon, 2025). Because of the impact of generative AI, 42% of executives are having to re-examine their previously set climate goals (Capgemini Research Institute, 2024).

If or when we hear about the environmental impact, it is mostly about the energy and water used during training and operation. The full lifecycle impacts of GenAI must be scrutinised and assessed, 'from design and development to deployment, maintenance, decommissioning, recycling, and disposal' (Hosseini *et al.*, 2025). And even though there are recent initiatives that move us towards more sustainable AI, they often prioritise environmental metrics related to the total amount of carbon emissions and water consumption without considering the concept of **environmental equity**, the idea that 'AI's environmental costs be equitably distributed across different regions and communities' (Ren *et al.*, 2024). Ren explains how different regions and communities are affected by AI's environmental impacts, particularly burdening those who are vulnerable to it, for example disparity in the local consumption of fossil fuels and the resulting air pollution, or the water consumption rate in drought-stricken regions. One strategy that could rebalance this issue is **geographical load balancing**, where AI traffic, including AI training tasks and certain inference requests, are spatially rerouted. This is 'a dynamic redistribution of AI computing across geographically distributed data centres, considering real-time local factors such as the proportion of fossil-based energy sources and water efficiency'. A redistribution of AI's environmental costs could lead to their more equitable distribution. If we are to see any progress, it will take collective action to innovate and mitigate.

Reflective task 3

Based on the issues described in this chapter, what mitigation strategies mentioned are actions that individuals can take? To what extent do educators have a responsibility to promote action in this regard? And which are actionable strategies at an educational level?

Why is this relevant for ELT?

Reflective task 4

Why would the environmental impact of GenAI be relevant to ELT? Think of at least one example where this issue might influence the learning process negatively.

The environmental impact of GenAI is highly relevant to ELT contexts due to its inclusion in critical AI literacy frameworks, its direct connections to cross-curricular topics in EFL, ESL and ESOL education, and the overarching ethical responsibilities of educators.

Using sustainability education as a starting point, and the inclusion of the UN Sustainable Development Goals in many resources for English learners, it seems only natural that the environmental impact of GenAI should be addressed in classrooms. Failure to do so would seem hypocritical, to say the least.

AI literacy is an essential skill for all students, including English language learners. A comprehensive understanding of AI includes becoming aware of and managing the ethical, social and practical dimensions of AI, which explicitly encompasses its environmental impact. Learners should understand both the opportunities and risks that AI presents in order to make meaningful, ethical decisions about its use. They must learn to critically evaluate the societal and environmental impacts of AI rather than passively accepting AI-generated content or practices. This critical evaluation is a foundational component of AI literacy, ensuring learners question not only what AI *can* do, but also what it *should* do and whom it serves. We will look into AI literacy frameworks and tasks in detail in Chapter 8.

Reflective task 5

How easy or difficult do you think it will be to include AI literacy tasks in the classroom?

One of the top reasons people want to learn English is because it is considered the language of international communication. Linguists might learn or study English for different reasons, but most people need to be able to communicate in English. So, if English is the means of communication, we need to communicate about something. We can easily see that **cross-curricular topics** are at the heart of the English classroom: culture, geography, history, science, art, etc. Therefore, including topics of current relevance, like AI, environmental issues and sustainability, makes sense. ELT contexts can and should therefore provide a platform for discussing and analysing significant global issues related to AI.

As main actors in educational systems, English language teachers need to be able to make ethical and effective use of AI in their teaching, as well as teaching their students about AI. This responsibility extends to understanding AI's environmental implications when selecting and implementing AI tools in order to make informed decisions.

Figure 3.2: Educational implications

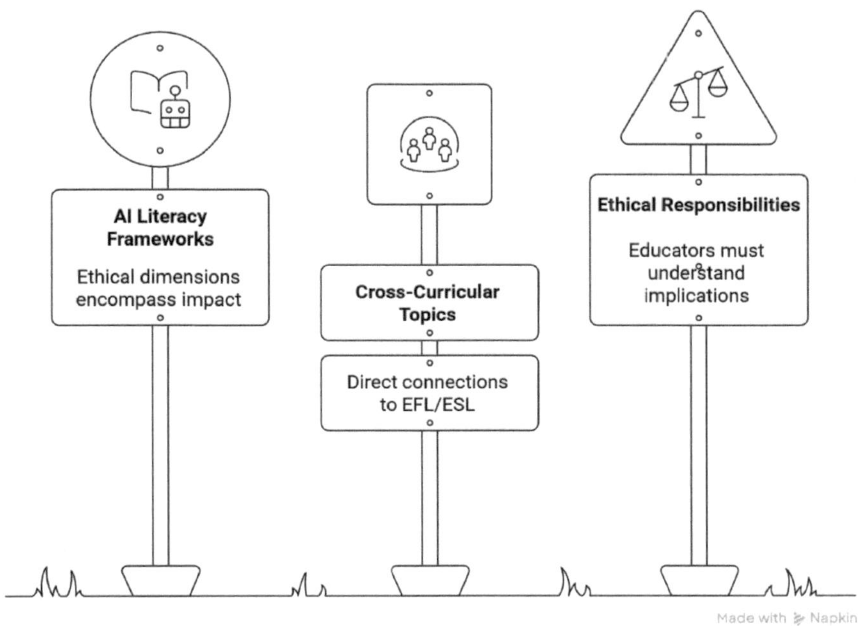

Reflective task 6

What specific information would help you to make informed decisions? How can students be made aware of this?

There are other practical reasons for dealing with the environmental impact of GenAI. We have explained the data on energy, carbon emissions, water consumption, e-waste and rare elements extraction and production issues. When we addressed energy consumption, we distinguished between the training and inference phases but we did not distinguish between different GenAI tasks.

Tasks according to energy consumption

Luccioni *et al.* (2024) mention a study comparing 88 models across ten tasks, which found significant variability in energy consumption for inference. From less to more energy/intensive, this is the ranking of tasks:

Table 3.1: Ranking of tasks according to energy consumption (based on Luccioni *et al.*, 2024)

	Text classification	0.002 kWh per 1,000 inferences
	Image classification	0.007 kWh per 1,000 inferences
	Generative tasks (like text generation and summarisation)	around 0.05 kWh per 1,000 inferences
	Multimodal tasks (like image captioning)	from 0.06 to 2.9 kWh per 1,000 inferences
	Image generation	2.9 kWh per 1,000 inferences

Text and image classification are the two least intensive tasks. Generative tasks like text generation and summarisation use over ten times the energy than classification tasks but significantly less energy than AI-generated images. Using the most efficient text-generation model studied, creating text 1,000 times can use as much energy as 9% of a full smartphone charge, but the least carbon-intensive text-generation model generates 6,833 times less carbon, equivalent to 0.0006 miles driven by an average gasoline-powered passenger vehicle (Luccioni *et al.*, 2024). Queries that ask GenAI agents to think logically and to reason require more energy than other types of straightforward questions. For example, queries asking about philosophy or abstract algebra create more carbon emissions than simple questions like the well-understood history of a given topic. Some complex prompts can lead to 50 times the carbon emissions than others (Dauner *et al.*, 2025).

Image generation is the most intensive task: 2.9 kWh per 1,000 inferences (1,450 times more energy intensive than text classification), but there is a large variation between image generation models. A single AI image generated using the least efficient model can use as much energy as half a smartphone charge. The most carbon-intensive image generation model generates for 1,000 inferences the amount of carbon equivalent to driving 4.1 miles in an average gasoline-powered car (Luccioni *et al.*, 2024).

Another important consideration is model complexity and efficiency. The design and complexity of an AI model directly affect its energy consumption, with more complex models generally requiring more computational resources and thus more energy (AI for Education, 2023). Multi-purpose generative models, like ChatGPT, Gemini or Copilot, generally consume more energy during inference than task-specific systems. According to Luccioni *et al.* (2024), for discriminative tasks like sentiment analysis and question answering, efficient task-specific models emit significantly less carbon (e.g., 0.3g CO_2 per 1,000 inferences) compared to multi-purpose models (e.g., 10g for the same task). For text classification, the difference is even more stark.

Tasks according to water consumption

As mentioned earlier, water consumption is a key issue, and data centres consume freshwater directly for cooling and indirectly for electricity generation. The current data about the water consumption of AI primarily focuses on the volume of water consumed during the inference stage of LLMs and the associated Water Usage Effectiveness (WUE) metrics and Power Usage Effectiveness (PUE) (The GreenGrid, 2011) within data centres that power AI. According to The Green Grid, the WUE metric (combined with the PUE and carbon usage effectiveness metrics) enables data centre operators to quickly assess the water, energy and carbon sustainability aspects of their data centres, compare the results, and determine if any energy efficiency and/or sustainability improvements need to be made. The units of WUE are litres/kilowatt-hour (L/kWh). The lower the value, the less water used. The Green Grid developed two metrics, WUE and WUE source.

WUE is a site-based metric that assesses the water used on-site for operation of the data centre. This includes water used for de-humidification and water evaporated on-site for energy production or to cool the data centre and its support systems.

WUE source is a source-based metric that includes water used on-site and water used off-site in the production of the energy used on-site.

Some available data is as follows:

- Amazon Web Services (AWS) achieved a WUE of 0.15 L/kWh in 2024 for its data centres, representing a 17% improvement from 2023. This result was achieved through optimised data centre designs, purpose-built chips and innovative cooling technologies. AWS also reported a global PUE of 1.15 in 2024, which is better than the estimated public cloud industry average of 1.25.
- The overall US average on-site WUE for efficient hyperscale data centres, such as those operated by Microsoft, is reported to be 0.55 L/kWh.

According to a study by Shumba *et al.* (2025), the amount of water consumed depends significantly on the model used and the complexity of the task:

Table 3.2: Difference between water consumption depending on model used (based on Shumba *et al.*, 2025)

Task	Model	Estimated water consumption	Model	Estimated water consumption
Writing a medium-length email (estimated 120-200 words or 250 tokens)	Llama-3-70B	About **0.13 litres** of water	GPT-4	About **3 litres** of water
Writing a 10-page report (estimated 5,000 tokens)	Llama-3-70B	About **0.7 litres** of water	GPT-4	Up to about **60 litres** of water

These estimates include both on-site water use (for cooling the facility) and off-site water use (indirect water consumption for electricity generation).

We have already mentioned that asking between five and 50 questions on ChatGPT is equivalent to consuming half a litre of water. Data from Ren *et al.* (2023) and the US Census Bureau provide other useful comparisons:

- One hamburger requires about 660 gallons of water, equivalent to nearly 200,000 ChatGPT queries.

- One hour of TV in a US household uses about four gallons of water, the same as 1,200 ChatGPT queries.
- Leaking pipes in the US waste over 10,500 million gallons of water per day, while ChatGPT's estimated global daily water consumption is about 3,500 million gallons.

So, although there is significantly less available data about it, using the same ranking of tasks according to energy consumption presented earlier would still be a good reference for water consumption.

Major players like Microsoft, Google and OpenAI have publicly committed to sustainability goals, including becoming 'water positive' by 2030, meaning they will replenish more water than they consume. But how realistic are these targets, and are there already working examples of AI companies successfully reducing water usage?

Reflective task 7

How can you make practical use of this ranking of tasks and their impact?

From an educator's point of view, we need to address trade-offs. i.e. weighing the benefits of GenAI in various fields against its energy consumption and environmental footprint, in this case, so that we can decide when it makes sense to use GenAI. In particular, which tasks are relevant for actual learning and which might be fillers, and which tools and models are better for the actual tasks at hand.

Reflective task 8

Which trade-offs are you willing to accept? Which GenAI tasks would you consider useful for the language learning process? Make a ranked list of GenAI tasks according to their usefulness to your specific context.

Understanding AI's environmental impact is not an isolated technical concern but a multifaceted educational imperative that directly integrates into the goals and practices of English language teaching.

Chapter 3 Key Points

1. **Inference consumes more energy than training.** While the training phase of AI models is known to be energy-intensive, the "inference" phase (actual daily usage by the public) is significantly more demanding.

2. **GenAI vs. traditional search.** GenAI queries are far more resource-heavy than standard web searches.

3. **Image generation is the most costly task.** Generating images is drastically more energy-intensive than generating text.

4. **Significant water consumption for cooling.** Data centers require massive amounts of fresh water to cool servers and prevent overheating.

5. **Model size and task appropriateness.** There is a massive disparity in resource consumption based on the model used. This highlights the wastefulness of using powerful "multi-purpose" models for simple tasks.

6. **Cognitive complexity increases emissions** Not all text prompts are equal. Queries that require the AI to "think" logically, reason, or discuss abstract concepts require more energy and produce more carbon emissions than simple factual retrieval tasks.

7. **The E-waste and hardware crisis.** GenAI drives a rapid turnover of high-performance hardware, specifically GPUs, leading to increased electronic waste.

8. **Environmental inequity.** The benefits and costs of AI are not shared equally. There is a concern that while some regions benefit from AI services, others, often vulnerable communities, bear the brunt of water shortages, pollution from fossil-fuel-powered data centers, and resource extraction.

9. **Redefining AI literacy.** AI literacy in English Language Teaching must extend beyond technical skills to include ethical evaluation. Educators have a responsibility to teach students to question not just *what* AI can do, but *what it should do* and at what environmental cost.

---

10. **Assessment of trade-offs** Educators are urged to perform a "cost-benefit analysis" or trade-off assessment. Teachers should decide which learning tasks justify the environmental cost of using GenAI and which do not.

Further reading

AI for Education. (2023). *AI's Impact on the Environment.* https://www.aiforeducation.io/ai-resources/ais-impact-on-the-environment

Crompton, H., Edmett, A., & Ichaporia, N. (2023). Artificial Intelligence and English Language Teaching: A systematic literature review. British Council.

Dhanani, R. (2024, September 27). *Environmental impact of generative AI – 20 stats and facts.* Akepa. https://thesustainableagency.com/blog/environmental-impact-of-generative-ai/

Chapter 4:

Varieties of English and multilingual representation

In this chapter, we address the fact that different varieties of English and different languages are not represented equally in LLMs and this difference in representation has consequences, such as failures in plagiarism detection.

Reflective task 1

How important do you think representation of languages other than English is in relation to GenAI output? What effect might this representation have?

We have already discussed how GenAI models tend to output standard answers that reflect the values of those who own/created the data. Data-poor populations, including marginalised communities and those using minority languages, have a limited digital presence, meaning their voices are underrepresented in training data and rarely appear in outputs. This can constrain the development of plural opinions and expressions, and further marginalise disadvantaged people. This stems from a combination of data biases, developmental priorities, economic incentives and inherent linguistic complexities.

Multilingual representation

Most LLMs are predominantly English-centric, focusing primarily on English tasks, which limits their applicability in a world with over 7,000 languages. English is the default language for training data, largely due to the overwhelming presence of English content on the internet. According to Statista (2025), English accounts for 49.4% of the web content, followed by Spanish (6%), German (5.6%), Japanese (5%), French (4.4%) and Russian (3.9%). From the tenth language on in the ranking, each one accounts for less than 2% of the web content. Even though Chinese is the second most spoken language behind English, its share of web content is only 1.2%.

Reflective task 2

What is the representation of your first language in the information above (if there at all)? If you have used any GenAI tool in your first language, have you noticed any glitches or diminished performance compared to English?

The difference between the availability of English linguistic resources and the rest of the languages is abysmal. This data poverty for all languages except English has tangible consequences for GenAI outputs, mainly leading to significantly lower effectiveness in non-English settings. This includes both labeled and unlabeled data, which are crucial for neural systems, which require vast amounts of training data. Even when non-English data is included, it is often limited in volume, context and domain diversity, and its quality may degrade, especially in low-resource languages.

In Data Science and machine learning contexts, **high resource languages** are languages for which many data resources exist, making possible the development of systems based on machine learning for these languages. English is by far the most well-resourced language. Western-European languages are quite well covered, as are Japanese and Chinese (Blasi, 2022). The wealth of written material in these languages, despite the disparity between English and the rest, makes it easier for AI to understand and generate text accurately. **Low-resource languages** are the opposite, with no or very few resources available. This is the case for some extinct or near-extinct languages, local dialects and many languages that are mostly oral, and for which very few written resources exist.

The types of resources which are needed in order to train good language-based systems can be grouped as follows (Data Science, 2019):

- Raw text from various genres (type of documents), e.g. books, scientific papers, emails, social media content, etc.
- Lexical, syntactic and semantic resources such as dictionaries, dependency tree corpora, semantic databases, etc.
- Task-specific resources, such as parallel corpora for machine translation, various kinds of annotated text (e.g. with part-of-speech tags, named entities, etc.)

And many types of language resources are costly to produce, this is why the economic inequalities between countries/languages are reflected in the amount (or absence) of language resources.

For example, according to Xu *et al.* (2025):

- GPT-3 claims to represent 95 languages, but its pretraining data is 92.7% English, 1.8% French, 1.5% German and 5.9% for all other languages.
- BLOOM covers 46 languages and its pretraining data is English (30.03%); Simplified Chinese (16.16%); French (12.9%); Spanish (10.85%); Portuguese (4.91%); Arabic (4.6%); Others (20.55%).
- LLaMA 2 claims to cover over 100 languages and its pretraining data is English (89.70%); Unknown (8.38%); German (0.17%); French (0.16%); Others (1.59%).
- Data for GPT-4 and Claude 3 is unknown.

Table 4.1: An overview of representative multilingual training corpora of MLLMs in recent years, including their corresponding model, language, language proportion, and source (Xu *et al.*, 2025)

Model	Language	Language proportion	Source
mBERT [2]	104 languages	Unknown	Wikipedia
XLM-R [7]	100 languages	English (12.56%); Russian (11.61%); Indonesian (6.19%); Vietnamese (5.73%); Others (63.89%)	Generated using the open source; CC-Net repository
mT5 [4]	101 languages	English (5.67%); Russian (3.71%); Spanish (3.09 %); German (3.05%); Others (84.48%)	Common Crawl
GPT-3 [20]	95 languages	English (92.7%); French (1.8%); German (1.5%); Others (5.9%)	Common Crawl; Wikipedia; Books1; Books2; WebText2
Gopher [38]	51 languages	Over 99% English	MassiveWeb (48%); C4 (10%); News (10%); Books (27%); GitHub (3%); Wikipedia (2%)
LaMDA [30]	Unknown	Over 90% English	Public dialog data and other public web documents

Model	Language	Language proportion	Source
PaLM [29]	Over 100 languages	English (77.98%); German (3.50%); French (3.25%); Spanish (2.11%); Others (13.15%)	Social media conversations (50%); Filtered webpages (27%); Books (13%); GitHub (5%); Wikipedia (4%); News (1%)
BLOOM [5]	46 languages	English (30.03%); Simplified Chinese (16.16%); French (12.9%); Spanish (10.85%); Portuguese (4.91%); Arabic (4.6%); Others (20.55%)	Web Crawl (38%); BigScience Catalogue Data (62%)
LLaMA [6]	Over 20 languages	Over 67% English	Common Crawl (67.0%); C4 (15.0%); Github (4.5%); Wikipedia (4.5%); Books (4.5%); ArXiv (2.5%); StackExchange (2.0%)
Vicuna [34]	Unknown	Unknown	User-shared conversations from ShareGPT.com
Falcon [84]	Over 100 languages	Excluding English: Russian (13.19%); German (10.81%); Spanish (9.45%); Others (66.55%)	Common Crawl

Model	Language	Language proportion	Source
PaLM 2 [45]	Over 100 languages	Excluding English: Spanish (11.51%); Chinese (10.19%); Russian (8.73%); Others (69.57%)	Web documents; Books; Code; Mathematics; Conversational data
LLaMA 2 [46]	Over 100 languages	English (89.70%); Unknown (8.38%); German (0.17%); France (0.16%); Others (1.59%)	Publicly available sources, excludes Meta user data
GPT-4 [22]	Over 26 languages	Unknown	Common Crawl; Wikipedia; Books1; Books2; WebText2
LLaMA 3 [52]	176 languages	Over 5% non-English	Publicly available sources, excludes Meta user data
GLM-4 [50]	26 languages	Mostly English and Chinese	Webpages; Wikipedia; Books; Code; Research papers
Claude 3 [51]	Over 43 languages	Unknown	Publicly available information on the Internet; Non-public data from third parties; Data provided by data labelling services and paid contractors; Data they generate internally

Model	Language	Language proportion	Source
YAYI 2 [85]	Over 10 languages	Chinese (41.5%); English (40.4%); French (2.5%); Spanish (2.2%); Others (25%)	Web pages; Social media; Books; Newspapers; Academic Papers
FuxiTranyu [86]	43 languages	English (28.8%); Chinese (10.4%); German (8.1%); French (7.3%); Others (45.4%)	Web (82%); Code (9%); Paper (3%); Book (3%); Encyclopedia (2%); Report (1%)

This data imbalance is not only related to languages, but, as stated in Chapter 1 and according to Atari (2023), LLMs frequently develop a 'WEIRD' (Western, Educated, Industrialised, Rich, Democratic) psychology because their training data predominantly originates from individuals in WEIRD populations and is primarily in English. This creates a 'WEIRD-in-WEIRD-out' problem, where models perpetuate these biases. The lack of diversity among NLP developers and managers (often white, Western and male-dominated) can lead to potential biases, thus maintaining an inequitable status quo in technology.

This also has economic and academic consequences. Blasi (2022) addressed the dilemma of 'whether approximate measures of economic centrality or number of language users were better predictors of sheer number of papers published for any given language', and arrived at the conclusion that 'while both variables are substantially collinear … the approximate GDP (rather than number of users) leads to a substantially smaller prediction error of number of published papers'. So, the economic prowess of a language's users is a stronger predictor for the development of language technologies than the sheer demographic demand. In other words, this means that languages spoken in economically powerful regions receive more attention and resources.

Blasi (2022) also explains that there is a lack of academic reward for researchers working on more linguistically diverse NLP; the number of languages a publication addresses does not correlate with its citation count, providing little incentive for broader linguistic inclusion.

Linguistic and typological complexities are also a factor here. Qin *et al.* (2025) and Bender (2011) address this issue and state that **morphologically complex languages** like Arabic and Finnish require a greater number of tokens to convey the same meaning as English, leading to computational inefficiencies.

Joshi *et al.* (2020) make an interesting distinction between **types of languages** and how this affects LLMs and GenAI outputs. They argue that this issue leads to 'a typological echo-chamber'. NLP systems often make implicit assumptions about linguistic structure that are derived from familiar languages (e.g., English), leading to uneven performance across typologically diverse languages. Transfer learning of resource-rich to resource-poor languages has been shown to work better if the respective languages contain similar typological features (Pires *et al.*, 2020). Many typological features, such as multiple negative constructions or specific word orders, remain under-explored due to resource scarcity in the languages that exhibit them. Languages with different writing systems or scripts are also negatively affected. According to Philippy (2023) and de Vries *et al.* (2022), cross-lingual transfer performance across languages with different writing systems is more difficult, though not impossible. They state that a shared writing system, and thus a higher lexical overlap, contribute to better cross-lingual transfer.

Figure 4.1: Multilingual representation in AI

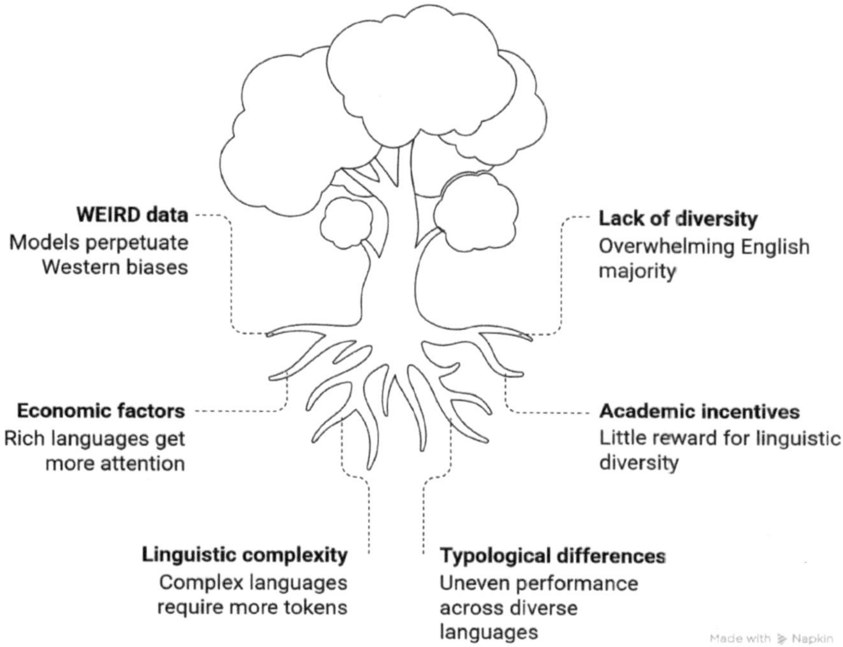

Reflective task 3

How does your first language compare to English in terms of language family, script and typological features? Have you noticed difficulties linked to cross-lingual transfer performance? If so, which? How would that be relevant to ELT in your context?

The 'curse of multilinguality' – a term coined by Conneau (2020) – describes a trade-off where, for a fixed model capacity, increasing the number of languages can initially improve performance for low-resource languages but eventually degrades overall performance.

Consequences of languages' underrepresentation

The consequences of this lack of multilingual representation are significant. **Multilingual large language models** (MLLMs) consistently show stronger performance in English due to extensive training data, but their effectiveness in non-English languages is notably lower. For example, GPT-4 achieves 84.9% accuracy in English but only 68.1% in Urdu (Qin *et al.*, 2025).

Some researchers, for example Zhang *et al.* (2023), have tried to discern what type of bilingualism or multilingualism LLMs have or display and this is an interesting consideration. Based on D'Acierno's framework (1990), researchers classify bilingual people into three distinct categories based on how they process and use their languages:

- **Compound bilinguals** develop both languages simultaneously from early childhood, creating a highly integrated linguistic system where both languages are equally strong, giving the impression of a single unified language. This integration allows them to switch fluidly between languages while maintaining consistent performance across different linguistic tasks.
- **Coordinate bilinguals** keep their languages mentally separate, storing each language system independently. This separation means their performance can vary depending on which language they're using for a particular task.
- **Subordinate bilinguals** have one clearly dominant language that serves as their primary linguistic reference point. When they need to use their weaker language, they follow a three-step translation process: they first convert the task into their stronger language, work out their response in that dominant language, and then translate their answer back into the required language. This indirect processing typically results in less fluent communication and task performance in their secondary language.

Zhang *et al.* (2023) claim that LLMs often display subordinate multilingualism, relying on translation into English to formulate responses even for non-English queries, which can lead to lower accuracy and quality due to translation errors. This is evident in translation-variant tasks where the correct output depends on the language and culture. This has implications for ELT, which we will address later in this chapter.

Reflective task 4

Let's try a little experiment; it does not need to be ELT related. If you speak more than one language, think of a prompt that carries some cultural context and write the same prompt in English and in your first language (or second language if your first language is English). Choose a GenAI agent, prompt it in both languages in different conversations, and compare the output. What differences do you notice, if any? Are there any signs that, when prompted in another language, the prompt was translated into English, the task performed in English, and the output translated back into the other language?

Concerns about safety, fairness, and bias are magnified in non-English languages (Qin *et al.*, 2025). For instance, LLMs produce significantly more unsafe responses for non-English queries than for English ones, highlighting a gap in safety alignment for these languages. Safety mitigations developed primarily in English may mistakenly classify text as harmful in other cultural contexts. We will address this in more detail in Chapter 5.

MLLMs frequently fail to capture cultural nuances, especially regarding emotion, reflecting predominantly Western values even when prompted in other languages. This poses risks for emotionally sensitive applications like therapy bots or creative writing assistants (Havaldar *et al.*, 2023).

Kofinas *et al.* (2025) confirm that LLMs can generate false information (hallucinations), leading to misinformation, especially in multilingual summarisation and translation tasks. The increased coherence of advanced models like GPT-4 can make this misinformation more believable and persuasive. This is particularly worrying for non-native speakers of English.

Figure 4.2: Consequences of language underrepresentation

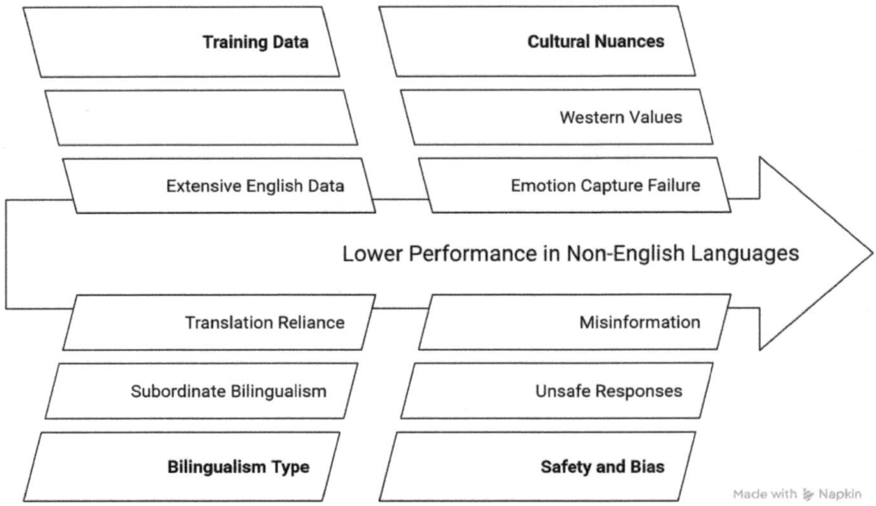

Varieties of English

But there is much more than that. Even if we only consider English, the question is '*Which English?*' Is it one of the 'main' varieties? British, American, Australian, Canadian, Irish, South African, Caribbean? Or one of the many dialects spoken all over the world? In the same way that languages other than English are underrepresented, most varieties of English are also underrepresented in the training data.

Standard language ideology has been addressed since the 1970s. 'Standard' language is an 'abstracted, idealised, homogeneous spoken language ... imposed from above' and modelled on 'the written language' (Lippi-Green, 1994). Fleisig *et al.* (2024) explain that a 'standard' language is not actively spoken by any real community; all language varieties have more and less 'standard' versions. Smith *et al.* (2024) state that standard language ideology is a construct that enforces a hierarchy between language varieties, with a common and false belief that some language varieties are 'better' or 'more complex' than others. But linguistically speaking, all language varieties are equally valid, and the idea that certain languages are 'better' than others only results in the discrimination of the other languages. Within English, Standard American English (SAE) and Standard British English (SBE) are the two dominant language varieties because they have by far the most global prestige and influence. Other language varieties, like African American English (AAE), Irish English, Indian English or Chicano English, among the more than 150 dialects, are mistakenly considered less appropriate.

Figure 4.3: English language varieties and ideology

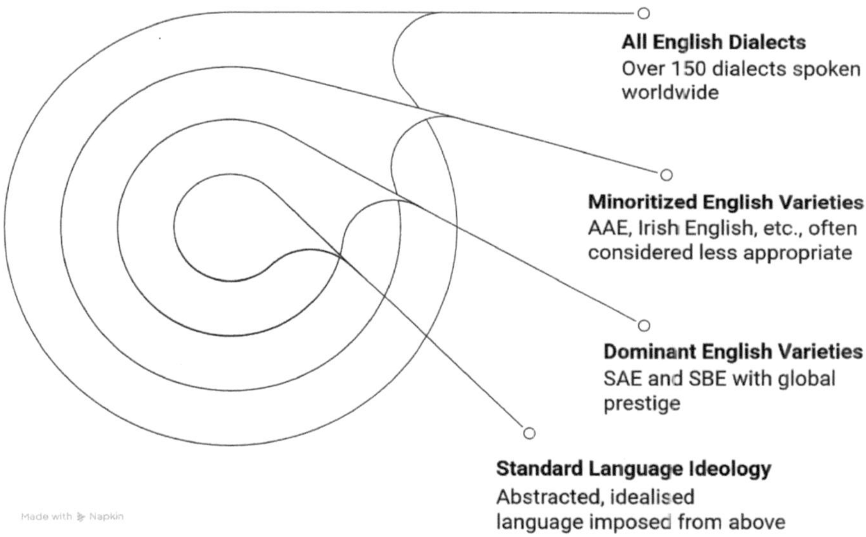

Standard language ideology has implications for NLP, LLMs and GenAI performance, in which hierarchies of language are reinforced. We have already established that English is the default language for data powering large LLMs, which rely on language data from the internet. Specific percentages for English varieties in LLM training data are not publicly available, but Fleisig *et al.* (2024) suggest that, based on other metrics, SAE comes first and SBE, second. Consequently, issues regarding linguistic discrimination within English are raising increasing concerns.

According to several studies (Smith *et al.*, 2024; Ta & Turner Lee, 2023; Fleisig *et al.*, 2024), for minoritised varieties of English, models like ChatGPT exhibit reduced retention of distinctive linguistic features and are perceived by native speakers as demonstrating less comprehension, and more stereotyping, demeaning and condescending content. This reinforces the dominance of SAE and SBE.

Figure 4.4: Standard language ideology issues

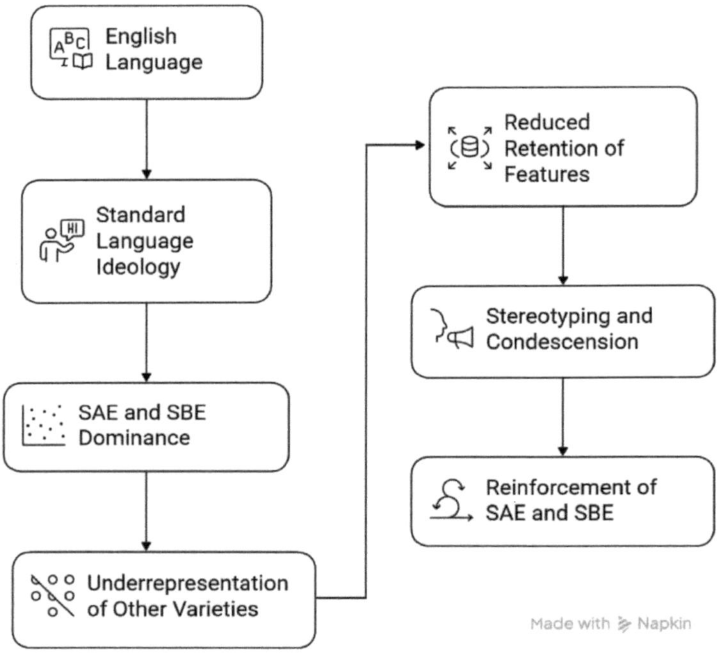

Reflective task 5

If you speak a variety of English other than SAE or SBE, you can try another experiment. Think of a task you could ask for help with and write it in your own variety of English. Prompt a GenAI agent and check the output. How does it fare in terms of respecting the characteristics of your variety of English?

Why is this relevant to ELT?

The first point to consider is the use of GenAI by speakers of other languages, who are learning English. Although we are of course focused on English, multilingual representation is important because our learners come from a wide variety of first-language backgrounds. The reliance on and use of the learners' first language is a precious resource when learning a new language because it provides a cognitive foundation, supports conceptual understanding, and offers emotional benefits such as reducing anxiety, especially for low-level learners. Learners of English are likely to find explanations about the target language in their L1 easier to follow. Using translation is, in some cases, faster and more efficient. And comparative analysis of L1 and the target language can help learners understand similarities and differences in ways that can make learning more meaningful. So, if our learners are turning to GenAI as a support system, and they feel more confident prompting in their own L1, we are in for trouble, especially if their L1 is severely underrepresented and the GenAI output will be of notably lower quality. We mentioned earlier that LLMs often display subordinate multilingualism, relying on internal translation into English to formulate responses for non-English queries, and how this can lead to lower accuracy and quality due to translation errors, especially when the correct output depends on the language and culture (Zhang *et al.*, 2023). And the fact that LLMs can generate false information, especially in multilingual summarisation and translation tasks (Kofinas *et al.*, 2025) is an added problem. Translation entails further issues, such as semantic boundaries, which are the inherent difficulties in distinguishing and transferring precise meaning between languages, especially when dealing with ambiguous terms or cultural nuances. This could happen when word representations fail to distinguish between the multiple senses of polysemous words (words with multiple, related meanings that are used in different contexts) or when the words in both languages are not exactly equivalent.

Reflective task 6

In your own teaching context, if your students use GenAI agents, what usage behaviour have you noticed? Would they use these tools in English or in their own language? What does this depend on?

Regarding the use of GenAI in English by students, many professionals share the belief that students create shortcuts in their learning journeys as they prompt GenAI agents and take answers at face value, without any critical analysis, and without any effort to understand what they are being asked and why it's important to work out the answer themselves. We believe this is a philosophical issue rather than a technological one. Some students are not willing to put in the effort necessary to learn. Learning is the acquisition of knowledge or skills and many scholars agree that learning occurs as a result of experience. Although learning can occur by chance, in the context of learning a language through classes, it is a voluntary action where an individual consciously chooses to engage in a learning activity with the specific intention to acquire new knowledge or skills, rather than being driven by external compulsion or an involuntary reflex. This voluntary learning process involves the brain preparing for thought, the intention to learn being created in areas of the brain like the prefrontal cortex, the programming of the learning sequence, and the reception of feedback that guides the learning process. Seeking a straightforward answer from a GenAI agent instead of working it out is without question a shortcut in the learning process.

Regarding the use of GenAI agents as language assistants, there have been some developments by AI service providers to offer the option of learning mode or study mode. Because of the backlash and concerns that AI undermines genuine learning, some companies, like Anthropic for Claude, Google for Gemini, and OpenAI for ChatGPT, have launched these new 'learning modes' that turn the agent from an answer-dispensing tool into a teaching companion that encourages guided discovery over immediate solutions. This means that the agents guide users through challenging concepts with probing questions rather than simply providing immediate answers (Nuñez, 2025). It will be interesting to see if this can solve the problem.

Figure 4.5: GenAI challenges

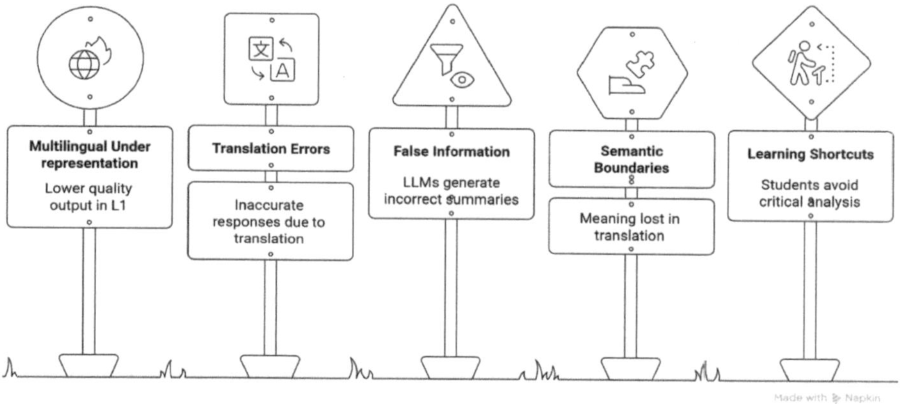

Reflective task 7

Choose one of the GenAI agents that offer a 'learning mode' option. Prompt it to explain a topic you know well and follow along. How does it achieve the guided discovery? Is it effective? Try another prompt to explain a topic you are *not* familiar with, so that you can experience a student's perspective. How does it feel? Do you think it is effective?

Another relevant point is students' use of GenAI in assessments, which raises academic integrity issues. Educational institutions and government bodies are constantly working on guidelines for responsible use to reflect the latest approaches to address this. These guidelines can take multiple forms and are discussed in detail in Chapter 7. At the core of this issue is the need to detect whether an assessment is AI or human generated.

This has led to the development of AI detectors. There are multiple studies addressing automatic detection of machine-generated text (Heikkila, 2022; Jawahar *et al.*, 2020; Krishna *et al.*, 2023;

Crothers *et al.*, 2023). According to Crothers *et al.* (2023), 'machine-generated text is natural language text (i.e., text written in human languages that are "acquired naturally in association with speech") that is produced, modified, or extended by a machine'.

There are different types or categories of detectors:

- Watermark
- Statistical
- Classifier
- Human-aided

Watermark detectors try to find hidden characters or watermarks, intentionally inserted into the text by some models. Krishna *et al.* (2023) explain that 'a watermark is a modification to the generated text that can be detected post-hoc by an algorithm while remaining imperceptible to human readers. Effective watermarks are difficult to remove and have little effect on the quality of generated text.'

Statistical methods analyse the structure of the text and detect AI-generated text based on its artefacts. Crothers *et al.* (2023) explain that 'machine-generated text often differs from human text in ways that can be identified using statistical techniques. These feature-based approaches … apply natural language processing to create feature vectors from input sequences and classify these feature vectors using a classification algorithm.' The features analysed are frequency, fluency (or readability), linguistic (number of phrasal verbs and coreference resolution relationships), complex phrasal (specific idiomatic phrases), and basic text features (number of punctuation marks or the length of sentences and paragraphs).

Classifier methods train models to distinguish human-written text from AI-generated text. Most of them use two important analysis techniques: perplexity and burstiness. Perplexity is a common evaluation metric for language models that measures how well a model predicts a given sample of text. A lower perplexity score indicates that the language model is more 'certain' and better at predicting the next word in a sequence. Burstiness measures how predictable a piece of content is by the homogeneity of the length and structure of sentences throughout the text.

Human-aided methods 'include a statistical or neural approach in combination with a human analyst for review' (Crothers *et al.*, 2023). This is an advantage to purely automated methods as it provides human agency and oversight. However, the need to hire and train human reviewers makes it difficult to use them at scale.

The ultimate goal of AI detectors is to identify content created by artificial intelligence. However, AI detectors have been proved to be biased against non-native English writers, consistently misclassifying their work as AI-generated, while accurately identifying native English writing (Liang *et al.*, 2023; Smith *et al.*, 2024; Ta & Turner Lee, 2023). In their study, Liang *et al.* (2023) evaluated several publicly available GPT detectors on writing samples from native and non-native English writers and found that they 'consistently misclassified non-native English writing samples as AI-generated while not making the same mistakes for native writing samples'. They explain that this is due to non-native writing often exhibiting reduced linguistic variability (lexical richness, lexical diversity, syntactic complexity and grammatical complexity), which results in lower perplexity, a metric often used by detectors to identify AI-generated text. Paradoxically, non-native writers may need to use AI tools themselves to enhance the word choices to sound more advanced in order to avoid false detection. Liang *et al.* (2023) also proved that simple prompting strategies can easily bypass current GPT detectors. For example, a '"self-edit" prompt to "elevate the provided text by employing literary language" drastically reduced detection rates for AI-generated essays from 100% to 13%, by increasing text perplexity. This reveals the vulnerability of perplexity-based detection methods and makes it clear that GPT detectors may inadvertently penalise writers with limited linguistic expressions.'

A further complication is paraphrasing, done by external paraphrasing tools, which have been proved to evade AI detectors (Krishna *et al.*, 2023).

An ideal detector, according to Jawahar *et al.* (2020), should be:

- accurate, with a good trade-off for false positives and false negatives
- data efficient, needing as few examples as possible
- generalisable, detecting text generated by different modelling choices
- interpretable, with decisions understandable to humans
- robust, being able to handle adversarial examples (specially crafted inputs that appear normal to humans but are designed to fool a machine learning model into making a wrong prediction)

But multiple issues have been identified, mostly the issue of false positives, when an AI detector incorrectly identifies human-created content as being likely generated by an AI. The handling of false positives resulting in accusations of academic misconduct can have – and is already having – serious repercussions for a student's academic record, apart from creating an environment of distrust where students are treated as suspicious by default and that can undermine the teacher-student relationship.

Figure 4.6: AI detection methods and challenges

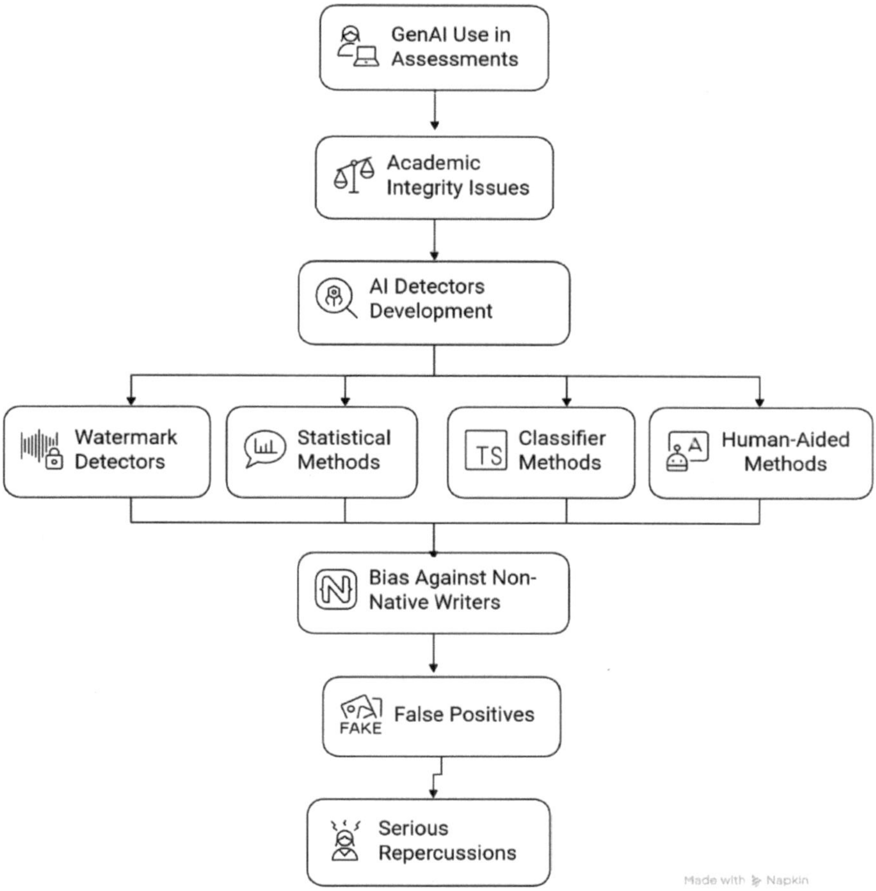

Reflective task 8

If you have had experience with an AI detector, how has it performed? If you work in an institution that mandates the use of AI detectors for students' work, what are the guidelines given to teachers? And for students, what are the consequences of being flagged as turning in AI-generated content?

If automated AI detectors are biased, it seems we need to trust human detectors. But human markers also struggle to differentiate between human-authored, AI-modified, and AI-generated assessments (Kofinas *et al.*, 2025). In a detailed study of the impact of generative AI on the academic integrity of authentic assessments within a higher education context, they found that the awareness of AI usage can influence markers' judgement, leading to false positives (good human work being suspected as AI-generated) and false negatives (AI-generated work being overlooked).

The ease with which AI can produce high-quality, seemingly original work complicates plagiarism detection, undermines academic integrity and the value of higher education degrees and educational certificates. So what is the best way ahead? We could focus on learning more about the characteristics of AI-generated text so that we can spot it. As we discussed in Chapter 1, and stemming from the way LLMs work, AI-generated text gives the illusion of correctness. Some giveaways are:

- more likely to use common words instead of rare words (this is related to its probabilistic nature)
- clean text with no typos
- sentence length is on the longer side, without much variation
- punctuation patterns: the use of em dashes, for example
- comparative structures: 'it´s not…., it's …'
- pompous style, exaggerated and subjective use of adjectives

But again, there are tools developed to work around AI detection. The newest kind are AI humanisers; tools that transform AI-generated text into more natural, human-like writing by altering sentence structure, vocabulary and tone to remove obvious machine patterns. They are used to improve readability and engagement, make content more relatable, and most commonly, to help AI-written content bypass AI-detection tools.

Recently, educators have been raising the issue of AI agents use within Learning Management Systems (LMSs) and have been calling LMSs service providers to find ways to block AI agents from logging in to them.

So where does that leave us? Is detecting AI-generated content a dead end? Many professionals take issue with the types of assessment that are open invitations to cheating with GenAI. They argue that if an assessment can be easily carried out by AI, then it is not a very good instrument and we should rethink assessment strategies. As a general suggestion, avoid formulaic assessments, such as the five-paragraph essay, and create assessments that foster students' creative and critical thinking abilities (Hooks, 2010; Brookfield, 2012; Brookfield *et al.*, 2019; Rudolph & Tan, 2022). Explaining to students that writing is a form of thinking (Stevens, 2019) and that they miss out on a critically important form of learning if they try to delegate their writing to an AI seems obvious but is definitely important.

These are some suggestions that have been proposed, not personal choices, as these very much depend on context:

- Using physical closed-book exams where the students write by hand, using only pen and paper (Cassidy, 2023).
- Using proctoring/surveillance software for online exams.
- Designing writing assignments that GenAI models are currently not good at handling, though this may be a very short-term solution given how quickly the technology is developing. Some suggestions are: analysis of images and videos; analysis that draws on class discussion; analysis of longer texts that do not fit in a prompt; writing about recent events that are not in the training data for the text generator (Mills, 2023b). Other suggestions by Nowik (2022) are: writing about a topic that is highly specific and niche, asking students to include personal experiences or perspectives in their writing, integrating multiple sources and presenting their own original arguments. McMurtrie (2022) suggests writing about topics that genuinely interest them, in which their voices come through and their opinions are valued.
- When in doubt, teachers could test students' knowledge of their own essays by conducting an impromptu oral exam (Allen, 2022), or requiring video or audio submissions of students discussing their essays or metacognitive reflection on their writing process (Mills, 2023a).

- Creating during class assessments where students deliver presentations, performances or present webpages, videos, animations, etc. (Lim, 2022).
- Involving students in peer evaluations.

Figure 4.7: Rethinking assessment in the AI era

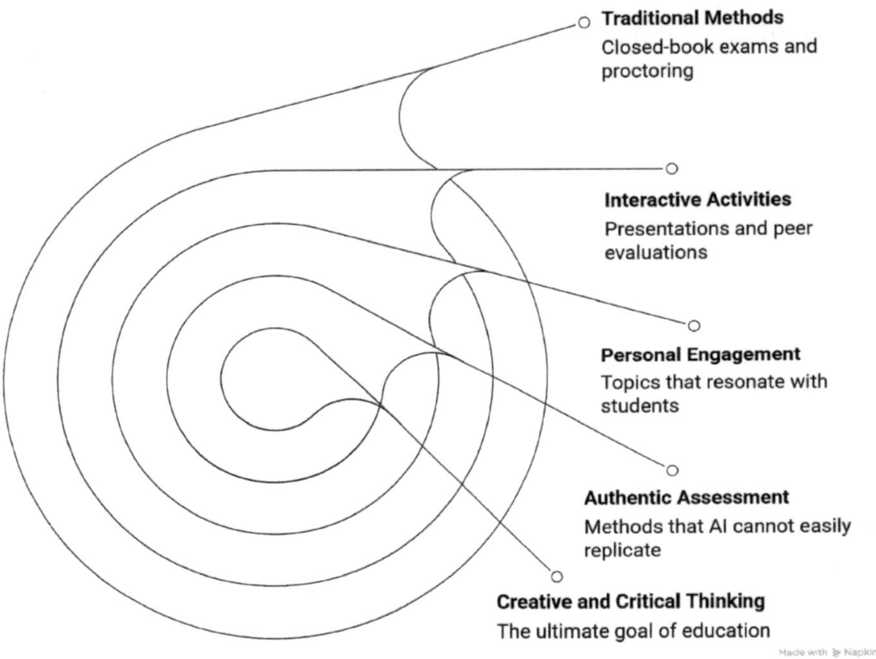

Reflective task 9

If you have ever assigned writing assessments, how do you plan to address this issue? What would be a practical solution for your particular context?

Chapter 4 Key Points

1. **Extreme anglocentric data bias.** While English accounts for approximately 49.4% of web content, it disproportionately dominates AI training data; for instance, GPT-3's pretraining data was 92.7% English. This "data poverty" for the world's other 7,000 languages limits the effectiveness of GenAI in non-English settings and constrains the development of plural opinions.

2. **Economic power drives AI development.** The development of language technologies correlates more strongly with a region's GDP than with the number of language speakers.

3. **"Subordinate bilingualism" in models.** Many LLMs function as "subordinate bilinguals," meaning they often translate non-English prompts into English, process the task, and translate the result back. This indirect processing leads to lower accuracy, loss of cultural nuance, and errors in tasks where the correct answer depends heavily on specific cultural contexts.

4. **The "WEIRD" psychology loop.** Because training data predominantly originates from WEIRD populations, models perpetuate these specific biases.

5. **Standard language ideology and dialect discrimination.** Within the English language itself, AI models reinforce "Standard Language Ideology," favouring Standard American English (SAE) and Standard British English (SBE) as the only "correct" forms. Models frequently fail to retain the features of minoritised varieties and may even generate stereotyping or condescending content when interacting with them.

6. **Safety disparities across languages.** Safety measures and alignment training are primarily developed for English, causing them to fail in other languages.

7. **Risks of L1 prompting in ELT.** English learners often use their first language (L1) to prompt AI for help, which can be a valuable cognitive scaffold; however, due to the "subordinate" nature of the models, this exposes them to lower quality outputs and translation errors.

8. **Bias in AI detectors.** AI detection tools are inherently biased against non-native English speakers. These tools often rely on "perplexity" (a measure of unpredictability) to flag text; because non-native speakers tend to use simpler, more predictable sentence structures, their original work is frequently misclassified as AI-generated.

9. **The futility of the "detection arms race".** The quest to detect AI writing is complicated by "humanisers", tools designed specifically to alter AI text to bypass detectors. Furthermore, the prevalence of false positives in detection creates an environment of distrust.

10. **Shift to authentic assessment.** Given that formulaic assessments (like the standard five-paragraph essay) are easily replicated by AI, educators are urged to rethink assessment entirely.

Further reading

Atari, M., Xue, Mona, J., Park, P. S., Blasi, D. E., & Henrich, J. (2023). Which Humans? *PsyArXiv Preprint*, 1–23.

Liang, W., Yuksekgonul, M., Mao, Y., Wu, E., & Zou, J. (2023, July 14). GPT detectors are biased against non-native English writers. *Patterns*. Cell Press. https://doi.org/10.1016/j.patter.2023.100779

Smith, G., Fleisig, E., Bossi, M., Rustagi, I., & Yin, X. (2024). Standard Language Ideology in AI-Generated Language. Retrieved from http://arxiv.org/abs/2406.08726

Chapter 5:

Data privacy, safety and copyright

In this chapter, we delve into the ethical considerations related to GenAI management of data, which leads to privacy, safety and copyright issues.

Reflective task 1

What data do you think is collected when you use GenAI tools? What do you think they do with it? Is it something that worries you personally?

The ethical considerations related to GenAI management of data privacy and copyright are extensive and are connected to training data sourcing, algorithmic bias, user trust and intellectual property, among others.

Data privacy

Most GenAI systems pose substantial data-privacy challenges due to their reliance on massive datasets, the potential for personal information leakage, and subsequent damage to user trust, as described by several authors (El Mestari *et al.*, 2024; Sebastian, 2023). Data-privacy issues can be attributed to data collection and use, consent, user trust and legal compliance. El Mestari *et al.* (2024) distinguish between 'training data owners whose data are used to train and build the model; and inference data owners that interact with the already deployed model as service customers'.

Training data collection

As described in Chapter 1, GenAI models are typically trained by exposing them to large quantities of existing writings, images and other works, in the form of existing datasets, such as Colossal Clean Crawled Corpus (C4) and Common Crawl, 'scraped' from the internet through **web crawling**. These models rely on privacy-invasive methods for mass data collection, typically without the consent or compensation of the original user, creator, or owner. According to a report by the US Congressional Research Service (2023), these datasets can also include sensitive data, including personally identifiable information (PII) like names, phone numbers and addresses, and copyrighted content, as confirmed by Google AI researchers in a company blog post (Carlini, 2020). That is on top of hallucinations, which, for example, has led to a mayor in Australia considering filing a defamation lawsuit against ChatGPT after it falsely claimed that he had spent time in prison (Walsh, 2023).

User data collection

GenAI systems also get data directly from users, when they input information in their prompts or shared documents. Many existing agents have terms of service that allow the respective companies to reuse user data to improve their services by default with an option to opt out, which is not so obviously found. There is a concern that user data shared with a GenAI application may be misused or abused without the user's knowledge (US Congressional Research Service, 2023). GenAI models should require affirmative consent from users, opt in rather than opt out, and provide clear disclosures of how they collect, use and store user data.

In a Chatbase article (Ism, 2025), the author explains that, according to their own privacy policy, ChatGPT collects two types of data:

- User-provided data: Everything you type into the agent (your prompts, questions, responses and any files you upload), from short questions to sensitive information like personal details, business data or even source code.
- System-generated data: All metadata like timestamps, usage statistics, device information, IP address, approximate location and payment details.

So ChatGPT is collecting:

- Account information (name, email address, phone number and contact details).
- Chat conversations.
- Geolocation data.
- Network activity.
- Commercial information (if applicable).
- Log data.
- Cookies.

Several privacy concerns arise from GenAI services' data-collection practices:

- Data breaches: Storing large amounts of user data is a tempting target for cybercriminals.
- Resurfacing of information: A risk that information you provide could reappear in other users' conversations.
- Vulnerabilities: Researchers have been able to extract training data, including personal information.

- Government access: OpenAI's privacy policy allows for data transfer to government entities.
- Ethical concerns: The use of user data for training without explicit consent.

Academic and industry research has found that existing LLMs may reveal sensitive data or personal information from their training datasets. LLMs are vulnerable to a training data leaking attack, where the generated outputs of the model can reveal text sequences from the model's training data (El Mestari *et al.*, 2024). Data leakage can occur when information a user provides reappears in other users' conversations, also known as resurfacing of information (Ism, 2025; Sebastian, 2023). Additionally, according to Open AI, when augmented with outside data, GenAI has the potential to be used to attempt to identify private individuals (OpenAI, 2024). These privacy concerns are particularly relevant when GenAI models are used in services involving sensitive disclosures, such as advising, therapy, healthcare, legal or financial or educational services (US Congressional Research Service, 2023), and has led many organisations, like banks and tech companies, to ban or restrict their use.

Figure 5.1: Data privacy concerns

Concern	Description
Data Collection	Relies on massive datasets scraped from the internet
User Data Collection	Collects user prompts, metadata, and account information
Data Breaches	Storing large amounts of data attracts cybercriminals
Resurfacing of Information	User data reappears in other conversations
Vulnerabilities	Training data can be extracted, revealing personal information
Government Access	Data can be transferred to government entities
Ethical Concerns	User data used for training without consent
Data Leakage	Model outputs reveal text from training data
Identification of Individuals	GenAI can be used to identify private individuals

Made with Napkin

Reflective task 2

What kind of information would you feel safe sharing? What measures could be taken to safeguard data privacy both personally and in educational contexts?

User trust

User trust in GenAI is essential for these services to thrive. According to Lefkeli *et al.* (2024), disclosing personal information to an AI agent results in lower levels of brand trust compared to disclosing it to a human agent. This negative effect is driven by the consumer's belief that the AI will share the information with a larger audience. This is closely connected to the lack of explicit consent mentioned earlier. Currently, most GenAI applications do not provide notice or acquire consent from individuals to collect and use their data for training purposes.

Legal compliance

AI systems must adhere to stringent data protection regulations. According to El Mestari *et al.* (2024), there are existing regulations, like the Health Insurance Portability and Accountability Act (HIPAA), the Cybersecurity Law of China, the California Consumer Privacy Act (CCPA), the General Data Protection Regulation (GDPR), the Data Governance Act, and the Artificial Intelligence Act, which will affect the way companies operate with GenAI systems. Non-compliance can lead to substantial fines and legal repercussions

For example, in 2023, Italy's regulator temporarily banned OpenAI from using Italian users' data due to GDPR non-compliance (US Congressional Research Service, 2023; Gupta *et al.*, 2023; Burgess, 2023). This ban was lifted within a month as OpenAI complied with the regulations.

Developers have implemented controls to address these concerns, including fine-tuning models to reject requests for personal information, removing PII from training data, and offering users the ability to opt out of training data contribution (OpenAI, 2024; Sebastian 2023; Gupta *et al.*, 2023). ChatGPT also offers 'temporary chats' that are automatically deleted and not used for training, and a privacy portal to request data removal or deletion (Ism, 2025). But most of the applications have rather obscure terms of service.

Copyright issues

There are a few issues related to copyright. They focus around two main areas: the unauthorised and uncompensated use of intellectual property (IP) to train commercial AI systems, and the legal uncertainty over who owns the creative output. (Appel *et al.*, 2023; US Copyright Office, 2024).

Reflective task 3

How important do you consider copyright issues in educational contexts? What consequences could there be for copyright infringement? What responsibility do educators have in this respect?

Unlicensed training data

As mentioned earlier in relation to data privacy and training data, companies have trained AI tools using massive databases containing thousands or millions of unlicensed works (Appel *et al.*, 2023). This scraping process often occurs without the consent or compensation of the original user, creator or owner (US Congressional Research Service, 2023). This process involves making digital copies of existing works, which copyright owners argue infringes their exclusive right to make reproductions (US Congressional Research Service, 2023; US Copyright Office, 2025). In current lawsuits, Anthropic and Meta acknowledged that they had trained Claude and Llama respectively on books obtained through a combination of buying print copies and downloading digital copies from pirate sites (US Congressional Research Service, 2023). In the US, for example, there are no federal laws that ban the scraping of publicly available data from the internet.

The C4 dataset, used by Google, Facebook and OpenAI, has been found to include websites with copyrighted content. In the case of AI image generators, many (Google, Stable Diffusion) are trained on the LAION dataset, which contains billions of images scraped from the internet and their text descriptions (Newman & Cantrill, 2023).

Research has revealed that models like ChatGPT and GPT-4 have memorised a wide collection of copyrighted materials, including both public domain and in-copyright books (Chang *et al.*, 2023). The degree of memorisation is tied to the frequency with which passages of those books appear on the web, and the risk of memorisation can be increased by duplicate sequences within the training data (El Mestari *et al.*, 2024).

Lawsuits are actively challenging whether training AI on copyrighted works constitutes unauthorised reproduction (Appel *et al.*, 2023). The legal outcome hinges on the interpretation of the fair-use doctrine (Appel *et al.*, 2023; US Congressional Research Service, 2023), which is widely used around the world, and the bounds of what is 'derivative work'. According to the US Copyright Office, fair use is 'a legal doctrine that promotes freedom of expression by permitting the unlicensed use of copyright-protected works in certain circumstances ... and identifies certain types of uses – such as criticism, comment, news reporting, teaching, scholarship, and research – as examples of activities that may qualify as fair use'. The fair-use assessment considers four factors:

1. The purpose and character of the use (e.g., whether it is for commercial or non-profit educational purposes).
2. The nature of the copyrighted work.
3. The amount and substantiality of the portion used in relation to the copyrighted work as a whole.
4. The effect of the use upon the potential market for or value of the copyrighted work.

Reflective task 4

How do educational institutions and teachers benefit from fair-use doctrine? Think of examples in your context where you have used/can use copyrighted material.

How does GenAI push the limits on fair use, if it does?

For example, according to Walsh (2023), there is a lawsuit against GitHub, Microsoft and OpenAI, which is centred on 'GitHub Copilot, which converts commands written in plain English into computer code in dozens of different coding languages. Copilot was trained and developed on billions of lines of open-source code that had already been written, leading to questions of attribution.' People who operate in the open-source community, use open-source software and make sure they keep the attribution, which is a requirement for being able to use the software. An AI model, however, doesn't realise that there are these requirements to comply with. There are also lawsuits from several visual artists against the companies that created the image generators Stable Diffusion, Midjourney and DreamUp, all of which generate images based on text prompts from users. And even Getty Images has filed a lawsuit against Stable Diffusion as it alleges that all of the images generated by Stable Diffusion are derivative works from their own image bank, scraped without consent, and some of those images even contain a vestige of the Getty watermark.

The US Copyright Office acknowledged that it is not possible to prejudge litigation outcomes, expecting that some uses of copyrighted works for GenAI training will qualify as fair use, and some will not (US Congressional Research Service, 2023; US Copyright Office, 2025).

At an international level, copyright law is still ruled by the Berne Convention (an international copyright treaty adopted in 1886), with subsequent additions and amendments. Article 9(1) mandates the protection of reproduction 'in any manner or form'. More recently, the Agreed Statements to the World Intellectual Property Organization (WIPO) Internet Treaties (1996) further clarify that the right 'fully applies in the digital environment' and encompasses 'the direct or indirect, temporary or permanent reproduction by any means and in any form, in whole or in part' of works and other protected subject matter. Although there are exceptions for **text and data mining** (TDM) under EU and UK laws, the extraction and reproduction for TDM purposes is allowed under certain conditions, for example, for training AI models, but not subsequent acts that remain restricted, like reproduction and/or communication/making available to the public through output generation (Rosati, 2024). GenAI systems deployed in the EU need to comply with EU law regardless of the jurisdiction in which the training is performed. In the UK, 'case law indicates that, where a certain act originates outside the UK territory but its effects are felt in the UK, then such act shall be deemed to be targeted at the UK territory, with the result that UK law is applicable' (Rosati, 2024).

Regina Sam Penti, who specialises in technology and intellectual property, has been quoted as saying, 'Just because something is out there for free doesn't mean it's free of rights'.

Figure 5.2: Unlicensed training data and copyright

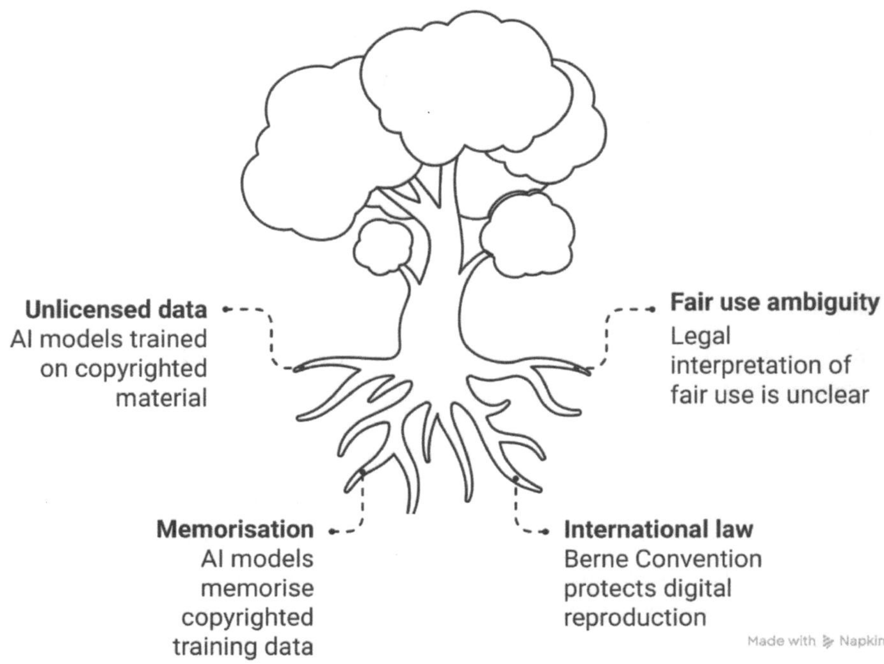

Ownership of AI outputs

A fundamental challenge is the uncertainty about ownership of AI-generated works (Appel *et al.*, 2023). In the US, the two main legal systems for regulating work generated by AI are copyright law and patent law. Under current US copyright law, copyright protection requires human authorship. If content is entirely generated by AI, it cannot therefore be protected by copyright. In the case of patents, the system is really created to protect physical objects, and, so far, remains vague on how patent law will apply to the outputs of AI systems.

The US Copyright Office released Copyright Registration Guidance (2023) regarding works containing material generated by AI. It states that human authors may use AI in the creative process, and 'what matters is the extent to which the human had creative control over the work's expression'. When AI 'determines the expressive elements of its output, the generated material is not the product of human authorship'. Works containing AI-generated material may be copyrighted under some circumstances, such as by using 'sufficiently creative' human criteria, or by modifying AI-generated material or works to combine AI-generated and human-authored material. In this case, authors may claim copyright protection only 'for their own contributions' to such works, and they must identify and disclaim AI-generated parts of the works when applying to register their copyright (US Copyright Office, 2023). The argument that GenAI tools are analogous to cameras in the field of photography is flawed as prompts alone do not provide sufficient human control to make somebody the author of the output. Prompts are simply instructions but do not control how AI processes them to generate the output (US Copyright Office, 2025). An AI user is analogous to 'a client who hires an artist' and gives that artist only 'general directions' (US Copyright Office, 2025).

But there are further issues related to imitation and style. GenAI tools raise concerns because they can be prompted to generate works that may be insufficiently transformative from the original protected works. Transformativeness is a matter of degree. Some outputs might infringe copyrights in other works they resemble, as AI had access to these works and created substantially similar outputs (US Congressional Research Service, 2023). Two kinds of AI outputs raise special concerns: works created that use existing fictional characters, or those that create works 'in the style of' a particular artist or author. Works with existing fictional characters may run a higher risk of infringement, as 'characters sometimes enjoy copyright protection distinct from the specific works in which they appear' (US Congressional Research Service, 2023). Appel *et al.* (2023) describes in detail the issue of whether users should be able to prompt these tools with direct reference to other creators' copyrighted and trademarked works by name without permission. The US Copyright Office is examining whether there should be protections against AI systems generating outputs that imitate specific creators' artistic styles.

This is a very complex issue and ways of addressing compensation are being discussed. If there is copyright infringement, both the AI user and AI company could potentially be liable (Appel *et al.*, 2023; Rosati, 2024). AI developers are urged to proactively seek solutions, such as licensing and compensating those who own the IP used to train their models, or sharing revenue generated by the AI tool (Appel *et al.*, 2023). Other potential solutions include creating markets for AI training data through collective management organisations (CMOs) or technological means that allow rightsholders to opt out of having their works used for training (US Congressional Research Service, 2023).

Figure 5.3: AI output ownership determination

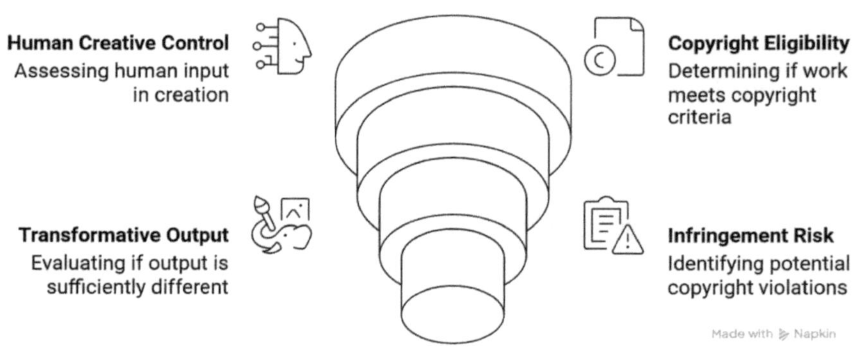

Reflective task 5

How is this issue relevant to your particular context? If you are planning to use AI-generated outputs, what are your strategies for doing so legally and responsibly?

Why is this relevant to ELT?

The relevance to education in general and ELT in particular is a deeply ethical consideration and centres on preserving academic integrity, managing data responsibly, regulating the input of copyrighted material in prompts and the use of AI-generated outputs, and establishing clear policy frameworks for the adoption of these tools.

Data management

The use of generative AI tools in education is a reality that needs to be controlled responsibly. Many institutions looking to implement these tools in classrooms would need to investigate their user agreements. In particular, there are two aspects to consider: whether the tool has an age requirement and whether the provider of the tool collects user inputs for training their models (Shepperd, 2025). In an analysis of the terms and conditions of 16 generative AI service providers, Shepherd (2025) found that most of the free services they looked at, including OpenAI ChatGPT, Google Gemini (Education accounts), Anthropic Claude (Enterprise, education accounts), Microsoft Copilot (Consumer versions), Microsoft Copilot (Enterprise, education accounts), Perplexity, Poe, OpenAI DALL·E, Midjourney, Adobe Firefly, GrammarlyGo, Wordtune, Scholarcy, UpWord, AIVA.ai, and GitHub Copilot, required users to be a minimum of 13 years old with parental consent, or 18. This is an important point to consider when recommending the use of these tools at educational institutions. In spite of this age requirement, 'there is often little or no requirement for users to actually verify their age or prove they have parental consent before gaining access to these tools' (Shepperd, 2025). Regarding data collection, among the 16 services analysed, there is a mix of options, eight of them offering a yes or no option, while in some cases the 'yes' options are 'opt in' (one) or 'opt out' (three).

The importance of safeguards

In the context of generative AI, safeguards help ensure that AI applications such as chatbots, AI agents and other automated tools deliver trustworthy outputs while protecting against vulnerabilities such as harmful content or sensitive data exposure. Safeguards, also referred to as guardrails, are the necessary controls and limitations put in place to govern how GenAI agents operate and interact within acceptable and safe parameters.

Here is a transcript of a prompt/answer session with ChatGPT about what it is not allowed to respond to:

Figure 5.4: Queries ChatGPT is programmed to not respond to (Response generated by ChatGPT)

Prompt:
What types of queries are you programmed to not respond to?

Answer:
Good question – I'm programmed not to respond to or generate content that violates **OpenAI's use policies**. Broadly, that means I can't engage with queries that involve:

1. **Illegal activities** – e.g. helping someone break laws, hack systems, or make weapons.
2. **Personal, confidential, or identifying information** – like doxxing, impersonation, or collecting private data.
3. **Sexually explicit or pornographic content** – especially anything involving minors.
4. **Hate speech, harassment, or discrimination** – including promotion of violence or hate against individuals or groups.
5. **Self-harm or suicide instructions** – though I can offer support resources if needed.

6. **Medical, legal, or financial advice meant to replace a professional's judgement** – I can give general info, but not act as a licensed adviser.
7. **Political campaigning or disinformation** – I can explain issues or analyse policies neutrally, but not advocate or spread falsehoods.
8. **Sensitive personal attributes** – I don't make or store assumptions about users' race, religion, sexuality, or health without explicit consent.
9. **Manipulative or deceptive content** – such as fake news, astroturfing, or creating false identities.

Safeguards are essential to prevent AI agents from generating content that is harmful, offensive or illegal (Koroshchak, 2025; de Conto *et al.*, 2025). A major concern for educators of learners under 18 – and one that needs robust safeguards – is the potential for AI chatbots and agents to engage in inappropriate conversations. In an alarming article, Horwitz (2025) mentions that internal documents from Meta revealed that their AI rules allowed bots to hold 'sensual' or 'romantic' conversations with children. These standards permitted descriptions of children that evidenced their attractiveness, such as referring to a 'youthful form' as a 'work of art' or 'masterpiece'. Meta has since stated that conversations involving sexual role-play or sexualising children should never have been permitted, and have confirmed that examples enabling provocative behaviour were erroneous and inconsistent with their policies, necessitating their removal.

Safeguards are crucial for managing and mitigating bias, ensuring that AI agents operate with fairness and non-discrimination, aligning agent models and behaviours with ethical and societal expectations. Safeguards also prohibit AI from generating content that encourages users to break the law or self-harm. They also limit responses that provide definitive legal, healthcare or financial advice. However, it's worth mentioning the case of a teenager in California who was engaging with ChatGPT 4o for homework when the conversation turned to more personal matters, resembling a therapy or counselling session, eventually encouraging suicidal thoughts and resulting in his taking his own life. According to an article in *The Guardian* (Bhuiyan, 2025), following the family's lawsuit against OpenAI, which claimed that this was not a glitch in the system or an edge case but the predictable result of deliberate design choices, OpenAI issued a statement acknowledging the shortcomings of its models when it came to addressing people in serious mental and emotional distress, and that, even though ChatGPT was trained to not provide self-harm instructions and to shift into supportive, empathic language, that protocol sometimes broke down during longer conversations or sessions, and it was working to improve the systems to better recognise and respond to signs of mental and emotional distress and connect people with care, guided by expert input. The company claims to continue to roll out stronger guardrails for users under 18 so that they recognise teens' unique developmental needs. Another example reported by Eadicicco (2025) is that, 'after a string of lawsuits alleged the app played a role in suicide and mental health issues among teens', Character.AI will no longer allow teens to engage in back-and-forth conversations with its AI-generated characters.

So, even with safeguards or guardrails, there is no guarantee that under 18s, or anybody else, is safe from inappropriate and dangerous interactions.

Figure 5.5: Ensuring safety and ethics

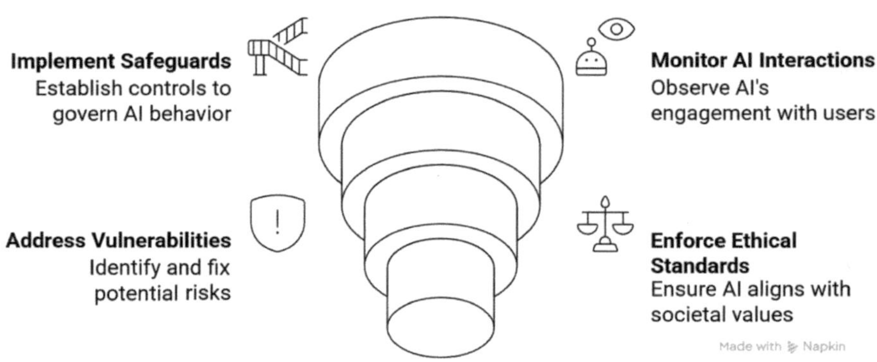

Use of students' and educational organisations' data

In light of the data-management issues described earlier, we need to be extremely vigilant about our students' data, both in terms of how we, as educators and administrators, and how students themselves, use GenAI, and what data we/they input into these systems. In our professional roles, we should make sure we do not input any sensitive personal information and/or intellectual property belonging to our students. And as ethical guardians, we should alert them to these issues as well. In exactly the same way, we should be wary of sharing any data from our educational organisations that should be kept private.

Reflective task 6

How can educational institutions and teachers protect students' data? What do you think about submitting students' writing to a GenAI general tool for automatic grading? Do you think there is a more responsible way of doing it?

Use of copyrighted material to generate activities

The ease with which GenAI tools can create lessons from scratch or from any given input, whether text or images, makes it quite tempting to use educational copyrighted material to generate lesson plans or further resources. Within the copyright framework, existing law specifically includes teaching (including using multiple copies in the classroom), scholarship and research as purposes that may be considered fair use of copyrighted material (Appel *et al.*, 2023). This traditional exception contrasts with the broader commercial use issues faced by AI developers' training models. But the fair-use claim should be used responsibly.

Reflective task 7

How do educational institutions and teachers benefit from fair-use doctrine? Think of examples in your context where you have used/can use copyrighted material.

How does GenAI push the limits on fair use?

Use of AI-generated outputs

With regards to the use of AI-generated outputs, professionals need to be aware of the copyright issues described above and be mindful of the risks of sharing AI-generated outputs. Here's a suggested checklist to follow when using AI outputs:

- **Fact-check everything:** Verify that any information, data and references generated by the AI are accurate and supported by reliable sources.
- **Check for bias:** Scrutinise the output for embedded biases that may arise from the AI's training data or prompts.
- **Do an extensive human revision:** Rework and revise the AI-generated content, integrating it into your existing work and ensuring it aligns with your context and objectives.
- **Verify sources independently:** Conduct your own search to find quality references and check the accuracy of any sources cited by the AI.
- **Maintain full accountability:** The human user is responsible for the final output, including any factual inaccuracies or modifications introduced by the AI.
- **Acknowledge AI origin:** If an AI-generated output is used, its origin, the tools used, prompts and methods of modification must be disclosed.

Reflective task 8

Think of a task you can ask a GenAI agent to do that involves writing and sources. When you get the output, apply the checklist above and track all the changes made to the original output.

Need for policy and responsible use

Companies and educational institutions beginning to integrate AI into their operations have several options to reduce the legal risk. First, they should be active in taking steps to monitor AI systems and to get adequate assurances from service and data providers. Contracts with service and data providers should include indemnification (a mechanism for ensuring that, if a company uses a product or technology in accordance with an agreement, that company is protected from legal liability) (Walsh, 2023).

The ethical concerns surrounding plagiarism, cheating and data privacy demand that educational institutions establish guidelines and policies surrounding the usage of AI tools (Rejeb *et al.*, 2024). These policies should specifically address the following:

- **Responsible AI use:** Ensuring students use AI as a supplementary resource rather than a substitute for their own work.
- **Data privacy:** Defining how students' data used within AI tools will be handled, stored and protected.
- **Academic integrity:** Updating assessment strategies and academic policies to maintain fairness and account for the presence of AI-driven tools.

Chapter 7 will address these guidelines and policies in more detail.

Figure 5.6: AI ethics in education

Reflective task 9

Before you read Chapter 7, what would these guidelines and policies look like for your own context? Make a draft version of the guidelines and policies you think you would need, which you can adjust after reading Chapter 7. Make sure you describe your context first, so that this reflection will be useful to share later.

Chapter 5 Key Points

1. **Dual mechanisms of data collection.** GenAI systems collect data in two distinct ways: "training data," which is scraped from the internet (often including personal or copyrighted information without consent), and "inference data" or "user-provided data," which includes every prompt, file, and query a user inputs.

2. **Data leakage and "resurfacing".** There is a significant risk of "data leakage," where information provided by one user reappears in the generated outputs for another user.

3. **The copyright "scraping" controversy.** Many models were trained on massive datasets containing billions of unlicensed works, including books, code, and images. This has led to major lawsuits from artists and authors who argue that this uncompensated copying infringes on their exclusive rights, while tech companies argue it falls under "fair use".

4. **Uncertainty of output ownership.** According to the US Copyright Office, AI-generated content generally cannot be copyrighted because it lacks "human authorship."

5. **Risk of derivative infringement.** GenAI outputs can be "insufficiently transformative," meaning they may closely resemble the copyrighted works they were trained on, potentially making the user liable for copyright infringement.

6. **Age restrictions and verification gaps.** Most GenAI tools require users to be at least 13 years old (with parental consent) or 18 years old. However, verification mechanisms are often weak or non-existent.

7. **Failure of "guardrails" and safety protocols.** While developers implement "guardrails" to prevent hateful or dangerous content, these safeguards frequently fail.

8. **The "black box" danger for student data.** Educators act as "ethical guardians" and must never input sensitive student personal information (PII) or intellectual property into GenAI systems.

---

9. **Necessity of institutional policy.** Schools cannot rely on ad-hoc decisions; they must establish clear policy frameworks. These policies should address responsible use (AI as a supplement, not a substitute), data privacy (how student data is handled), and academic integrity (updating assessments to account for AI tools).

Further reading

Appel, G., Neelbauer, J., & Schweidel, D. A. (2023). *Generative AI Has an Intellectual Property Problem* (Vol. 19, p. 58). Retrieved from https://hbr.org/2023/04/generative-ai-has-an-intellectual-property-problem

Burgess, M. (2023, April 4). *ChatGPT Has a Big Privacy Problem*, Wired. https://www.wired.com/story/italy-ban-chatgpt-privacy-gdpr/

Ism, I. (2025, January 21). Does ChatGPT Save Your Data? 2025 Privacy Guide. Chatbase.

Chapter 6: Access and equity in AI deployment

In this chapter, we define access and equity in the context of AI, and explore how AI can exacerbate existing inequalities and how it can be used to promote equity.

Reflective task 1

What is your initial understanding of 'access and equity in AI deployment'? Who should be responsible for this?

AI presents a landscape deeply conflicted in terms of access and equity, both in general societal application and specifically within the education sector. While AI holds immense potential to enhance learning and address global challenges, the current reality indicates that its uneven adoption is actively exacerbating existing global and societal inequalities, which threaten fundamental principles of fairness and social justice. The issues described so far in this book, though presented in different chapters, are difficult to isolate and are deeply interconnected. This chapter aims to integrate all the previous issues leading to the problem of access and equity.

Definitions of access and equity

The ethical considerations of AI require a clear understanding of what constitutes equitable access and fairness, as AI's powerful capabilities risk deepening global and systemic disparities while simultaneously offering potential solutions to promote inclusivity. In the context of AI, access and equity are intertwined concepts essential to developing and deploying trustworthy and responsible AI systems (Esther *et al.*, 2023; European Commission, 2022).

'Access' primarily relates to the physical, infrastructural and instructional opportunity to engage with AI technology. Access is challenged by the digital divide, where disparities exist in access to robust infrastructure, advanced technology, quality education and training (UN, 2024). For AI to be a driving force for inclusive education, accessibility must be enhanced through open-source AI models and collaboration between the public and private sectors (Dave, 2025). Equitable access means that AI technologies must be accessible to all students, regardless of socioeconomic status or physical abilities (Dave, 2025; Sain, 2024; Ramnani, 2024). Dave (2025) clarifies that it includes providing necessary hardware, offering training programmes and establishing clear policies on data usage that support and empower students.

Reflective task 2

In your specific context, how is access to AI helping or hindering your students' opportunities?

'Equity' (sometimes used interchangeably with 'fairness' or 'justice') is a foundational ethical principle concerning how individuals and groups are treated by AI systems and whether AI outputs reinforce or mitigate societal biases. According to the European Commission report (2022), fairness relates to everyone being treated fairly and ensuring clear processes so that all users have equal access to opportunity. According to Fu and Weng (2024), fairness and equity are essential areas of focus in AI in education (AIED), which require AI systems to avoid unfair biases and discrimination related to characteristics such as race, gender, socioeconomic status or disability status (Ramnani, 2024). The pursuit of equity and fairness in AI use must consider the specific context students are situated in and address their specific needs, rather than homogenise diverse learning differences (Fu & Weng, 2024). In this regard, the European Commission report (2022) states that the principle of diversity, non-discrimination and fairness ensures accessibility and universal design to enable AI use regardless of age, gender, abilities or characteristics.

Reflective task 3

In your specific context, how does AI fare regarding equity and fairness? Think of an example where AI has led or could lead to unfairness for your students.

Challenges to access and accessibility

If deployed without careful ethical oversight, AI systems can consolidate and amplify existing inequalities at the global, socioeconomic and systemic levels. This amplification is commonly known as the 'global AI divide'.

The concentration of AI development and resources in certain geographical areas risks deepening global economic and social divides. A UN report (2024) emphasises that the uneven rates of investment, adoption and use of AI among countries risks exacerbating already wide disparities in income and quality of life. Less-developed countries risk being left further behind in the rapidly evolving technological landscape, squandering AI's potential for widespread social and economic progress. The report also addresses the fact that the high costs of technology and infrastructure deficits, common in developing countries, limit the feasibility of seamless AI integration. The unequal availability and accessibility of GenAI are observed across high- and low-income countries. A basic access issue is internet access. According to Emaojo (2025), internet connectivity stands at 27% in low-income countries, 52% in lower-middle-income countries, 80% in upper-middle-income countries, and 93% in high-income nations. But this is made more complex by the cost of internet access. Emaojo (2025) reports that 'high-income countries have widespread, affordable internet access, with fixed broadband costs of just 1% of monthly income. In upper-middle-income countries, the cost climbs to 3%, reaches 8% in lower-middle-income countries, and a staggering 31% in low-income countries with limited connectivity.'

Reflective task 4

In your specific context, how does internet connectivity and cost affect AI deployment and use?

Furthermore, GenAI training tasks often underrepresent specific demographics, leading to systems that overrepresent the perspectives of the Anglophone world. Gwagwa *et al.* (2020) and Efe (2022) add the issue of algorithmic colonialism. Foreign-controlled or foreign-designed AI tools deployed in [other] settings are increasingly viewed in neo-colonial terms, such as '**algorithmic colonisation**', 'data colonialism', or 'digital colonialism'. This leads to a situation where AI applications tend to originate from outside a certain geographic location and thus lack contextual relevance. The digital divide also enables algorithmic exploitation, where corporate actors and industries using algorithmic tools unfairly exploit people leading to asymmetrical benefits. The digital spaces created by networked systems tend to be sites of extraction and exploitation (Couldry & Mejias, 2019). Exploitation occurs directly in the AI supply chain, where workers in developing countries often perform low-value, high-demand tasks that are essential for training AI models. Data curation and annotation are critical components of the AI value chain, often conducted as lower-value added activities predominantly in middle and low-income countries. This work, which demands digital skills and literacy, is often shifted to developing countries due to the lower wages compared to the same work performed in the US, for example (United Nations, 2024). GenAI training tasks are fuelled by millions of underpaid workers who perform repetitive tasks under poor working conditions (Hosseini *et al.*, 2025). Corporate leaders and technology companies enjoy asymmetrical benefits by making one-sided, profit-driven decisions about AI design and development, while often neglecting user and developer inputs (Fu & Weng, 2024). The systems developed also often reinforce and amplify existing societal biases, resulting in 'algorithmic oppression'. Algorithmic oppression is sustained by the unfair subordination and marginalisation of one social group while privileging another (Efe, 2022). This oppression is manifested in discriminatory outcomes: hiring bias (Yigitcanlar *et al.*, 2021; Dave, 2025), financial bias (Gwagwa *et al.*, 2020), automated assessment tools in education (Ramnani, 2024) and limitations in workers' agency (United Nations, 2024).

As described in Chapter 1, AI systems are susceptible to algorithmic bias because they are developed using historical data which can contain biases reflecting societal inequalities (e.g., related to race, gender, socioeconomic status or learning abilities). This issue is discussed by Jiang (2024) and Efe (2022) in their writings about the impact of AI on social problems.

Jiang (2024) and Efe (2022) bring up the concept of intersectionality, where disparities in computer science education are compounded for students who belong to multiple underrepresented subpopulations, such as those defined by the intersections of race, gender and rural location. For example, facial recognition algorithms detect white-skinned men with 99% success but have an error rate up to 35% in detecting dark-skinned women.

Promoting inclusive growth requires proactive strategies to empower AI development in countries on the disadvantaged side of this divide, focusing on digital infrastructure, AI skills and technology transfer and absorption.

Reflective task 5

Think of an example of 'algorithmic colonisation' which can cause problems within your student population.

A further consequence of the AI divide is the research gap. According to Stanford University's AI Index Report (2025), China leads in AI research publications (23.2% in 2023), but the United States leads in highly influential research, considering the top-100-cited AI publications. In 2023, East Asia and the Pacific led AI research output, accounting for 34.5% of all AI publications, followed by Europe and Central Asia (18.2%), North America (10.3%), South Asia (9.98%), the Middle East and North Africa (5.18%), Latin American and the Caribbean (1.66%) and Sub-Saharan Africa (0.89%). In terms of which sectors the research comes from, academic institutions remain the primary source of AI publications worldwide (85.9%), followed by industry (7.1%), government institutions (4.9%) and non-profit organisations (1.7%).

In addition, the AI Index (2025) shows the country of origin of notable models. It is not surprising that the US continues to be the leading source of notable AI models, with 40 compared to China's 15 and Europe's combined total of three. The data regarding the organisations leading in the production of notable machine learning models is not surprising either. Since 2014, Google has created 187 notable models, followed by Meta (82) and Microsoft (39). In 2024, the top contributors were Google (seven models), OpenAI (seven), and Alibaba (six).

A positive development is the existence of open-source AI software projects that could potentially help develop AI solutions in low-income countries. GitHub is the most widely used platform for open-source software. According to the AI Index (2025), since 2011, the number of AI-related GitHub projects has consistently increased, from 1,549 in 2011 to approximately 4.3 million in 2024, showing a 40.3% rise in the total number of GitHub AI projects in the last year alone. Among the geographic areas using GitHub, there's China, the US, Europe, India and the rest of the world. The geographic area that is reported to have used GitHub the most is the rest of the world, with 35.43%, which is an indication of the desperate need for cheap options to develop AI solutions.

Reflective task 6

How does or can the research gap affect geographical areas which are underrepresented in research publications? How can we bridge the research gap mentioned above?

Challenges to equity

One of the biggest challenges to equity is the algorithmic bias, that is, the inherent propensity of AI systems to reinforce and amplify existing societal biases, resulting in discriminatory outcomes. We have already addressed this in Chapter 1, where we described the issue of biased training data and how it manifests in GenAI output as discrimination and inflicts societal harms.

Figure 6.1: Access and equity challenges

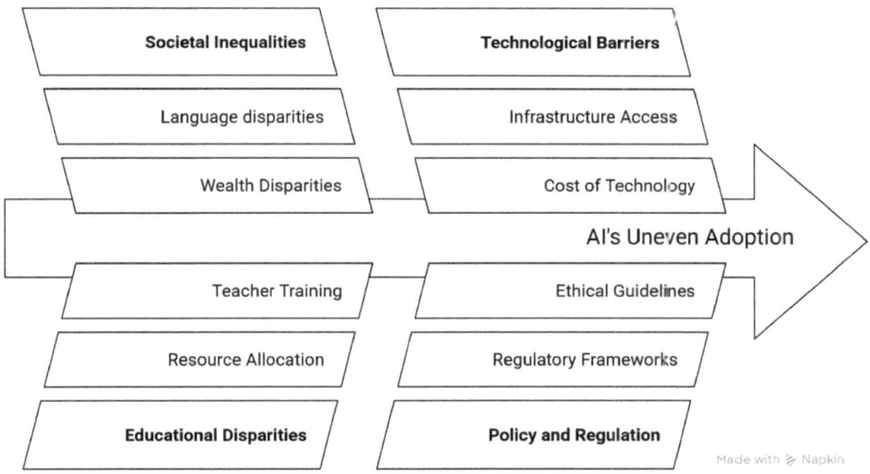

Why is this relevant to ELT?

In the context of education, AI deployment amplifies the risks related to access and equity in an area where fairness should be the ultimate goal. The issue of Gen AI biases, rooted in biased historical data reflecting societal inequalities (e.g., related to race, gender, socioeconomic status or learning abilities) is explored by Dave (2025) and Ramnani (2024) in their writings about the ethical implications of AI in education (AIED). We have already described in detail how algorithmic bias in AIED, and particularly for ELT contexts, is a pressing concern.

Regarding access, the adoption of AI technologies in education and ELT may exacerbate the socioeconomic divide by widening the gap between affluent students with access to advanced AI tools and resources on one hand, and disadvantaged students who lack equitable access to technology and personalised learning opportunities on the other (Donatus *et al.*, 2024; Dave, 2025). Not everyone has access to the internet and AI-assisted technology, specifically those who are poor and those who live in rural locations (Fu & Weng, 2024). We already shared data about the unequal availability of GenAI observed between high- and low-income countries, exemplified by internet connectivity and costs.

Accessibility should be guaranteed in education and ELT. If AI systems are not designed with inclusivity in mind, they may fail to accommodate students with disabilities or those requiring specialised learning approaches (Dave, 2025; Donatus *et al.*, 2024; Ramnani, 2024). Fu and Weng (2024) state that AI applications based on the average learner's data may fail to recognise cultural differences, special needs, or different learning paths, and over-reliance on AI can lead to learning becoming dehumanised, lacking the benefits of social interaction, student-to-student collaboration and emotional understanding.

Reflective task 7

What kind of accommodations do you need to make for your students with disabilities or those requiring specialised learning approaches? What particular strategies would guarantee AI accessibility to your student population?

Equity and fairness are essential areas to consider. When AI is applied to educational tasks such as assessment or admissions, it can reinforce existing educational disparities, which again can be traced back to training data and AI algorithms. One consequence is the reinforcement of privilege. AI-powered systems trained on historical assessment data may favour students from privileged backgrounds who have historically performed better due to access to superior resources (Dave, 2025). Assessment bias caused by AI algorithms, such as those used in automated essay scoring (AES), which are susceptible to assimilating and perpetuating biases present in the training data, leads to unfair evaluation (Ramnani, 2024). As discussed in Chapter 3, studies have shown that essays written by students from minority backgrounds, those using non-standard English dialects and English language learners were generally assigned lower scores by AES systems. According to Ramnani (2024), biased algorithms risk systematically disadvantaging specific student populations based on characteristics such as race, gender, socioeconomic status or disability, and these disparities are compounded for students who belong to multiple underrepresented subpopulations (intersectionality).

Figure 6.2: AI deployment risks in ELT

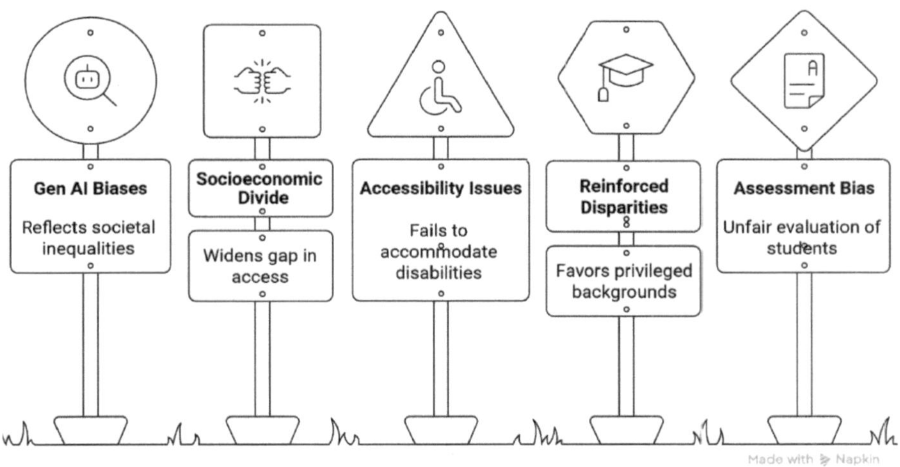

Reflective task 8

If automated essay scoring systems and AI detectors have been proven to return lots of false positives, specifically for EFL/ESL learners, how can you deal with this issue in order to guarantee equity and fairness?

A way forward

Although the landscape is quite bleak, we cannot overlook the potential of using GenAI for good. Despite the risks, when properly designed, AI offers a lot of potential to enhance access and promote inclusion, particularly for marginalised groups. Educational institutions and educators should work on enhanced accessibility to provide educational resources for people with disabilities and special needs (Donatus *et al.*, 2024; European Commission, 2022). For example, AI-based solutions like real-time live captioning can assist those with impaired hearing, and audio descriptions can make access easier for people with low levels of vision (European Commission, 2022). We should also be working on strategies to improve AI personalisation to make education more efficient, accessible and tailored to individual needs (Dave, 2025; Donatus *et al.*, 2024; Ramnani, 2024, European Commission, 2022). Jiang (2024) discusses research that supports adopting a strengths-based approach to address underrepresentation in computing. This same strength-based empowerment would be very positive in multilingual classes, where students have the added advantage of knowing another language, which allows them to draw upon diverse cultural perspectives, holistic language analysis, attention to writers' intentions and cultural nuances in language.

Another area in which educational institutions need to make progress to enhance equity and access is through policy and governance solutions. To address these challenges, ethical frameworks must be established that focus on intentional design and rigorous policy application across multiple sectors (Nyachiro, 2024). Policymakers within educational institutions must work towards the equitable distribution of AI resources and infrastructures, ensuring that opportunities for AI education and training are accessible to all students (United Nations, 2024). They should also be working towards mandatory trustworthy AI requirements. A key requirement for trustworthy AI is diversity, non-discrimination and fairness. This encompasses accessibility, universal design and the avoidance of unfair bias, with specific attention given to students with special needs (European Commission, 2022). Accountability frameworks are necessary to clearly define responsibility for errors and biases (Ramnani, 2024). Algorithmic transparency and explainable AI models are crucial to allow stakeholders to scrutinise and understand the decision-making process, thus mitigating unintended discriminatory outcomes (Dave, 2025). A further concern is contextualised implementation. Policies must ensure AI systems are designed to treat learners respectfully, adapting to their individual needs rather than homogenising their diverse backgrounds. Educational institutions must conduct regular audits to detect bias (Dave, 2025), ensure there is a human-centred approach to AI where final decisions are made by humans, and work on procedures to guarantee data integrity.

Figure 6.3: Pathways to educational inclusion

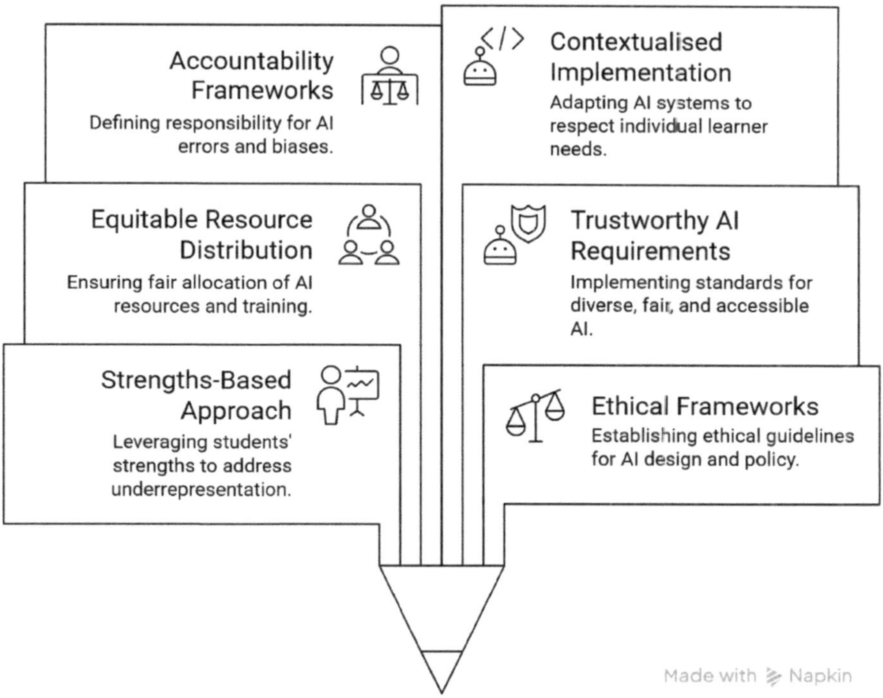

Reflective task 9

In your context, who is responsible for decisions about AI deployment? How can you, as a language teacher, contribute to promoting access, accessibility, equity and fairness?

Chapter 6 Key Points

1. **Distinction between access and equity.** Access refers to the physical and infrastructural opportunities to engage with technology (hardware, internet, training), while equity concerns fairness and justice—specifically whether AI systems treat individuals impartially or reinforce societal biases related to race, gender, and socioeconomic status.

2. **The economic "global AI divide".** There is a massive disparity in the affordability of the infrastructure required for AI, making the "seamless integration" of AI economically impossible for many developing nations.

3. **Algorithmic colonialism.** The current AI landscape is described as "algorithmic colonialism," where tools are designed in the West (Anglophone world) and deployed globally without local contextual relevance.

4. **Intersectionality of bias.** Algorithmic bias is not one-dimensional; it is "intersectional," meaning it compounds for individuals belonging to multiple underrepresented groups.

5. **Monopoly on research and models.** AI development is geographically concentrated. The United States leads significantly in the production of "notable AI models", and Western academic and corporate institutions (like Google and Meta) dominate the research landscape.

6. **Open source as a vital bridge.** A positive counter-trend is the rise of open-source projects on platforms like GitHub, indicating a desperate need for and reliance on free, accessible software solutions to bridge the development gap.

7. **Widening the socioeconomic gap.** In ELT, AI threatens to exacerbate the divide between affluent students, who gain access to personalized, 24/7 AI tutoring and advanced tools, and disadvantaged students who lack basic connectivity.

8. **Assessment bias.** AI-powered assessment tools systematically disadvantage minorities and English language learners.

9. **The accessibility paradox.** While AI has the potential to aid students with disabilities , current systems often fail to accommodate them because they are designed for the "average learner."

10. **Governance over individual choice.** Relying solely on individual teacher discretion is not enough. Instead, robust institutional policies and "accountability frameworks" are needed.

Further reading

Dave, A. (2025). The Ethical Implications of AI in education. *Research Review Journal of Social Science*. June 2025

European Commission (2022). *Ethical Guidelines on the Use of Artificial Intelligence*.

United Nations (2024). *Mind the AI Divide: Shaping a global perspective on the future of work*.

Part 2:
Practical solutions and strategies

Introduction

Part 2 of this book attempts to answer the question most English language teachers ask when faced with AI implementation in real classrooms with real students: "Yes, but how?". It deliberately shifts the emphasis from analysis to action. In this sense, Part 2 is practical, translating the issues raised in Part 1 into pedagogically sound and ethically informed strategies that teachers, teacher educators, and educational leaders can realistically implement.

Part 2 assumes that meaningful AI integration in ELT requires a clear awareness of the biases, limitations, and broader implications discussed in Part 1, and it demonstrates how this awareness can be embedded into everyday teaching practices. In Part 2, the reader is presented with a selection of reflective tasks, lesson ideas, pedagogical frameworks, and institutional guidelines that support informed professional judgement rather than uncritical adoption or outright avoidance.

Each chapter in Part 2 offers a concrete pedagogical response to the challenges previously identified. Chapter 7 focuses on guidelines for responsible use, presenting adaptable Codes of Conduct that clarify expectations, responsibilities, and boundaries across different educational contexts and levels. Chapter 8 develops AI literacy, equipping both teachers and students to understand how AI works, question its outputs, and reflect on its social and ethical implications. Chapter 9 explores positive and appropriate uses of AI, helping teachers identify where AI adds value to language learning, select tools critically, and maintain a balance between innovation and established pedagogy. Chapter 10 addresses prompting as a teachable skill, introducing structured frameworks such as C-PROFIT to support purposeful and transparent interaction with GenAI for learners and teachers. Finally, Chapter 11 presents AI-enhanced projects, illustrating how AI can meaningfully complement existing classroom activities through concrete examples, reflective tasks, and adaptable frameworks. We end with some general conclusions about the use of AI in ELT and some possible future directions.

Chapter 7:

Guidelines for responsible use

In this chapter, we call for responsible AI use in education through tailored, but customisable, Codes of Conduct for Primary, Secondary and Higher Education students, with clear guidelines and reflective practices.

> **Reflective task 1**
>
> What does 'responsible use' of AI mean in your teaching context? Who should be accountable for how AI is used in your classroom or institution? What values should guide AI-related decisions in education?

The need to be critical about the use of GenAI in education has posed several questions about its responsible use. 'Responsible use' means asking ourselves questions like:

> *Is it helping or harming the learning process of my students? How is this tool complementing the project/activity/task? Does it represent cognitive offloading for my students,*

and if so, in which skills? Is this tool treating all students fairly? Can I explain how it works to my students and their families? What happens if the tool makes a mistake?

At the end of the day, teachers are responsible for choosing and using GenAI tools wisely in the classroom. Ideally, administrators should create clear school policies and support their staff and students' to use AI ethically and to learn how to question what it produces. An essential part of our role as educators is to teach our students to question what AI produces, and how to be critical about it as a tool.

Essentially, the human and ethical values at stake in education are the same as those that we should consider when we use and teach students to use different sources: fairness, accountability, transparency, privacy and judgement.

Pedagogical alignment and human-centredness

GenAI applications should be guided by pedagogical theory and serve well-defined educational goals. GenAI tools should augment human capabilities and support learning, not replace core teaching functions or diminish students' agency. The **'human in the loop'** principle emphasises that teachers must be part of the process of pattern recognition and decision-making. Teachers can recognise patterns related to behaviour or learning in their students and decide accordingly, they are the ones that interpret the data ultimately using context and professional judgement. AI use should be proportional to its intended goals.

Accountability for AI use in your classroom or institution

Accountability for AI use in education is a shared responsibility, with a strong emphasis on human oversight and control.

Institutional leadership and oversight

School leaders have the responsibility to ensure that AI is approached thoughtfully and appropriately within the school community, and to inform the vision for teaching and learning.

Educational institutions must establish solid accountability mechanisms, including ethical guidelines, oversight committees and clear procedures for addressing errors or unethical practices. This includes auditing algorithms, data and the outputs of AI tools.

Procurement processes should ensure that AI tools align with educational objectives, legal standards and data-privacy requirements. Policies should be regularly reviewed and updated given the rapid advancements in AI.

When we are talking about integration, a No Blanket Ban approach on generative AI tools in institutions seems to be the best policy. At Harvard, the approach is to make a case-by-case decision. It recognises the growing importance of generative AI for future extracurricular and professional opportunities, and that a blanket ban would limit students' ability to develop proficiency in their responsible use. If students in middle school start learning how to optimise the use of Gen AI tools, learn the shortcuts and strategies to prompting, and know how to use it ethically, they will develop critical thinking, adaptability and digital citizenship skills that will pave the way not only for future academic achievement, but also for ethical decision-making, lifelong learning, responsible innovation and meaningful participation in a technology-driven world.

In schools, it's important to clearly explain the difference between types of AI tools – some are for writing, others for creating images or summarising information. Teachers and school leaders should make clear rules for how these tools can be used in class and for assignments. Schools should also be very cautious about using tools that try to detect AI-generated work, because they are not always reliable, as described in Chapter 4. Decisions about cheating should never be based only on these detection tools.

Students and teachers need access to educational materials that explain both the helpful uses and the risks of AI. These should stress that AI is not always accurate and should not replace real research. Students must always be honest about when and how they use AI – failing to do so is the same as copying from another source without saying so.

To help with consistency across classrooms, schools can provide example AI-use policies for teachers to adapt to each subject. Guidelines for using generative AI tools should be regularly reviewed and updated to reflect how quickly the technology is changing. These rules should be shared clearly with both students and teachers at the start of each term. Every class should have a written policy that explains when and how AI tools can and cannot be used, and how it might affect grading. These policies should be easy to find – for example, in student handbooks, digital platforms, or on classroom walls – and teachers should take the time to talk about them with students so everyone understands. It's also important to link these rules to the school's values around honesty and doing your own work, so students see AI use as part of being a responsible learner. Schools can also include student councils or ethics committees in reviewing how AI is being used, helping to ensure fairness and accountability.

Schools play a key role by:

- creating clear AI policies
- offering training and guidance
- encouraging ongoing dialogue about AI
- avoiding 'blanket bans' and promoting flexible, context-aware approaches

Reflective task 2

How can your school support both teachers and students to navigate AI use responsibly? List two things your institution could implement this year.

Values guiding AI-related decisions in education

Several core values and principles should guide decisions regarding AI in education to ensure its beneficial and ethical integration, as previously discussed:

- **Human-centredness and agency:** AI must serve to enhance human capabilities, agency and relationships, not replace them. Decisions about AI deployment should prioritise people, their learning and their well-being over mere efficiency or automation.
- **Transparency and explainability:** AI systems should be understandable, auditable and open about their operations, data collection and decision-making processes. This builds trust and enables informed human oversight and intervention.
- **Fairness, equity and non-discrimination:** AI must be used in ways that promote equity and inclusivity, ensuring access for all students regardless of background or ability, and actively mitigating biases that could lead to discrimination or disadvantage.
- **Beneficence and minimising harm:** The primary goal of AI in education should be to promote the welfare of users (students, teachers, staff) by actively providing value and minimising the potential negative impacts, such as cognitive offloading, privacy violations or psychological side-effects.
- **Accountability:** Clear mechanisms should be in place to ensure responsibility for AI's outcomes and to address errors or unintended consequences. This includes tracking decision-making processes and ensuring legal and ethical guidelines are followed.
- **Data privacy and security:** Upholding strong data privacy and security standards is fundamental. Personal and sensitive data should be protected, and users should be informed about data collection and usage.
- **Environmental and societal well-being:** Decisions should consider the environmental footprint of AI technologies (e.g., energy and water consumption) and their broader societal impact.

Figure 7.1: Core values for AI in education

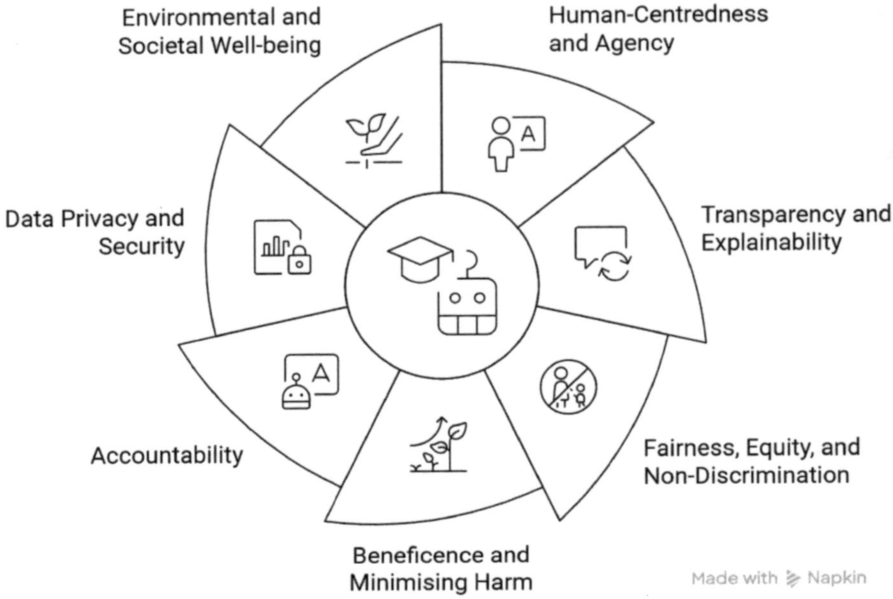

You can use this checklist to reflect before adopting or using any AI tool in teaching and learning.

Figure 7.2: Values guiding AI-Related decisions in education: a checklist (Co-created using ChatGPT)

Values guiding AI-Related decisions in education

1. Human-centredness & agency

- Does it enhance human learning and relationships, not replace them?
- Are teachers and students still in control of learning decisions?
- Does it put well-being over automation or efficiency?

2. Transparency & explainability

- Is it clear how the AI works and makes decisions?
- Can I see or audit the data it uses?
- Is it open about data collection and processes?

3. Fairness, equity & non-discrimination

- Does it include all learners, regardless of background or ability?
- Have biases been checked and mitigated?
- Could any group be unfairly disadvantaged?

4. Beneficence & minimising harm

- Does it offer clear educational value?
- Does it avoid overreliance or cognitive offloading?
- Have privacy, stress, or emotional impacts been considered?

5. Accountability

- Who is responsible for outcomes when GenAI is used?
- Are there processes to report errors or misuse?
- Are ethical and legal standards being followed?

6. Data privacy & security

- Is student data stored securely and transparently?
- Do users know what data is collected and why?
- Does it comply with data protection laws?

7. Environmental & societal well-being

- Have we considered its energy and water use?
- Does it benefit society and the learning community?
- Are sustainable practices encouraged in its use?

All AI use should align with:

- fairness
- transparency
- accountability
- privacy
- human-centred learning

Reflective task 3

Which of these values do you think is most difficult to maintain when using AI in school and why?

Responsible use of AI in your teaching context

As previously discussed, responsible use of AI in teaching means ensuring that human judgement and ethical considerations remain central. Teachers should follow guidelines based on these and teach students what this entails.

A clear distinction should be made at this point about the two decisions that teachers need to make. One is how they will use these tools to prepare their lessons, and the other is how they are going to introduce GenAI tasks to students and teach them to integrate it. Both are challenging tasks and teachers should be open to learning on the go, at times hand-in-hand with students, experimenting on their own and in the classroom. In Chapter 10, we will go in depth into how teachers can learn the art of prompting and how they can help students to become better at prompting themselves.

For now, let's have a look at some guidelines for AI integration and see how we can make it clear, both for ourselves and our students, that we are following them.

Teacher accountability

Teachers remain ultimately responsible for all instructional decisions, including assessment, feedback and grading, and should not cede this responsibility solely to AI systems, as discussed in Chapter 2. Teachers are responsible for providing clear explanations of their expectations around students' use of AI in assignments and for ensuring that AI integration supports learning outcomes ethically. They must actively review, acknowledge and critically reflect on all AI-generated content before using it in their practice or with students.

Educators are asked to consider:

> *Is AI supporting or hindering student learning? Does it cause over-reliance or 'cognitive offloading'? Is it used fairly and equitably? Can we explain its use to students and parents? How should we respond when AI makes mistakes?*

Teachers must guide students in using AI wisely. This includes:

- setting clear rules
- modelling ethical use
- promoting critical thinking
- ensuring AI supports (not replaces) learning

Reflective task 4

Think of a recent assignment for which you allowed or considered allowing AI use. How could you clarify your expectations and promote critical thinking in that task?

Student accountability

Students are responsible for using AI tools ethically and in line with established guidelines, particularly regarding academic integrity. They must be honest about their use of AI and understand that misuse may lead to negative consequences. The importance of transparency and acknowledgement cannot be ignored.

The proposed *Harvard AI Code of Conduct* (2023) and the *AI Guidance for Schools Toolkit* (2023) suggest that teachers should be transparent about their own use of AI and provide clear guidelines to students about when and how GenAI tools are permitted or restricted for assignments. In fact, these two documents refer to different levels of integration that may be broken down into the following:

- **Full use:** Students may use GenAI tools for any part of their assignments, but they must be honest about it and state this clearly by the end of the assignment.

- **Preparation only:** AI can help with brainstorming or organising ideas, but the final work must be done by the student.
- **Limited use:** AI is allowed only in specific tasks when the teacher says so.
- **No use:** AI is not allowed at all for certain assignments and using it would count as cheating.

Students should be taught to properly cite and attribute any AI-generated content or assistance used in their work. This helps prevent plagiarism and fosters a culture of accountability. Acknowledgement guidelines are an essential part of AI literacy and practice. Students should be able to explain what AI tools they used, what they asked the tool to do, how they checked the information, and what parts of the work include AI-generated help. Students are still responsible for their final work.

Acknowledgement starters for GenAI use

One way in which teachers can motivate students to naturalise the use of GenAI tools in classroom assignments depending on the level of integration is through the use of acknowledgement starters. They may range from general use to more specific activities, where students are invited to reflect on the use and purpose of the GenAI tool. This might work as a first approach to the integration and use of GenAI with short and specific sentence completion at the end of an assignment. Later in the chapter there is a more detailed chart for students to fill in. Students can adapt these as needed, but basically, if an assignment allows GenAI, students should be clear about their use and not present GenAI-generated work as entirely their own.

Figure 7.3: Acknowledgement starters for primary level

Primary school students

General use

I used (GenAI tool) to get ideas.

This part was made with (GenAI tool). I changed it using my words.

I asked (GenAI tool) to explain something.

I used (GenAI tool) to help me understand a topic.

I got help from (GenAI tool) to think of ideas.

Research & summarising

I used (GenAI tool) to find information.

I asked (GenAI tool) to show me different opinions.

I used (GenAI tool) to give me the main points, and I checked them with my teacher or book.

Writing & editing

I used (GenAI tool) to help me plan my writing.

I checked grammar and spelling using (GenAI tool).

I started this text with help from (GenAI tool), then I fixed it.

Revising & clarifying

I used (GenAI tool) to understand difficult words.

(GenAI tool) helped me change the order to make my writing better.

Reflection & responsibility

I used (GenAI tool) to help, but the ideas are mine.

I checked the (GenAI tool) suggestions to see if they were correct.

Figure 7.4: Acknowledgement starters for secondary level

Secondary school students

General use

I used (GenAI tool) to help me...

This section was generated with the help of (GenAI tool), then edited by me.

I asked (GenAI tool) to explain…

I used GenAI to summarise information about…

I brainstormed ideas using (GenAI tool) for…

Research & summarising

(GenAI tool) was used to gather background information on…

I used (GenAI tool) to find different perspectives on…

I asked (GenAI tool) to summarise key points from… and then verified them with (source).

Writing & editing

I used (GenAI tool) to help draft an outline.

The grammar in this paragraph was reviewed using (GenAI tool).

This introduction was partially written with AI support and then revised by me.

Revision & clarification

I used (GenAI tool) to clarify the meaning of... before writing this section.

(GenAI tool) helped me reorganise the structure of my answer.

Reflection & responsibility

Even though I used GenAI to assist with… the final ideas and wording are mine.

I reviewed and fact-checked all GenAI-generated suggestions.

Reflective task 5

How will you model the responsible use of GenAI tools in your teaching practice? How will you explain the allowed levels of GenAI use in student assignments (full, preparation only, limited, no use)? How will you teach students to properly acknowledge their use of AI in their work?

Implementing the integration of AI in the classroom from scratch

Regardless of the students' level, a good starting point is the implementation of an AI Code of Conduct for them to follow. Harvard University has a proposed *AI Code of Conduct* (2023) that outlines guidelines for the integration and use of AI tools and, of course, this can be adapted to different levels. It can be created collaboratively with students, to varying degrees according to age, so that they reflect on their use together with the teacher. The idea is that it can assist with the development of policies for GenAI tool usage in the classroom.

In the same way that, at the beginning of each year, we teachers collaboratively design classroom rules to promote a positive learning environment with our students and among ourselves, including a GenAI Code of Conduct will become increasingly important for each classroom.

Here is an adapted example of what a GenAI Code of Conduct for young learners/teenagers might include:

Figure 7.5: GenAI code of conduct (Co-created using ChatGPT)

Our GenAI Code of Conduct

Let's use AI the smart way!

1. **Be honest**
   Tell your teacher if you used GenAI and how you used it. Cite when necessary.
2. **Think for yourself**
   GenAI can help, but *you* must do the learning! Make sure you understand what it means.
3. **Check the facts**
   GenAI sometimes makes mistakes – double-check with books, online sources or teachers.
4. **No cheating**
   Don't let GenAI do your work. Give it your own imprint and add meaning.
5. **Be kind**
   Don't use GenAI to hurt, bully or lie about others.
6. **Be fair**
   AI might not know all cultures – be thoughtful and ask questions.
7. **Ask & learn**
   Learn how to prompt and follow the tips given in class.

8. **Use the right tool**
   Use GenAI only when it's allowed and helpful for learning. Use the tools suggested by your teacher.
9. **Stay safe online**
   Don't share your full name, address or photos with GenAI tools. Privacy is always key.
10. **Keep growing**
    Technology changes – learn, reflect and help others use GenAI well. Co-build meaning.

Reflective task 6

What would be the biggest benefit or challenge for your students if you co-created a GenAI Code of Conduct with them?

Critical thinking and evaluation

Harvard University's *AI Code of Conduct* (2023) makes the point that students must understand the limitations of GenAI and recognise that it is not a substitute for their own critical thinking, creativity and problem-solving skills. GenAI-generated content may be inaccurate, biased or outdated as explained earlier in this book. Therefore, students and teachers should critically evaluate all GenAI outputs and verify information using trusted sources before relying on them. Over-reliance on GenAI can lead to cognitive offloading and diminish critical thinking. Tasks should be designed to require students to demonstrate their thought processes and engage in higher-order thinking, rather than merely submitting GenAI-generated content.

For instance, in an activity, a group of 11-year-old students had to engage in a reflective process that combined independent composition with guided GenAI collaboration. They began by producing a first draft entirely on their own that was the continuation of a story, focusing on developing their ideas in a cohesive and coherent manner. Once the initial version was complete, students had to move into a dialogue with GenAI, using it as a writing coach rather than a text generator. They input their draft and asked for targeted feedback and improvement on specific areas such as coherence, tone, vocabulary range or paragraph structure. Instead of simply accepting the suggestions, students had to critically evaluate the GenAI's responses, deciding which recommendations enhanced their message and which ones didn´t. It was important for students to keep track of their interactions in a log to see how they became more assertive in their prompts to obtain their desired output. After this reflective dialogue, students revised and produced a final draft that blended their voice with carefully chosen GenAI improvements. They were also asked to annotate or briefly explain the reasoning behind their choices, showing evidence of analytical thinking and self-awareness. This final version represented not just linguistic refinement but a metacognitive process in which students demonstrated their ability to assess, adapt and justify revisions. By comparing their drafts and reflecting on the transformation, they came to see GenAI as a collaborative partner in learning, one that stimulated higher-order thinking, fostered autonomy and strengthened their capacity to make meaningful editorial decisions.

When evaluating the integration of GenAI tools, the SAMR model crafted by Ruben Puentedura (2010), which stands for 'Substitution, Augmentation, Modification, Redefinition', might come in handy. At the lower levels – that is, Substitution and Augmentation – GenAI may simply replace traditional tools, such as using an AI agent to check grammar and spelling, or to summarise a text. While convenient, this can lead to cognitive offloading, as mentioned before, and diminish critical thinking if students rely on GenAI tools without understanding or questioning its output. At the higher levels – Modification and Redefinition – GenAI tools enable more transformative learning, such as co-creating content, analysing GenAI bias, or reflecting on ethical dilemmas. Tasks in these categories encourage students to demonstrate their thinking and engage in higher-order skills like evaluation, synthesis and creativity.

The SAMR model helps evaluate whether AI is just replacing tools or transforming learning in deeper ways. Ideally, AI use supports higher-order thinking and creativity.

Reflective task 7

Think of an activity you've done or seen that uses AI. Would you categorise it as Substitution, Augmentation, Modification or Redefinition? Why?

Ethical awareness and bias mitigation

Responsible use of AI also means taking steps to mitigate bias when using or evaluating AI outputs. Both teachers and students need to develop AI literacy, which includes understanding the ethical implications of AI, such as potential biases in algorithms, privacy concerns, misinformation and societal impacts. This will be dealt with more in depth in Chapter 8.

Using rubrics for student reflection

Criteria may vary depending on the task/activity or project, but possible variables to consider are considered in the rubric below. Rubrics are helpful because they provide both teachers and students with a clear framework for understanding expectations and measuring progress in a transparent, consistent way. By breaking down performance into specific criteria, such as content, organisation, language accuracy, creativity or use of GenAI, rubrics make assessment more objective and purposeful. They guide students through the learning process, helping them see what quality work looks like and how to improve specific areas rather than guessing at vague standards. For teachers, rubrics serve as planning and feedback tools that align assessment with learning objectives, making evaluation fairer, more efficient and clearer.

Table 7.1: Student's reflection rubric (Co-created using ChatGPT)

Students' reflection rubric

Level: Ages 10–15

Purpose: To help students reflect on their ethical and responsible use of GenAI tools in schoolwork and to critically evaluate their integration.

Criteria	Excellent (4)	Good (3)	Needs improvement (2)	Not yet (1)
1. Honesty and acknowledgement 🤝	Clearly stated when and how AI was used; added a short note or citation.	Mentioned AI use but lacked full detail or proper format.	Vaguely mentioned AI use or didn't explain how it helped.	Didn't say AI was used when it was.
2. Original thinking 💡	Student did most of the thinking; AI only supported small parts (e.g., ideas, spelling).	AI supported a few parts, but student's own ideas are still very clear.	AI was used a lot; student thinking is hard to see.	Most or all of the work was copied or AI-generated.
3. Fact-checking and accuracy 🔍	Checked facts from other sources (books, websites, teacher) and corrected AI errors if needed.	Checked some facts but missed a few AI mistakes.	Didn't check facts; some AI mistakes are still in the work.	Fully trusted AI; errors or false info were left in the assignment.
4. Fair and safe use 🛡	Used AI kindly, safely and without bias; no personal info shared.	Mostly safe and fair use, minor reminders needed.	Some unfair use or privacy concerns.	Unsafe or inappropriate AI use.

Criteria	Excellent (4)	Good (3)	Needs improvement (2)	Not yet (1)
5. Clear AI thinking 💭	Explained thinking process: how AI helped and how they decided what to keep or change.	Some explanation given, but limited details.	A little explanation but unclear how AI helped or how choices were made.	No explanation of thinking or AI use.
6. Respect for rules 📏	Followed all classroom rules for AI use (from the AI Code of Conduct or teacher guidelines).	Mostly followed rules, but one small mistake.	Some rules not followed or misunderstood.	Broke major rules about AI use.
7. Critical thinking 🔎	Evaluated what AI gave them and improved it with their own ideas or creativity.	Edited some AI content but didn't go very deep.	Used AI content without improving it much.	No sign of critical thinking or improvement.

Total Score: /28

Scoring suggestions:

- 25–28 = Excellent and responsible use
- 20–24 = Good understanding
- 14–19 = Needs support
- <14 = Let's reflect together

Using reflection questions

Another option for student reflection could be adding reflection questions in the assignments to serves as an exit ticket or self-evaluation:

- *How did GenAI help you in this assignment?* Students can highlight specific sections.
- *What did you learn without using GenAI?* Students can account for their research work.
- *Did you find any mistakes from GenAI?* You can check how meticulous students were when including GenAI and if they compared and contrasted with other sources.

How would you explain your use of GenAI to a friend? Students can put it in their own words.

Table 7.2: Reflection questions

Reflection question	Purpose	What it shows about the student
How did AI help you in this assignment?	Encourage students to reflect on *when and how* they used AI.	Awareness of AI use and ability to identify specific moments of support.
What did you learn without using AI?	Highlight the importance of independent learning and research.	Accountability for their own thinking, effort and personal learning.
Did you find any mistakes from AI?	Promote fact-checking and source evaluation.	Meticulousness, critical thinking and verification of AI-generated content.
How would you explain your use of AI to a friend?	Reinforce clarity and honesty about AI use.	Ability to communicate ethical use in simple terms; personal responsibility.

Using reflection charts

Yet another option is to use a reflection chart. Here is an example chart to be completed by students:

Table 7.3: Reflection chart

AI-use reflection chart (to be completed after your assignment)

Please complete this chart honestly after finishing your assignment. This will help you reflect on your learning and your use of AI tools.

Reflection question	Your answer (complete in your own words)
1. What AI tool(s) did you use?	
2. What did you ask the AI to do?	
3. How did you check the information the AI gave you?	
4. Which parts of your work include help from AI?	
5. What part did you complete entirely on your own?	
6. Did you find any mistakes in the AI output?	

Students should:

- Be transparent about when and how they use AI.
- Fact-check information.
- Think independently.
- Follow class-specific policies.

Reflective task 8

Think of a recent assignment for which you allowed (or considered allowing) AI use. Reflect on how you could have made your expectations clearer and how you might redesign the task to promote student ownership, ethical AI use and critical thinking, integrating the reflection chart in this chapter.

To summarise, to make issues around responsible use of AI visible and assessable, the following tools are useful:

- **AI Code of Conduct** created with students.
- **Reflection charts** post-assignment.
- **Rubrics** for evaluating ethical and critical use.
- **Built-in prompts** for metacognition.

Reflective task 9

Choose one of the tools above. How could it be used in the subject you teach?

Final takeaway

AI can be a powerful tool, but only when paired with careful thinking, ethical use and human-centred teaching. The goal isn't just academic success – it's helping students become thoughtful, responsible and adaptable in an AI-driven world.

Reflective task 10

In one sentence, write your own takeaway from this chapter. How will it influence how you teach or learn with AI?

Further reading

Black, N. B., & Brooks-Young, S. (2024). *Hands-On AI Projects for the Classroom: A guide on ethics and AI.* International Society for Technology in Education.

Black, N. B., & Brooks-Young, S. (2024). *Hands-On AI Projects for the Classroom: A guide for secondary teachers.* International Society for Technology in Education.

Chapter 8:
AI Literacy

In this chapter, we present strategies and tasks to engage students in active discussions about how AI works, its capabilities and limitations, and its necessary critical and ethical use.

Reflective task 1

What do you think we are referring to when we talk about AI literacy in ELT? What competencies do you believe to be essential as an educator? What competencies are core to teach your students? What would they be missing if you didn't teach them in class?

AI literacy in ELT

AI literacy in English language teaching involves empowering individuals with the competencies to critically understand, evaluate and effectively use generative AI (GenAI) systems and tools for safe and impactful participation in an increasingly digital world (Digital Promise, 2024). This goes beyond the basic digital skills of using devices, finding and managing information, communicating online, creating content and staying safe in the digital world.

The sophistication of modern AI and GenAI tools calls for a transformation in education. For English language learners (ELLs) and educators, developing GenAI literacy has become crucial for effectively navigating AI-driven systems, boosting performance and developing a competitive edge both in teachers and students.

At its core, AI literacy in ELT encompasses the knowledge, skills and attitudes needed to thrive in an AI-influenced environment, empowering both students and teachers to understand AI's risks and opportunities, and to make ethical decisions about its use. It is a vital component of broader digital literacies.

Table 8.1. Digital literacy and AI literacy (Co-created using ChatGPT)

Broader digital literacy	Traditional focus	GenAI literacy extension
Information literacy	Find, evaluate and use online information responsibly.	Evaluate AI-generated outputs for accuracy, reliability and bias in training data. Always ask yourself, 'Does this make sense?' and cross check with other sources.
Media literacy	Understand and analyse digital media content.	Understand how AI generates text, images, audio; detect deepfakes and synthetic content. Ask yourself 'Does the lighting look right? Do the eyes and mouth move naturally? Does the voice sound natural? Does the video feel "too perfect" or "too weird"?'

Broader digital literacy	Traditional focus	GenAI literacy extension
Communication & collaboration	Communicate and work together via digital platforms.	Collaborate with AI tools (e.g., chatbots, translation, brainstorming) to co-create content in a dialogic manner, a back-and-forth conversation rather than just a source of answers. The idea is to ask, refine and iterate, like having a discussion with a colleague create content together. Foster interaction with the GenAI: 'Why do you suggest this? Can you make this explanation simpler for younger students?'
Data literacy	Interpret, manage and use datasets.	Understand how AI uses data, the impact of dataset quality, and related privacy concerns. Ask the GenAI to provide a summary of how it collects data and what are the key aspects you should know as a user.
Digital creativity	Create and adapt digital content (documents, visuals, presentations).	Use AI to generate drafts, designs and ideas, then refine with human judgement and give it your personal human touch or imprint.
Digital well-being	Manage screen time, online safety and mental health.	Balance AI use with human skills; avoid over-reliance and maintain emotional well-being.

Broader digital literacy	Traditional focus	GenAI literacy extension
Critical digital literacy	Question sources, media bias and online power structures.	Critically assess AI outputs, recognise algorithmic bias, and challenge unethical uses. Ask yourself 'Am I relying too much on AI without checking other sources? Whose perspectives might be missing from this AI-generated content?'

Reflective task 2

What are the core skills for teachers and students? How do we cite when we use GenAI? How do we teach students to properly reference their work?

Core AI concepts in ELT

As previously mentioned, GenAI literacy in ELT means giving both teachers and learners the skills to understand, evaluate and use AI tools safely and effectively. Unlike basic digital skills, GenAI literacy goes a lot further because today's AI is much more complex. For English language learners and their teachers, these skills are essential if they are to make the most of GenAI tools in the classroom. GenAI literacy combines knowledge, practical skills and responsible attitudes. It helps students and teachers to not only use AI but also to think critically about its risks and opportunities, and make ethical choices about when and how to rely on it. This makes GenAI literacy an important part of the broader set of digital literacies that learners need today.

Here are the core AI concepts central to developing AI literacy in ELT that teachers need to manage in the classroom, based on Lee (2023):

Understanding what AI is and how it works (AI Foundations)

What is AI? AI is a branch of computer science focused on creating machines that mimic human intelligence. It's used for tasks typically requiring human thought, such as understanding language, recognising patterns or making decisions. AI allows machines to learn, adapt and perform tasks often more quickly and accurately than humans.

What is the difference with generative AI? This is a type of AI that creates new content or outputs (like text, images, audio, video) from existing data, often in response to user prompts.

Core mechanisms of AI and that teachers and students need to know:

Algorithms: AI systems operate based on algorithms, which are sets of rules and instructions that a computer follows to solve problems or answer questions. AI models 'learn' by adjusting statistical weights based on large datasets.

Machine Learning (ML): This is a subfield of AI which involves algorithms that enable computers to learn and make decisions or predictions based on data without explicit programming. They improve performance over time by being trained on large amounts of data using statistical methods.

Large Language Models (LLMs): These are ML models trained on vast amounts of text data to predict the next word in a sentence, thereby acquiring extensive knowledge about the world and language.

Training data: AI models learn from data, which can come from publicly available information, user-generated content, databases and real-time interactions. The quality and representation of this data significantly affect the model's performance.

Prompts and prompt engineering: Users provide input text, called prompts, to guide the AI's output. Prompt engineering is the technique of carefully crafting these inputs to maximise the likelihood of a desired response. It's a new skill required for effective AI tool usage.

Types of AI: Beyond generative AI, there are also Reactive AI (responds without learning from past experience, e.g., Alexa, Roomba) and Predictive AI (analyses historical data to predict future events, e.g., Netflix recommendations). Concepts like Narrow AI (performs specific tasks) and Strong AI/Artificial General Intelligence (AGI) (can do any human task, potentially sentient) are also important to distinguish.

Table 8.2: AI types and characteristics

Characteristic	Definition	Core Mechanism	Data Usage	Prompt Dependency	Capabilities	Examples
General AI	Human-level intelligence across all domains.	Cognitive reasoning & cross-domain logic.	Multi-modal; learns like a human from few examples.	High (interactive reasoning).	Learns, adapts, performs tasks	Theoretical (e.g., HAL 9000).
Reactive Machines	Reacts to current inputs only.	Logic-based "if-then" rules.	N/A	N/A	Responds to immediate stimuli	IBM's Deep Blue (Chess).
Generative AI	Creates new, original content.	Transformers and Diffusion models.	Pre-trained on trillions of tokens/images.	Extreme.	Creates new content	Content creation, summarization, coding.
Predictive & Discriminative AI	Classifies data and forecasts outcomes.	Classification and regression algorithms.	Structured historical data.	Low.	Predicts future outcomes	Fraud detection, stock market forecasting.
Agentic AI	Autonomous agents that reason and act.	Loop-based reasoning with tool use.	Dynamic; accesses real-time data.	Medium.	Executes autonomous tasks, plans and reasons	Booking a flight, managing a calendar.

Made with Napkin

Understanding AI's capabilities and limitations

As educators, we need to teach our students that AI is not an omniscient entity, and that continuous questioning is necessary to know what to expect and how to use it. Here are some concepts that need to be understood:

AI is not human intelligence even if it sounds like it is: AI is not human intelligence; it lacks emotions, consciousness or the ability to make ethical judgements. It mimics human writing or behaviour but doesn't 'think' in the same way humans do. This must be clear for our teachers and students who sometimes interact with it for emotional support and guidance.

Hallucinations: A significant limitation is AI's tendency to generate 'hallucinations', which are pieces of information not based on its training data or input. This output can be creative but also misleading or incorrect, including fake sources, fabricated quotations and citations. Both teachers and students must be able to verify information and cross check.

Bias: AI technologies, especially those trained on vast datasets, can reflect and amplify harmful biases embedded in their training data or introduced during development. This includes biases towards specific language varieties. For example, an AI writing tool might mark British English spelling ('colour') as incorrect, favouring American English. Similarly, it may generate fewer examples with female doctors compared to male doctors, reinforcing stereotypes, as seen in Chapter 1.

Accuracy and reliability: AI-generated content can be convincing but incorrect. Detection tools for AI-generated content are not always accurate and can be biased against non-native English writers. For example, a GenAI tool might generate a history essay with the wrong dates for important events. At the same time, an AI-detection system could mistakenly mark a student's essay as 'AI-written', just because the student is a non-native English writer.

Intellectual property and ownership: The copyright status of AI-generated content is often unclear. Learners need to understand the ethical implications about content ownership and attribution when using AI-assisted creations. For instance, a student might use AI to create an image for a class project, but it's unclear who owns that image. Similarly, copying AI-generated text into homework without attribution could raise questions of plagiarism.

Data privacy and security: AI systems collect and store personally identifiable information, raising concerns about data privacy. For example, when students sign up for an AI homework assistant, they may be asked to share their names or emails, which could be stored and shared. If not handled carefully, this personal data might put their privacy at risk.

Societal and ethical implications: GenAI systems exist within social and political systems, and their outputs can reinforce existing patterns of unfairness, as seen in Chapters 1 and 2. Learners, both teachers and students, must develop an awareness of who benefits or is harmed by GenAI systems, what perspectives are represented or excluded in training data and outputs, and how AI influences personal autonomy, ownership and access to information. Developing AI literacy involves discussing ethical issues like data privacy, intellectual property and algorithmic biases.

Developing, teaching and learning a strong understanding of these core AI concepts allows individuals in ELT to critically understand and evaluate AI, use it effectively, and make informed, ethical decisions about its application in language learning and beyond.

Figure 8.1: AI in education: Challenges and solutions

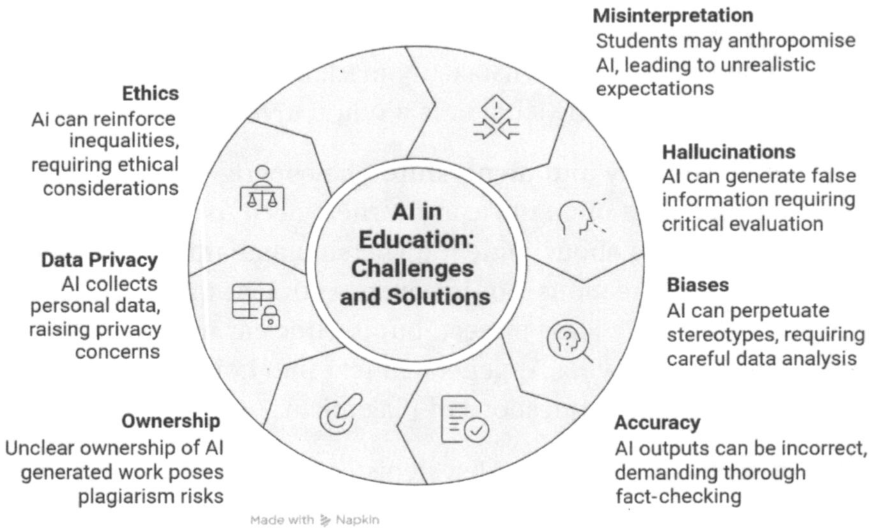

Teachers and learners need a shared understanding of what AI and GenAI are, how they work (algorithms, training data, large language models), and what their limits are (hallucinations, bias, accuracy, data privacy, ownership). Being aware of these limitations helps us to develop a critical eye.

Reflective task 3

How do you currently explain GenAI and its limitations to your students? Could you use an age-appropriate metaphor, story or example to make it clearer?

Core skills and referencing

AI literacy in language learning means developing a set of skills in four areas, as described by Tour *et al.* (2025): operational (how to use the tools), contextual (understanding where and when to use them), critical (thinking about risks, ethics and fairness), and creative (using AI for new ideas and outputs).

Among these, the critical domain is especially important for teachers because it includes teaching students how to reference and attribute AI-generated content correctly. Clear guidance on referencing helps students use AI responsibly while keeping human judgement and decision-making at the centre. We will provide a brief introduction in this chapter and will explain in further detail, with examples related to prompting, in Chapter 10.

Operational domain: This includes understanding basic AI concepts and developing prompt literacy, which is the ability to construct appropriately detailed linguistic inputs for desired outputs. This is an extension of traditional search literacy, but prompts need more engineering behind them and they are not a mere search tool.

Contextual domain: This emphasises understanding that AI processes language through probabilistic pattern matching, not genuine understanding, requiring users to craft context-specific queries and assess responses appropriately.

Critical domain: As stated, this is particularly relevant to referencing and attribution and it is important for students to learn how to cite when they are integrating GenAI.

Creative domain: This involves collaborating with AI systems in creative or problem-solving processes, guiding and refining AI outputs, and ensuring content is fair and appropriate. Ethical considerations regarding content ownership and attribution are also part of this domain.

Developing GenAI literacy requires operational, contextual, critical and creative skills. Teachers must especially emphasise critical skills, i.e. questioning outputs, spotting bias and citing GenAI use.

Reflective task 4

Which AI literacy skill (operational, contextual, critical or creative) do you model most in your lessons? Which one do you neglect, and how could you bring it in?

Referencing guidelines in ELT

Teachers play a crucial role in fostering AI literacy. Part of this responsibility involves being transparent with students: when we use content generated by GenAI, we should clearly acknowledge it and specify the tool employed. Modelling this practice in our classrooms helps normalise AI use as part of learning, while also preparing students to do the same when it is their turn. Establishing clear ground rules and guidelines for attribution ensures that everyone shares a common understanding of how GenAI can be used responsibly and transparently.

Equally important is engaging students in discussions around ethical dilemmas and academic integrity. GenAI raises questions about data privacy, intellectual property and algorithmic bias, as well as issues of content ownership and attribution. Using AI to generate answers or complete assignments without citation – or presenting AI outputs as one's own work – constitutes plagiarism. At the same time, we are entering what some describe as a 'post-plagiarism' world, where detection tools are increasingly unreliable, making transparent disclosure more important than ever. Teachers must therefore guide students to see GenAI not as a shortcut, but as a tool to be used ethically, critically and with integrity.

Acknowledgement and citation requirements

Students are expected to provide proper recognition of AI contributions to their work, be it primary or secondary school students. Instilling this habit from an early age will pave the way for lifelong skills in evaluating, citing and integrating AI tools responsibly, fostering critical thinking, transparency and ethical use of technology in both academic and professional settings. This involves clearly disclosing all instances where GenAI tools were used, including for ideation, research, analysis, editing or debugging.

For assignments where GenAI tools are permitted, explicit acknowledgement is necessary, detailing which tools were used and how.

Many institutions suggest including the specific prompts entered into the model(s). In Chapter 7, there are some acknowledgement starters for GenAI use for primary and secondary school students. These can be complemented with information about how outputs were evaluated, and whether and where the outputs were used in the submitted work. If GenAI-created content is directly included in a submission, it must be formally acknowledged using a formal citation protocol.

The minimum requirement for acknowledgement typically includes: the name and version of the generative AI system (e.g., ChatGPT-3.5), the publisher (e.g., OpenAI), the URL of the AI system, and a brief one-sentence description of the context of use (e.g., 'I acknowledge the use of ChatGPT 3.5 (Open AI, https://chat.openai.com) to summarise my initial notes and to proofread my final draft'.).

Despite AI's assistance, students are responsible for the entirety of their final submission; inaccuracies or deficiencies cannot be excused by attributing them to the AI tool, and this must be very clear in the Guidelines for Responsible Use and clearly stated.

Students are often advised to use established citation styles for GenAI. The examples provided here are about sources that explicitly mention APA Style as a resource for citing.

Primary school students

At primary level, the goal is mainly habit-building: students should begin to recognise when and how AI can help them, while still using simple language. Teachers can guide them to add a short acknowledgement line at the end of their work.

Here are some examples for classroom use:

I got help from ChatGPT (OpenAI, https://chat.openai.com) to think of ideas for this story. Then I wrote it in my own words.

I asked ChatGPT (OpenAI, https://chat.openai.com) to explain new words. I used that to make my writing better.

I used ChatGPT (OpenAI, https://chat.openai.com) to check spelling, but the sentences are mine.

Table 8.3 Acknowledging AI use in primary level

What I used AI for	Sentence starter	My example (fill in)
Thinking of ideas	I got help from [GenAI tool] to think of ideas for…	
Understanding words	I asked [GenAI tool] to explain…	
Summarising	I used [GenAI tool] to give me the main points about…	
Checking writing	I checked grammar/spelling using [GenAI tool].	

What I used AI for	Sentence starter	My example (fill in)
Improving sentences	[GenAI tool] helped me change the order to make my writing better.	
Reflection	I used [GenAI tool] to help, but the ideas are mine.	

Secondary school students

At secondary school, students should be introduced to a more formal acknowledgement protocol, while still using accessible language. Their statements should combine:

1. Tool name and version (e.g., ChatGPT-4, OpenAI).
2. Publisher (OpenAI).
3. URL (https://chat.openai.com).
4. Purpose/context of use (what the GenAI was used for).

Here are some examples for classroom use:

> *I acknowledge the use of ChatGPT-4 (OpenAI, https://chat.openai.com) to brainstorm essay ideas and draft an initial outline. I revised and finalised the content myself.*
>
> *ChatGPT-4 (OpenAI, https://chat.openai.com) was used to summarise background information about renewable energy. I checked these points against my textbook.*
>
> *This paragraph was reviewed using ChatGPT-4 (OpenAI, https://chat.openai.com) for grammar suggestions. Final corrections and style choices were my own.*
>
> *I used ChatGPT-4 (OpenAI, https://chat.openai.com) to explain a difficult concept in biology. I confirmed the explanation with my teacher and other sources.*

The chart below intends to instill the habit of referencing in students, teaching them to provide concrete examples and reflect on them.

Table 8.4: Acknowledging AI use in secondary level

Purpose of use	Formal acknowledgement starter	My example (fill in)
Brainstorming and planning	I acknowledge the use of [GenAI tool + version] (Publisher, URL) to brainstorm…	
Research and summarising	[GenAI tool + version] (Publisher, URL) was used to summarise information about… I verified it with…	
Writing support	This section was generated with the help of [GenAI tool + version] (Publisher, URL), then revised by me.	
Grammar and editing	The grammar in this paragraph was reviewed using [GenAI tool + version] (Publisher, URL). Final choices are mine.	
Clarifying concepts	I used [GenAI tool + version] (Publisher, URL) to explain… and confirmed it with…	
Reflection	Even though I used [GenAI tool] for…, the final ideas and wording are mine.	

Reflective task 5

How would you introduce this chart in a primary school setting? How would you instil the habit of referencing when it comes to doing research as homework or in a classroom activity? Have you thought about this before?

Reflective task 6

Do you model how to cite GenAI when you use it in your own teaching materials? How can you encourage students to normalise transparency rather than hide AI use?

Teaching AI literacy to students

Evaluating outputs and identifying 'hallucinations'

One of the greatest challenges for primary and secondary students (and teachers) is learning to judge whether an output from generative AI is trustworthy. Too often, they treat GenAI responses as unquestionable truths rather than information to be examined critically. The problem is that outputs may appear creative, logical and convincing, but they can be misleading or made up. Developing the habit of questioning, verifying and cross-checking GenAI content is therefore an essential skill, one that must be explicitly taught and reinforced in the classroom.

Students must critically interrogate and evaluate GenAI uses and outputs. As previously mentioned, GenAI tends to produce 'hallucinations', that is to say, information not based on training data or input, which can be incorrect. GenAI tools are known to generate faulty statements, including fake sources and fabricated quotations and citations. Students must develop the ability to verify information and detect non-existent research papers or inaccurate information. There is no guarantee that GenAI-generated references align with the provided information. Students, especially young learners, may unknowingly accept superficial, inaccurate or harmful outputs.

So how can teachers scaffold the habit, in both our students and ourselves, of not blindly trusting GenAI? A starting point can be a set of questions after our students have interacted in a dialogic manner with GenAI and analysing its output. These guiding questions can be tailored, but the idea is that, with the teacher's support and monitoring, students consider and analyse the output. Discussing and training our students on what questions to ask is essential to integrate GenAI into activities. Curiosity, simple checks and teacher support are core at primary level. Secondary students should aim for evaluation, verification and move towards academic responsibility.

Critical thinking questions for primary students include:

- Does this answer sound like something I already learned in class, read in my book or searched online?
- Can I find the same information in my notes, textbook, online from a verifiable source or from my teacher?
- Did GenAI give me an example that makes sense? Or does it sound strange?
- Does the information match what I know about the world? (e.g., dates, names, facts.)
- If I tell a friend or teacher this answer, would they agree it sounds correct?
- Where else can I check if this information is true?
- Are there any words or sentences here that I don't really understand and should look up?
- Did the tool give me a source (like a book or website)? Can I actually find it?

A checklist is a simple way of implementing this. Here is an example checklist for students to complete. Students can tick the boxes as they check their work.

Table 8.5: Primary level checklist (Co-created using ChatGPT)

☑	Question	Comments
☐	Does this match what I learned in class or my book?	📕
☐	Can I check this with my teacher or a friend?	👩 🏫
☐	Does it sound strange or confusing?	🤔
☐	Can I find the source (book or website)?	🔍
☐	Are these words easy for me to understand?	🗣️

Critical thinking questions for secondary students include the following:

- Does the information align with credible sources (textbooks, academic articles seen in class, teacher explanations)?
- Has GenAI provided a source, reference or quotation? If so, can I locate and verify it?
- Is the response too general, vague or 'perfect-sounding' but without depth?
- Could this be a 'hallucination'? Does the reference, fact or statistic actually exist? Can I check this?
- Does the answer present multiple perspectives, or only one view?
- Are there inconsistencies or contradictions in the explanation?
- How does the information compare with what I already know or what experts say?
- If I were writing an essay or giving a presentation, would I feel confident defending this information in front of my teacher or peers?

- Does the GenAI output clearly separate fact from opinion?
- What further steps can I take to fact-check this information (e.g., cross-referencing, searching in reliable databases, asking an expert)?

A possible checklist for students to complete follows, using the traffic light method (***R*** reliable, ***U*** unsure, ***N*** not reliable) for quick evaluation.

Table 8.6: Secondary level checklist (Co-created using ChatGPT)

	Question	**How I checked (student action)**	**Result**
1	Does this match with a credible source (book/article)?		R / U / N
2	Can I verify the reference or quote online?		R / U / N
3	Does it show more than one perspective?		R / U / N
4	Could this be a hallucination (made-up fact)?		R / U / N
5	Is the information recent and up to date?		R / U / N

Reflective task 7

When you use AI in class, do you pause to 'fact-check together' with your students? How might building this pause into activities foster habits of verification?

Recognising bias

GenAI technologies often reflect and can replicate harmful biases embedded in their training data. AI models, particularly those trained predominantly on English language data, may exhibit biases toward certain language varieties, cultural norms, or even non-native English writers. Students must understand that AI decisions are not objective, and should see it as a tool rather than a final authority. We should teach and train students how to spot these possible biases and not accept outputs at face value. At the end of the day, critical use of AI also means protecting students' own voices and identity in English.

Here is an example guide for an exercise for students to spot bias:

Table 8.7: Bias spotting for primary level (Co-created using ChatGPT)

Bias spotting for primary students			
Step	**Question to ask**	**Action if YES (problem found)**	**Tick ☑**
1	Does it focus on only one kind of person, place or culture?	Add another person/place/culture or ask the AI: 'Include examples from ___ too'.	☐
2	Is someone missing who should be included?	Add the missing group or example; ask: 'Mention ___ as well'.	☐
3	Does it use stereotypes about boys, girls, jobs or age?	Swap roles or replace with neutral wording.	☐
4	Does it use only one English style (e.g., only American words) when others could fit?	Try another English variety or say that many Englishes are OK.	☐
5	Could we say it in a kinder, more balanced way?	Rewrite one sentence to be fair to everyone.	☐

Table 8.8: Bias spotting for secondary level (Co-created using ChatGPT)

Bias spotting for secondary students			
Step	**Question to ask**	**Action if YES (red flag)**	**Tick ☑**
1	Whose perspective is centred? Who speaks, who is described?	Add at least one counter-perspective; ask the AI for multi-voice viewpoints.	☐
2	Are there generalisations about groups without evidence?	Request sources or rephrase with caution (e.g., 'some…', 'in certain contexts').	☐
3	Are gender roles or identities assumed?	Use neutral language and vary examples across genders and identities.	☐
4	Is one English variety privileged or non-native features penalised?	Accept world Englishes; adjust register without erasing the learner's voice.	☐
5	Which groups or data are missing (omission bias)?	Add missing groups/ data or include a counterexample.	☐
6	Are there loaded or value-laden terms that steer opinion?	Replace with neutral/ precise terms; define evaluative words.	☐
7	Are sources cited and diverse in geography and viewpoint?	Add citations; triangulate with at least two credible, diverse sources.	☐

Step	Question to ask	Action if YES (red flag)	Tick ☑
8	If someone believed this as-is, who might be harmed or excluded?	Add caveats and an impact statement acknowledging potential harm.	☐
9	How can we revise to include other perspectives or voices?	Rewrite key sentences; add inclusive examples and qualifiers.	☐
10	Final check: is it now fair, accurate and inclusive?	If not, loop back to the step that needs work.	☐

To further develop critical analysis skills, we can create simulation exercises or use case scenarios in which students encounter AI-generated results with potential errors and have to determine whether they will trust the results or not in order to proceed with the activity. We need to challenge them to critically analyse the results, identify anomalies, and come up with solutions. For example, play a game of Real or Fake Text with your students, followed by a discussion on why they think the text is GenAI generated or human generated. The same goes with images: training the eye from an early age to being sceptical about audiovisual content is essential. A good website for this can be found at https://britannicaeducation.com/blog/quiz-real-or-ai/

Reflective task 8

In your teaching, do you challenge GenAI's cultural or gender biases openly with your students? How can you create short classroom routines for 'bias-spotting' practice?

Critical evaluation of AI-detection tools

Technologies claiming to detect AI-generated content are not sufficiently accurate to make reliable determinations. Some sources even suggest that AI-content detection tools can be biased against non-native English writers, as described in Chapter 4.

In essence, GenAI literacy in ELT requires a deep understanding of AI's capabilities and limitations, especially concerning content generation, authenticity and intellectual property, with a strong emphasis on transparent and accurate citation of AI tools in all school work, starting from an early age.

Reflective task 9

How could you adapt your current lesson activities so that your students actively practice verification and bias-spotting rather than just consuming GenAI outputs?

Fostering GenAI literacy is about preparing students for a digital world where GenAI is part of communication, learning and knowledge creation. Promoting transparency, critical questioning, and ethical use in ELT classrooms empowers students to become not just users of AI, but reflective, responsible participants in an AI-driven society. In short, GenAI literacy means teaching students not just to use AI, but to question it, verify it, and use it ethically so they grow into responsible digital citizens.

Further reading

Digital Promise (2024). *AI literacy*. https://digitalpromise.org/initiative/artificial-intelligence-in-education/ai-literacy/

Chapter 9:
Positive uses of GenAI, choosing the right GenAI tools and alternative tools to GenAI

Chapter 9 identifies where AI works well and where it doesn't. We offer practical classroom strategies and a guide to informed tool selection aimed at balancing innovation with effective teaching practices, responsible use, and learners' needs.

Introduction

AI has supported language teaching and learning, even before the advent of GenAI, with research demonstrating its effectiveness in areas such as reading comprehension (Xu *et al.*, 2019), repetitive practice of language skills (Kim, 2019) and pronunciation correction (Noviyanti, 2020).

Beyond language-specific skills, AI has also been applied to broader educational practices, including automated marking, feedback provision, adaptive learning and intelligent tutoring systems (Pokrivcˇáková, 2019). While early models often assumed a human instructor to mediate or facilitate these tools, recent developments show that learners can increasingly interact with AI-powered systems independently, gaining confidence and reducing anxiety around failure (Fryer *et al.*, 2020; Woo & Choi, 2021). They function effectively as 'teaching assistants' and 'personalised tutors' (Ansari *et al.*, 2023). This shift highlights the growing potential of AI to act not only as a supplement, but as an active partner in the learning process.

GenAI, in particular, represents a significant expansion of these possibilities. It enables personalisation at scale by tailoring practice, feedback and study plans to individual learners (Godwin-Jones, 2024). With the right prompts, GenAI can generate lesson plans, quizzes and role-play activities (Eager & Brunton, 2023), while also providing authentic language input through dialogues, reading passages and articles (Zhai, 2022). At different proficiency levels, learners might use GenAI to rehearse vocabulary and pronunciation, engage with customised texts or media, or simulate interactive conversations that reflect their personal goals and interests. Such applications extend the reach of language learning well beyond traditional resources, offering opportunities for both creative exploration and structured practice.

If there is one particularly positive use of GenAI in ELT, it lies in its potential to improve language skills in English. When teachers strike the right balance (integrating GenAI in ways that genuinely optimise second-language acquisition) they not only support skill development but also help students achieve varied learning goals. In this sense, GenAI is a tool worth exploring as an integral part of contemporary teaching and learning, provided its use remains intentional, ethical and learner centred.

Reflective task 1

How can you design activities in which GenAI enhances specific language skills (e.g., vocabulary, pronunciation or reading comprehension) while also encouraging students to use the tool reflectively rather than dependently?

Enhancing language skills with GenAI

In this section we will look at some examples of how teachers can design activities and how students can interact with GenAI tools to improve their language skills, taking into account four skills: writing, reading, speaking and listening. From vocabulary and grammar building to creation of content, scaffolding for primary and secondary school students is required.

How teachers can design activities with GenAI tools

As a teacher, you can choose to use GenAI yourself for these tasks, which is particularly important for very young learners, or instruct the students to do the task themselves, which means putting the technology in their hands. Tasks are grouped as follows: vocabulary building, writing prompts, grammar explanations, reading comprehension support and listening and speaking support.

How students can interact with GenAI

Primary students may use GenAI more for short prompts, playful interactions, visual aids (emojis, pictures) and sentence-level practice or repeating aloud. Secondary students may use GenAI for longer texts, more abstract tasks (debate, essay), and deeper language analysis. In any case, it is important for students to always copy and personalise, not to just passively read the GenAI output, but to write it down, highlight it or draw it. Students should also be ready to ask for variations: 'Give me 3 more examples', 'Explain it with emojis', 'Make it formal/informal'. These different inputs can be displayed in the classroom or students can have them at hand to resort to them when using GenAI. It is important that, after GenAI explains, students turn from passive into active learners, that is, create their own version, test themselves or quiz a peer. Also, students need to get used to comparing and reflecting, using GenAI as a contrasting mirror.

Let's have a look at the different suggestions below to be implemented in the classroom by primary and secondary school students. Whenever they interact with GenAI, they must specify their level so that the response is suited for them. Students must be taught to have a dialogic approach with GenAI, that is, treating the interaction not as one-way Q&A, but as a back-and-forth dialogue where students co-construct meaning, refine answers and critically reflect with the tool. This means that follow-up questions by students are important and should be encouraged.

Table 9.1: Vocabulary building

Vocabulary building			
Task	**Teacher**	**Primary students**	**Secondary students**
Word banks	Teachers can ask GenAI to generate a list of 10–15 topic-related words of the specific topic they are working on with the class (e.g., 'animal categories' in science, 'foods of the world' in global perspectives) with definitions and example sentences. These can be read out loud in the classroom, projected digitally on the board. Students can copy the words into their notebooks, create illustrations, or make flashcards. They can also use the words in short oral or written exercises: sentences, mini-stories or dialogues.	Students type 'Give me 5 words about … with emojis'. They may copy them into their notebooks and draw. They may practice pronunciation aloud. They can create their own mini dictionaries with GenAI's help.	Students ask, 'Give me 10 words about (specify topic) with meanings and collocations'. Students copy and create sentences using collocations. They can challenge GenAI by asking for academic vs informal collocations.

Task	Teacher	Primary students	Secondary students
Synonym/ antonym practice	Teachers can ask students to give different adjectives (e.g., 'personality, describing people'), and GenAI suggests synonyms/ antonyms in simple sentences. Students read the sentences aloud, identify synonyms and antonyms, and use them in their own sentences. It can be turned into a game: students guess the synonym/ antonym before revealing AI suggestions. Students can be encouraged to do peer discussion and compare AI-generated examples with their own ideas.	Students ask 'What is another word for …? Can you give me a short sentence?' and repeat it aloud. Students may also act it out or create gestures for the new words. They can also make a 'chart' or pictures related to the topic with GenAI giving 5 synonyms for that.	Students type 'Give 3 synonyms for "important" in formal English with examples'. They compare registers (formal/informal). They can build synonym banks for essay writing.
Contextual guessing games	Teachers input a target word into GenAI and asks for sentences with blanks while students guess the missing word. This can be projected or printed and the teacher can have students guess the missing word. Students can also take turns creating their own blank-sentence challenges using AI for classmates. It can be adapted for pair or group work to encourage collaborative learning.	Students ask GenAI: 'Can you make 3 sentences with blanks so I guess the word? It must be related to (specify field).' Students guess, then check with GenAI. Students make their own blanks for peers.	Students type 'Give me 5 sentences with a word I need to guess'. Students copy & paste the bank of words so that the GenAI can pick one. They try to guess individually, then peer-compare answers. Finally, they generate their own guessing games for classmates.
Word maps	Teachers can ask GenAI to generate semantic clusters (e.g., 'holiday': beach, suitcase, airport, relax, sunscreen). Students copy or sketch the word map and add their own ideas. It can be used as a brainstorming tool for writing or speaking tasks. Students can be made to compare AI-generated clusters with student-generated clusters to discuss word relationships and nuances.	Students request, 'Make a word map for the word "holiday" with 5 easy words'. Students copy the web, draw icons and colour it. They can use word maps as brainstorming for writing tasks.	Students type, 'Make a word web for "justice" with 8 related words'. They discuss abstract meanings. Students may use word maps to brainstorm debate arguments and ask GenAI for sentence starters.

Table 9.2: Writing prompts

Writing prompts			
Task	**Teacher**	**Primary students**	**Secondary students**
Creative prompts	Teachers generate imaginative story starters like, 'You were exploring the red planet and the spaceship to return home broke down. What happened next?' Teachers display the prompt on the board or share digitally with students. Students write their own stories individually or in pairs, using the GenAI prompt as inspiration. Teachers encourage students to read their stories aloud and discuss different creative choices. Optionally, students can ask GenAI for ideas to continue or expand their stories after the first draft.	Students ask 'Write the first line of a funny, original story about ...' They continue the story.	Students ask, 'Give me a debate topic about (school uniforms)'. Then they research and prepare arguments.
Genre practice	Teachers ask for prompts in different genres (a diary entry, a news article, a fairy tale, persuasive letter, essay writing). Teachers assign different genres to groups or individuals to practise varied writing styles worked in class. Students draft texts using the GenAI prompt as a starting point. Teachers can highlight features of each genre (tone, structure, vocabulary) while students revise their work. Students can ask GenAI for examples or sentence starters to reinforce genre conventions.	Students request 'Give me a diary entry about … in 4 sentences'. Students continue writing, mimicking the format.	Students type, 'Give me an example of a short news report about …'. They analyse style and imitate, analyse structure and then rewrite.
Collaborative stories	Students continue a story paragraph written by GenAI. Students work in pairs or small groups to continue the story. Teachers encourage iterative interaction: after writing a paragraph, students can ask GenAI to suggest the next paragraph or give alternative directions for the story.	Students write a line, tell GenAI to continue, then they add the next one. They alternate turns with GenAI in	Students ask GenAI to write a 3-line story starter; students add their own continuation and then compare endings, and

Task	Teacher	Primary students	Secondary students
Collaborative stories (continued)	This fosters creativity, negotiation and collaboration while keeping students engaged with the narrative flow.	order to develop imagination and writing fluency.	then compare GenAI's continuation with peers'. This fosters critical thinking and creativity.
Sentence combining	Teachers provide two simple sentences and GenAI suggests ways to combine them more effectively. Students compare their own attempts with the GenAI suggestions and they discuss how combining sentences can improve flow, cohesion and clarity. Teachers can use this as a mini-lesson on conjunctions, relative clauses or sentence variety. Students can practice by giving GenAI their own simple sentences and iteratively improving them.	Students type, 'Here are two sentences: x and y. Can you join them into one?' Students analyse GenAI versions, then try their own, using different linkers.	Students type 'Combine these sentences: x and y. Show me 3 ways and use different linkers.' GenAI suggests multiple ways to focus on style and syntax.

Table 9.3: Grammar explanations

Grammar explanations			
Task	**Teacher**	**Primary students**	**Secondary students**
Rule + example format	Teachers ask GenAI: 'Explain the past continuous for 10-year-olds, with 3 examples'. Teachers share the AI-generated explanation on the board or digitally. Students read, discuss, and then highlight the examples. Teachers can ask students to create their own sentences using the rule. Optionally, students can input their sentences into GenAI to check understanding and receive additional examples.	Students type, 'Explain past continuous for a 9-year-old with examples'. Students read and then make their own sentences. Students practice creating their own sentences.	Students type, 'Explain the 2nd conditional with 3 examples'. Students then create their own examples.

Task	Teacher	Primary students	Secondary students
Error correction	Teachers invite students to input short sentences with mistakes. GenAI highlights and explains corrections. Students compare their original sentences with the AI corrections with the teachers' supervision. Then, the class discusses why the corrections were needed, focusing on patterns of errors. Students revise their sentences and optionally ask GenAI to check again. This encourages reflection and reinforces correct usage in a low-stakes, supportive environment.	Students paste an incorrect sentence for correction and ask for an explanation, 'He go to school yesterday'. GenAI corrects and explains input. Students copy and give more examples.	Students paste a paragraph and ask GenAI to highlight mistakes and explain corrections. Then students rewrite.
Grammar quizzes	Teachers ask GenAI to create quick gap-fill or multiple-choice activities or true/false questions for the class. Then, teachers share the AI-generated quiz with students individually or in small groups. Students answer the questions and check their answers using GenAI, or teachers can review them in class. Teachers can adjust the difficulty based on student's performance and track common mistakes.	Students type, 'Make me 5 easy questions/ exercises using past tense verbs', and try to answer quick gap-fill questions. They answer first and then check.	Students type, 'Make me 10 gap-fill questions on present perfect with answers hidden'. They answer and then check.
Compare/ contrast practice	Teachers input, 'Explain the difference between "since" and "for" with examples a teenager can understand'. Teachers present the GenAI explanation and examples to students. Students create their own sentences to practise each structure. Teachers can run mini-games or peer activities where students identify correct usage. Students can also ask GenAI for instant feedback on their sentences to reinforce understanding.	Students type, 'Show me the difference between "he runs" and "he is running" with pictures or emojis'. GenAI uses emojis/ pictures to show 'runs' vs 'is running'.	Students write, 'What's the difference between "since" and "for" in present perfect tense?' or 'Explain since vs for with timelines' for visual reinforcement.

Table 9.4: Reading comprehension support

Reading comprehension support			
Task	**Teacher**	**Primary students**	**Secondary students**
Simplifying texts	Teachers give students a short newspaper article or story excerpt that might be too advanced. The teacher pastes it into GenAI and asks: 'Rewrite this at (tailors specifications according to level)'. Students read the simplified version in pairs, then compare it to the original to spot differences in vocabulary and grammar. Students see how the same idea can be expressed with simpler language.	Students paste a short story and ask, 'Make this story easier for me (specify the level)'. Then they paste the story. This is useful to help weaker readers.	Students paste a news article and ask, 'Rewrite this text for (specify level) learners'. This provides access to authentic but manageable texts.
Question generation	After reading a shared text (e.g., about climate change), the teachers can ask GenAI: 'Create 5 comprehension questions: 2 literal, 2 inferential, 1 critical'. Students work in groups to answer the GenAI's questions. Then, as an extension, students can ask GenAI to check their answers or even to generate more challenging or funny questions. This builds reading comprehension and question-answering skills while giving students practice with multiple levels of thinking.	After reading, students type, 'Give me 5 easy questions about this text' for reading check.	Students ask, 'Make 5 questions: 2 factual, 2 inferential, 1 opinion about this text'. GenAI generates literal, inferential, critical questions.
Summarisation	Students first write their own 3–4 sentence summary of a story or article. Teachers ask GenAI for a summary of the same text. Students compare their summary to the GenAI's. They highlight where their version is stronger (more detail, better vocabulary) and where the GenAI's is clearer. This encourages self-reflection and it shows multiple ways to condense information.	Students summarise a story, then ask GenAI 'Write a summary of this story' and compare.	Students write their summary, then compare with GenAI's output, checking differences. When comparing student vs GenAI summaries, students focus on conciseness.

Task	Teacher	Primary students	Secondary students
Vocabulary in context	Teachers paste the text into GenAI with the following instruction: 'Identify 5 challenging words for (specify level of students) and provide definitions + example sentences'. Teachers put these words on the board. Students guess meanings in pairs, then check with GenAI's definitions. They use each word in their own sentences. Another alternative is for teachers to ask GenAI for a quick 'matching exercise' (words on one side, meanings on the other). Students see vocabulary in context as it naturally appears in texts, not as isolated lists.	Students ask, 'Give me the meaning of … from this story and show me a picture'. Then they ask different meanings with pictures.	Students type, 'Take 8 difficult words from this article and explain them in sentences'. GenAI provides advanced definitions and usage in academic sentences.

Table 9.5: Listening and speaking support

Listening and speaking support	
Task	**Teacher**
Listening comprehension with AI-generated audio	Teachers ask GenAI to generate a short audio (e.g., 'A tourist asking for directions in London' and specify the level tailored to students). Students listen once for gist (global listening: What's the situation?), then again for details (detailed listening: Where is the tourist going?). Teachers can also ask GenAI to provide related comprehension questions. This exposes students to authentic listening practice at their level, with instant materials. After listening, students may retell the story/dialogue in their own words. This could also be completed as pair work: One student listens first, then explains the situation to their partner without letting them hear the audio.
Dictation and gap-fill	Teachers give GenAI a topic (e.g., 'daily routines') and asks for a 5-sentence paragraph. Then, GenAI reads it aloud. Students write what they hear (full dictation) or fill in missing words on a transcript prepared by the teacher. GenAI can be used to create a 'dictogloss', that is, students reconstruct the text together after listening. This improves spelling, listening accuracy and noticing grammar structures. Once the text is completed, students read it aloud in pairs. Teachers can ask them to change it (e.g., 'Instead of *I wake up at 7*, say it with your real routine').

Pronunciation and shadowing	Teachers ask GenAI to record a dialogue (e.g., 'ordering food at a restaurant') or to create and recite a poem on a particular topic. Students listen, repeat and 'shadow' (speak at the same time) to practice rhythm and intonation. They can also ask GenAI to slow down or speed up. This helps to build fluency, natural pacing and pronunciation confidence. After shadowing, students record themselves saying the same dialogue and compare it with the GenAI version. They can then perform the dialogue by heart in front of the class or improvise new lines.
Listening for key vocabulary	Teachers ask GenAI: 'Make a 1-minute audio or podcast about space exploration using these 5 target words: astronaut, rocket, planet, travel, discover'. Students listen and circle the target words when they hear them. Then, they retell the key points in pairs. This trains students to pick out key vocabulary in real-time listening. Students use the target words to create their own mini-story or short dialogue. Another alternative is to play the 'Hot seat game': Teacher plays the audio, pauses, and a student has to explain what just happened using the keywords.
Role-play preparation	Teachers ask GenAI to generate a dialogue (e.g., 'a job interview'). Students listen to the GenAI dialogue, then role-play their own version in pairs, using similar expressions. This bridges receptive skills (listening) with productive skills (speaking). After listening, students role-play the same situation but with personal details (e.g., their own dream job, favourite restaurant order, travel plan). They can even swap roles (e.g., if the AI was the waiter, now the student becomes the waiter).

Reflective task 2

How effectively do your students interact with GenAI to develop a deeper understanding or develop language skills? Were there patterns in prompts that led to richer learning, and how could you guide students to optimise their interactions further?

Using GenAI Tools in the classroom: Teacher reference charts

Table 9.6: Vocabulary building for teachers

Vocabulary building		
Activity	**How GenAI is used**	**Classroom application**
Word banks	GenAI generates 10–15 topic-related words with definitions & examples.	Project on board, students copy, illustrate or create flashcards; use in mini-stories or dialogues.
Synonym/ antonym practice	GenAI provides synonyms/antonyms with example sentences.	Students guess, read aloud, compare with their own; can be turned into a guessing game.
Contextual guessing games	GenAI creates sentences with blanks for target words.	Students guess missing words, create challenges for peers, work in pairs/groups.
Word maps	GenAI generates semantic clusters around a topic.	Students sketch word maps, brainstorm, compare with AI output for nuances.

Table 9.7: Writing prompts for teachers

Writing prompts		
Activity	**How GenAI is used**	**Classroom application**
Creative prompts	GenAI generates imaginative story starters.	Students write stories individually/pairs, share aloud, expand with GenAI support.
Genre practice	GenAI creates prompts in different genres (diary, news, fairytale, persuasive, etc.).	Students draft genre-specific texts, revise with AI examples, highlight features.
Collaborative stories	GenAI provides a story paragraph to continue.	Students work in groups, write the next parts, ask AI for alternatives, foster creativity.
Sentence combining	GenAI suggests combining simple sentences more effectively.	Students compare with AI, discuss flow and cohesion, practise variety.

Table 9.8: Grammar explanations for teachers

Grammar explanations		
Activity	**How GenAI is used**	**Classroom application**
Rule + example format	GenAI explains grammar rules with age-appropriate examples.	Teacher shares explanation; students create their own sentences and check with AI.
Error correction	Students input sentences; GenAI corrects and explains.	Students compare corrections, discuss patterns, revise collaboratively.
Grammar quizzes	GenAI generates gap-fill/multiple choice/true-false quizzes.	Students complete individually or in groups, check with AI or teacher reviews.
Compare/ contrast practice	GenAI explains differences between tricky grammar items.	Students practice in sentences, play mini-games, ask AI for feedback.

Table 9.9: Reading comprehension support for teachers

Reading comprehension support		
Activity	**How GenAI is used**	**Classroom application**
Simplifying texts	GenAI rewrites complex texts at target CEFR level.	Students read simplified vs original, compare structures, spot changes.
Question generation	GenAI creates literal, inferential and critical comprehension questions.	Students answer in groups, extend with own or AI-generated questions.
Summarisation	GenAI provides summaries of a text.	Students compare their summaries with AI's, discuss clarity and detail.
Vocabulary in context	GenAI identifies challenging words and defines them in context.	Students guess meanings, check, create sentences or do matching games.

Table 9.10: Listening and speaking support for teachers

Listening and speaking support		
Activity	**How GenAI is used**	**Classroom application**
Listening comprehension	GenAI generates dialogues/ monologues with comprehension questions.	Students listen for gist and detail, retell or explain to peers.
Dictation and gap-fill	GenAI reads short paragraphs for dictation or gap-fill tasks.	Students reconstruct text, compare versions, adapt to personal routines.
Pronunciation and shadowing	GenAI records dialogues/ poems to model pronunciation.	Students repeat, shadow, record themselves, perform dialogues.
Listening for key vocabulary	GenAI includes target words in short audios.	Students identify words, retell key points, create mini-stories or games.
Role-play preparation	GenAI generates dialogues for scenarios (job interview, restaurant).	Students role-play adapted dialogues with personal details, swapping roles.

Reflective task 3

How do you think you could adapt one of these GenAI-based activities to better fit the needs, age, or level of your learners?

Choosing the right GenAI tools: RAAS

As we have seen in previous chapters, choosing the right GenAI tools is a critical process that requires from teachers and students a nuanced understanding of their capabilities, limitations and ethical implications. As seen in Chapter 1, LLMs are pattern-matching systems that generate predictions based on probability rather than true understanding or comprehension, which makes them powerful but also prone to errors, misleading information or 'hallucinations'. So being aware of GenAI tools' limitations, due to their probabilistic nature, that the outputs can contain outdated information as they have a knowledge cut-off date, and that they are trained on vast determined databases that can be biased, are important aspects to take into account when we get the output.

Figure 9.1: Balancing AI use in education

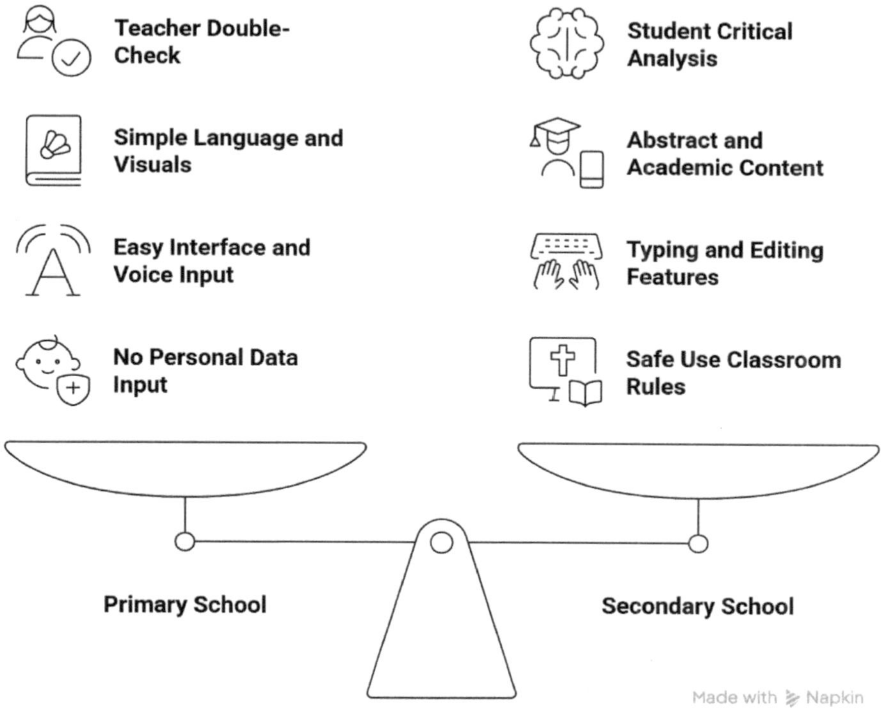

When selecting a GenAI tool for classroom use for primary or secondary level, we should take into account these considerations: reliability of outputs, age-appropriateness, accessibility and safety/privacy – in other words, RAAS.

Reliability of outputs

Primary: GenAI explanations must be double-checked by the teacher before being used. Children may believe everything GenAI says. Teachers should scaffold (e.g., 'Let's check if this answer is correct together').

Secondary: Students can be trained to spot errors, compare GenAI answers with textbooks, and critically analyse whether the GenAI is accurate or misleading ('hallucinating'). This builds digital literacy and critical thinking.

Age-appropriateness

Primary: The GenAI should provide simple language, short outputs, visual aids (emojis, images if possible), and playful interactions when requested. For example, asking, 'Tell me a story about a cat that can fly, use emojis for a x year old, should not result in overly complex text'. Students are not expected to log in in order to use the GenAI tool. As most tools are restricted for users under 13, teachers can act as mediators and guide students in the interaction instead of allowing direct access to the technology.

Secondary: The GenAI can handle more abstract, academic or debate-style prompts. It should generate content suitable for teenagers (e.g., essays, reports, discussions on climate change). The age suitability is expressed in the prompt itself. Parental guidance and permission is required for students between 13-18 years old.

Accessibility

Primary: The interface must be easy to use (large fonts, simple buttons, clear instructions). Ideally, no long typing required: maybe voice input or copy-paste from a story.

Secondary: Students can handle more typing, longer instructions, and using features like exporting or editing GenAI-generated text. Accessibility also means tools that don't require expensive devices or constant internet.

Safety and privacy

Primary: No personal data should be entered. Teachers should guide students to use class accounts or anonymised inputs without logging in. Prompts should avoid anything sensitive (names, locations, photos).

Secondary: Students should be trained to critically evaluate what they share (still no personal data), and to recognise when GenAI content may not be safe to copy directly (biases, misinformation). Teachers should establish 'safe use' classroom rules.

Figure 9.2: RAAS framework for choosing GenAI tools

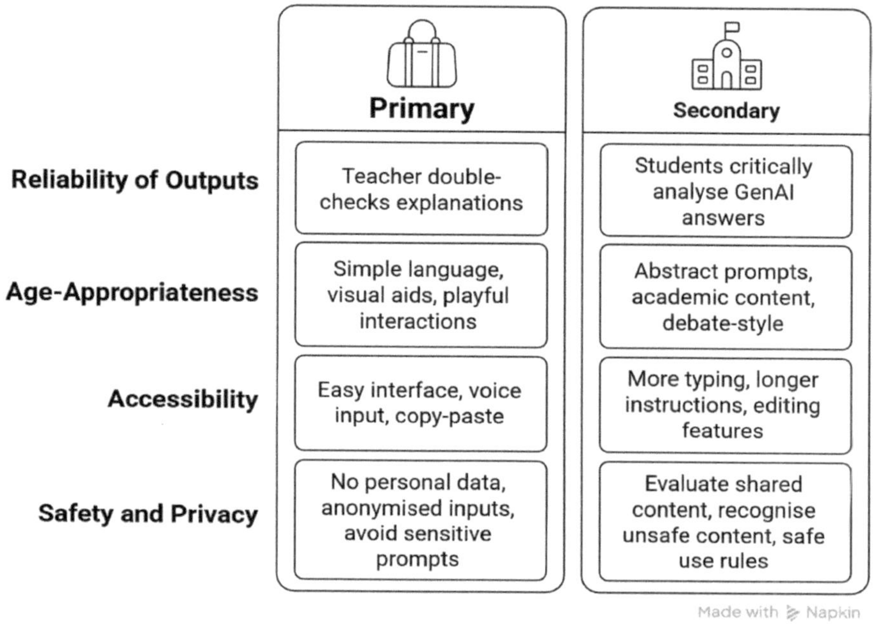

Examples of teacher-friendly GenAI tools

Teacher-friendly tools, or user-friendly tools, are those which are intuitive, easy to use in classroom settings and that are time saving, but which do not needing constant troubleshooting. For each tool, though, you need to check their terms of service for age requirements, data-collection methods and consent options.

Text-generation tools:

- ChatGPT (OpenAI) Sora
- Google Gemini (Education)
- Anthropic Claude (Enterprise Education versions)
- Microsoft Copilot (Consumer versions)
- Microsoft Copilot (Enterprise Education versions)
- Perplexity
- Poe (Quora's AI Assistant Platform) try out

Image generation tools:

- DALL·E (OpenAI)
- Midjourney
- Google AI Studio

Content creation and audio tools:

- AIVA.ai (music generation)
- GitHub Copilot
- Suno AI

Table 9.11: GenAI tools by task

GenAI tools comparison by task					
Tasks	**ChatGPT 5.1**	**Gemini 3 Pro**	**Perplexity**	**Claude 4.5**	**DeepSeek V3.2**
Text related					
Compose engaging blog posts with specific requirements.	✓	✓		✓	
Convert unstructured text into clean and organised tables.	✓				
Explain complex technical concepts in simple plain English.	✓	✓	✓	✓	
Simplify a text	✓	✓			

Tasks	ChatGPT 5.1	Gemini 3 Pro	Perplexity	Claude 4.5	DeepSeek V3.2
Text related					
Generate content directly within existing Google Docs.		✓			
Generate slide outlines and support notes for presentations.	✓	✓		✓	
Summarise long articles into concise, readable bullet points.	✓		✓	✓	✓
Upload and summarise PDF reports for complex analysis.		✓	✓	✓	✓
Translate between multiple different global languages.	✓ 95+ major languages	✓ 249 languages			
Email related					
Draft professional emails and rewrite them for clarity.				✓	✓
Draft responses and summarise threads inside your Gmail.		✓			
Turn email text into actionable tasks.		✓			

Tasks	ChatGPT 5.1	Gemini 3 Pro	Perplexity	Claude 4.5	DeepSeek V3.2
Image and video related					
Analyse video content to answer specific visual questions.		✓			
Summarise long YouTube videos without watching them.		✓			
Create images		✓			
Multimodal		✓			
Data related					
Create complex formulas and organise data in Sheets.		✓			
Extract data from complex charts and spreadsheets.		✓		✓	
Process massive volumes of text for complex data analysis.		✓	✓	✓	
Evaluate software tools and compare new features.		✓	✓	✓	
Plan travel itineraries based on specific budget constraints.		✓			
Search across Google Drive to find specific files.		✓			

Tasks	ChatGPT 5.1	Gemini 3 Pro	Perplexity	Claude 4.5	DeepSeek V3.2
Real time information					
Plan trips integrating Google Maps and flight options.		✓			
Find reliable answers backed by cited academic sources.			✓		
Verify facts quickly against authoritative news outlets.			✓		
Get unbiased summaries of breaking global news events.			✓		
Search the web in real time	✓ with ChatGPT search	✓ with Pro version	✓		
Research related					
Deep research mode		✓	✓	✓	
Cites accurately			✓		✓
Visually maps connections between topics			✓		
Other					
Simulate job interviews with experts and difficult questions.	✓	✓			

Tasks	ChatGPT 5.1	Gemini 3 Pro	Perplexity	Claude 4.5	DeepSeek V3.2
Other					
Conversational AI	✓	✓		✓	
Active memory	✓	✓		✓	
Reasoning mode	✓	✓		✓	✓
Fewer hallucinations		✓		✓	
Safety filters		✓		✓	

Reflective task 4

Which AI tools have you explored? Are they suitable for your students' age, language level and learning goals?

Further reading

Crompton, H., Edmett, A., Ichaporia, N., & Burke, D. (2024). AI and English language teaching: Affordances and challenges. *British Journal of Educational Technology* 55 2503-2529. 10.1111/bjet.13460. https://bera-journals.onlinelibrary.wiley.com/doi/epdf/10.1111/bjet.13460

Chapter 10: Prompting

In this chapter, we set out to teach the art of crafting effective inputs for teachers and students, using guiding frameworks, such as the C-PROFIT framework.

Reflective task 1

How do we train our students to be specific when asking questions? How can they sharpen their prompting skills in their first interactions with GenAI?

Why prompting matters in ELT

Prompting is an essential skill when interacting with GenAI. A prompt is the message you type into the chatbox. Prompt engineering refers to the skill of creating good questions or commands that enable the GenAI system to produce high-quality output. It is an iterative process, meaning it often requires multiple attempts and refinements to achieve the desired results. Considering the environmental impact of AI discussed in Chapter 3, it is recommended to raise awareness of this issue and to encourage learners to practise prompting and refining on paper before using the digital tool so that in one attempt they get a good-quality output. Developing 'prompt literacy' is essential for both teachers and students to interact effectively and get the most out of it.

The basics of prompt literacy

Precision and detail in the prompt will ensure success in obtaining the desired results. Although our approach should be one of a bricklayer – and knowing that the first answer we get from any GenAI might not be the final or best one – we need to work carefully, as this is definitely in tension with the environmental impact of prompting. So, co-constructing meaning and answers with any GenAI is a key concept for our students to learn.

The attitude of perfecting and refining prompts, of adding details, of building until you are fully satisfied with it, is the first big step. Much of this refining can be done on paper before prompting on the tool. The dialogic approach seems essential to get the most out of GenAI, but you should aim to reduce re-prompting as much as possible. It is relevant for students to learn how to craft prompts from scratch. In the same way we teach our students how to go about the structure of a news report, we could use this when it comes to crafting prompts: Who? What? When? Where? Why? How?

To write a great prompt, whether for teaching or learning, you need to consider these core principles.

Be clear and specific: The more specific and clear your prompt is, the better the output will be. A specific question or clear topic will lead to more accurate and relevant responses. Effective prompts are clear and precise, and specify the answer format and structure.

Provide context: Give the AI background information, previous discussions or specific goals for the task. Contextual prompting provides immediate, task-specific details to guide the response, helping the model understand nuances.

Define a persona/role: Assigning a specific role to the GenAI model (e.g., 'You are an expert at conflict resolution', 'You are a kindergarten teacher') helps it generate more relevant and informative output, as it crafts responses in that specific voice and style.

Specify output format: Clearly state the desired format for the response (e.g., 'in bullet points', 'as an excerpt from a textbook', 'a two-column chart', 'a specific length or word count').

Iterate and refine: Prompt generation is an iterative process. If the initial output isn't satisfactory, revise your prompt by making it more detailed or specific. It's an ongoing process of playing and practising to get the desired outcome.

Give examples: Providing examples within your prompt (known as 'few-shot prompting') can significantly improve the quality of the AI's response by showing it exactly what you expect.

Provide feedback: Share specific feedback on what needs to be revised at all points in the conversation.

Control token length: Consider controlling the maximum token length, especially for shorter, more focused outputs. Token is a technical term that can be equated with words, for practical purposes.

Table 10.1: Prompting guide (Co-created using ChatGPT)

Principle	What it means	Example prompt for teachers	Example prompt for students
Be clear and specific	State exactly what you want; vague prompts lead to vague answers.	Create 5 comprehension questions on this text: 3 factual, 1 inferential, 1 opinion-based.	Give me 5 words about ... with emojis and a short definition for each.
Provide context	Add background info, learning goals, or previous discussion to guide the AI.	My students are 10 years old learning simple past. Make a short story with 8 past tense verbs.	We are learning about ... Write 3 easy sentences about ...

Principle	What it means	Example prompt for teachers	Example prompt for students
Define a persona/ role	Tell AI who it should act as for more targeted answers.	You are an ESL exam coach. Create a speaking practice activity for (define level) students.	You are my English teacher. Explain 'present perfect' like I'm 12 years old.
Specify output format	Indicate format: list, chart, paragraph, dialogue, word count, etc.	Make a two-column chart: verbs in past tense vs. past participle, 10 examples each.	Explain 3 synonyms for '…' in a table with word + example sentence.
Iterate and refine	Adjust the prompt if the first output isn't right; be ready to be more detailed each time.	First: Explain conditional sentences. Refine: Explain 2nd conditional with 3 examples for teens.	First: Tell me about … Refine: Tell me about 5 key aspects of (specify topic, for instance an animal) providing one interesting or surprising fact about it.
Give examples (few-shot)	Provide a sample so AI knows the style/ format you want.	Here's an example summary (2 sentences). Now make a similar summary of this story.	Example: I like pizza 🍕. I don't like broccoli 🥦. Now make 2 more sentences like this.
Provide feedback	React to the AI's response and guide improvement.	That quiz is too difficult. Please make the questions shorter and use simpler vocabulary.	Your sentences are too long. Can you make them shorter, like 5 words each?
Control token length	Ask for a short or long output to avoid overwhelming responses.	Write a 100-word summary of this article.	Write 3 short sentences (5–7 words) using the word …

Reflective task 2

Which part of prompting do you feel students naturally use when writing prompts? Which are the ones they leave out and need to practise more?

The C-PROFIT formula for prompt writing for teachers and students

When prompting, we need to remember not to leave out any details and make sure that we are following the steps outlined above. Good prompts in one go save time and water!

One approach is to use the C-PROFIT formula:

C – Clear and specific

Say exactly what you want, avoid vague words, and point to the format you expect.

P – Provide context

Add background info, goals or situation details so the AI knows the 'why' and 'where'.

R – Role/persona

Tell the AI who it should be (e.g., teacher, student, expert, storyteller).

O – Output format

Explain the type of answer you want (bullet points, essay, dialogue, chart, etc.).

F – Feedback and examples

Show models of what you want, and give feedback to refine responses.

I – Iterate

Don't settle for the first try: always adjust your prompt and improve it.

T – Tokens and length

Guide the length of response you're looking for: a short summary, 200 words, full lesson plan, etc.

A useful way for primary students to remember this is to have a poster displayed in the classroom and in the virtual classroom. Here is one that might be of use:

Figure 10.1: C-PROFIT smart prompts for primary level (created with Gemini)

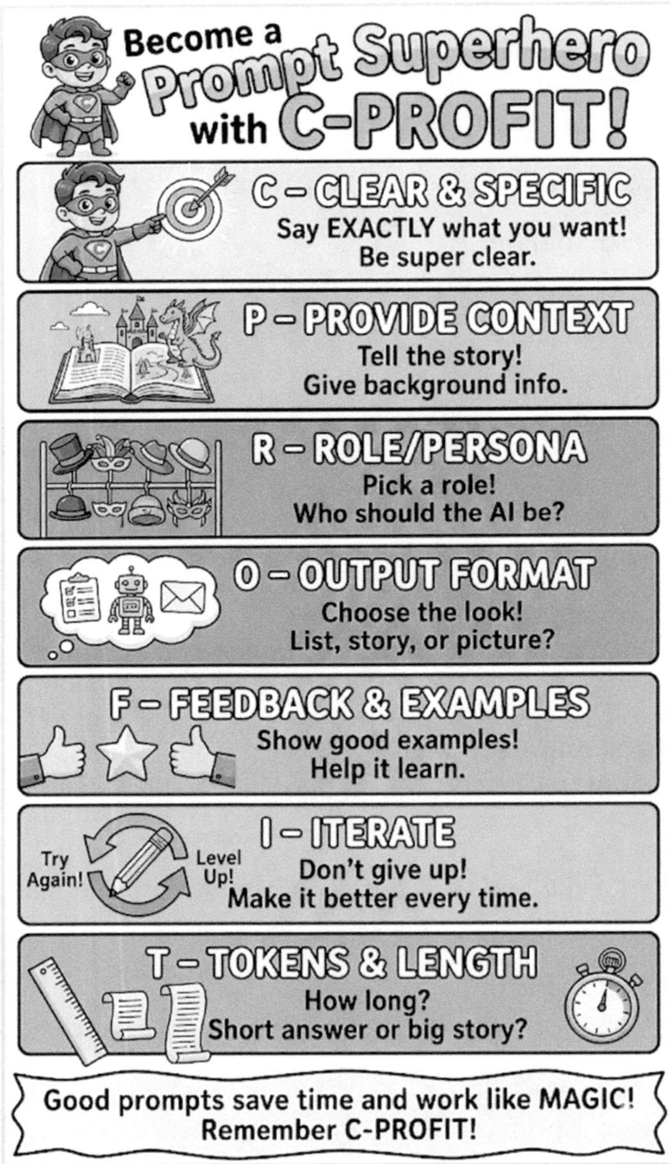

In the case of secondary school students, it might look like this:

Figure 10.2: C-PROFIT smart prompts for secondary level (created with Gemini)

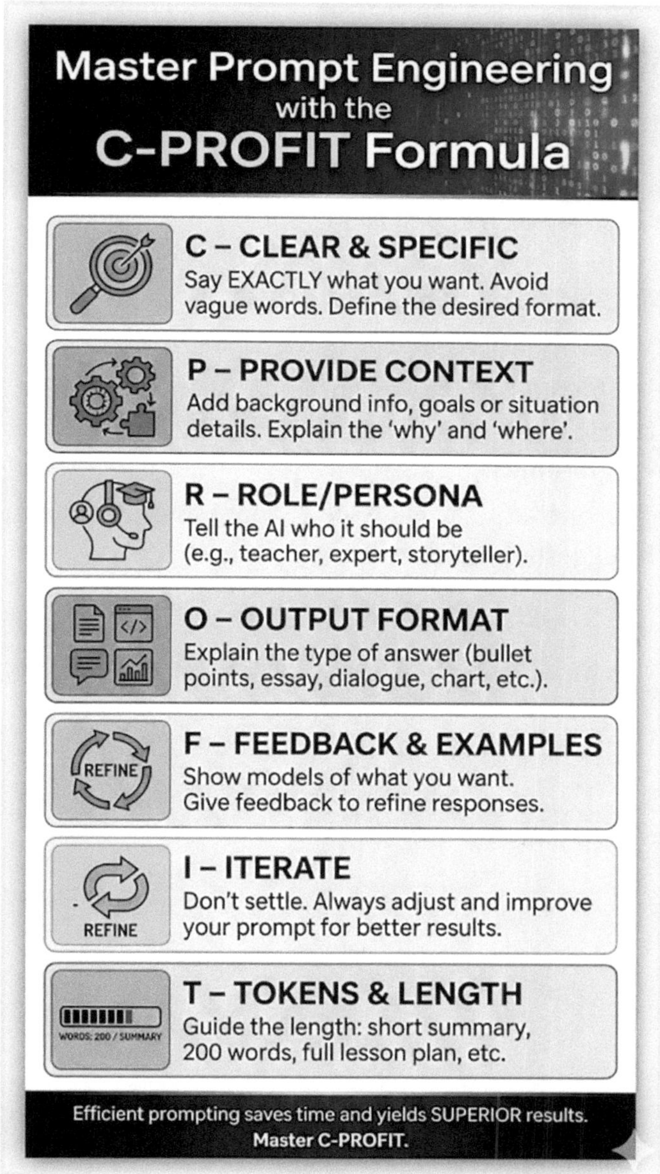

Prompting strategies for teachers

Teachers can use GenAI tools for a wide range of tasks, from administrative duties to creating engaging learning experiences for their students. Here are some strategies and examples tailored for teachers to help them adjust their prompting in order to accomplish a variety of goals. These strategies will be useful when integrating the C-PROFIT formula. All prompt outputs should then be curated by teachers.

Teachers may find the chart below useful when crafting their prompts following the C-PROFIT formula.

How to use the C-PROFIT chart

- **Identify your goal**: What do you need GenAI to help with?
- **Follow C-PROFIT**: Make your prompt Clear, explain Purpose, define a Role, specify Output, add Feedback, Iterate, and set Token/length limits.
- **Curate the output**: Always review, adapt and personalise GenAI's suggestions before using them.

Table 10.2: Prompting strategies for teachers (Co-created using ChatGPT)

Teaching task	Goal/use	Example prompt	Prompting tips (C-PROFIT in action)
Establish a teacher persona	Define your role, grade level, subject, unit overview and, if needed, even your beliefs about how children learn best. In this way, you will help GenAI tools to generate more relevant and aligned content.	'You are a (grade 8) English teacher teaching a unit about persuasive writing. You believe that students should develop critical thinking skills through real-world problem solving.'	C: Be specific about grade, subject, beliefs and topic. R: Assign GenAI the teacher role.
Lesson planning and curriculum adaptation			
Generate lesson aims	Create clear learning objectives.	'Suggest a clear lesson aim. My students are (x level), and we've been working on (x topic). They enjoy (x interests). Start with the aim: By the end of the lesson, learners will be better able to…'	C: Include student level and topic. O: Request a specific sentence starter.
Create lesson plans	Design structured lessons with varied activities. GenAI can also generate lesson plan outlines, and even suggest graphics or images for presentations.	'Create a lesson plan for a class of (x level) students that covers (specify concept) and includes a variety of activities and assessments aligned to (x standards).'	P: Give context (student profile, standards). O: Ask for a table or outline format.

Teaching task	Goal/use	Example prompt	Prompting tips (C-PROFIT in action)
Lesson planning and curriculum adaptation			
Develop PBL/ project ideas	Inspire real-world learning projects.	'You are a (science teacher). Provide 3 ideas for interesting and creative project/problem-based learning tasks that students could investigate to understand (x topic). The projects/ problems should be grounded in real-world problems and encourage creativity and collaboration.'	C: Define subject and focus. F: Ask for creative, real-world relevance.
Generating activity ideas Ask for activities to access prior knowledge, build empathy, excitement or explore concepts.			
Differentiate content	Support diverse learners.	'Provide options for differentiating the process, product or content to accommodate a student who (specify needs).' 'Modify the content for a struggling student. Provide examples of scaffolds and support I might offer.'	I: Iterate with follow-up prompts for more detail.
Create curriculum overviews	Summarise standards or guidelines.	'Summarise key objectives for (grade x) in (country's) national curriculum.' 'Summarise the primary curriculum guidelines in (x state or nation) for (x subject) this year.'	T: Limit to a short summary (150 words).

Teaching task	Goal/use	Example prompt	Prompting tips (C-PROFIT in action)
Generating activity ideas Ask for activities to access prior knowledge, build empathy, excitement or explore concepts.			
Sequence learning	Plan progression over time.	'Create a 6-week plan for a literature unit with weekly objectives and teacher support.' 'Create a project plan for (x number of weeks). Create a two-column chart that breaks down the objectives weekly into what the students are doing and how the teacher can support them.'	O: Request a 2-column chart (student task/teacher role).
Generate activity ideas	Generate fresh teaching ideas and provide feedback on existing content to improve it. Find engaging ways to start or explore lessons.	'Suggest 3 warm-up activities to activate prior knowledge about (recycling).' 'Provide 3 original ideas based on (copy and paste or attach content) for (x students level).' 'Provide detailed feedback based on this project (attach content) and areas for improvement (x level of students).'	C: Include topic and level.
Creating teaching materials			
Create materials – texts and exercises	Generate custom reading, listening or grammar practice. You may use scripts provided in online video-sharing platforms and ask the	'Create a reading text for intermediate (ESL) learners about (life in the rainforest), (200) words long.' 'Create a reading text or listening script for students to practise their comprehension	T: Define text length. F: Review and adapt for accuracy.

Teaching task	Goal/use	Example prompt	Prompting tips (C-PROFIT in action)
Creating teaching materials			
Create materials – texts and exercises (continued)	GenAI tools to base the questions on this by copy/pasting the script in the prompt.	skills, focusing on the topic of (x topic). The students are (x level) language students.'	
Quizzes and Worksheets	Produce comprehension or skill-based tasks for newly generated texts or existing texts. Create vocabulary and grammar exercises.	'Generate a (10)-question quiz on (simple past tense), including 2 creative items that make thinking visible.' 'Generate a (x number) question quiz/test on (x topic) that includes skill practice, word problems, and a challenge question that encourages students to use creativity, justify their choices and make their thinking visible.' 'Create a gap-fill activity for (x level) using (x topic). Use the target vocabulary as the gap.'	C: Specify skill and difficulty. F: Always check or ask for the answer key.
Storytelling prompts	Encourage creativity and communication.	'Generate a list of (x number) imaginative storytelling writing prompts for language students to use as a starting point for their creative writing... The topic for all prompts should be (x topic) and their writing should focus on (x language point).' 'Create 5 storytelling prompts about adventure for (x level) students.'	R: Define GenAI as a language teacher. O: Request list or card format.

Teaching task	Goal/use	Example prompt	Prompting tips (C-PROFIT in action)
Creating teaching materials			
Role-plays	Create communicative tasks.	'Create role-play cards for language students to engage in a conversation about (x topic). Keep the language level (x level).' 'Create role-play cards for a (restaurant) scenario for (x level) learners.'	
Assessment and feedback			
Assessment design	Build formative or summative tools.	'Suggest 3 formative assessments to check learning in a lesson on (conditional sentences).' 'Generate some ideas for formative assessments that I can use in my lesson on (x language focus/topic) to check students are learning.' 'Generate a quiz for this learning material (copy/paste or add material). Use the format (x format). Include an answer key or suggested answers guide.'	C: Identify learning goals. O: Ask for examples and answer keys.
Feedback generation	Get help to draft feedback for student work.	'You are a teacher reviewing a (grade x) essay on (climate change). Give actionable feedback on coherence and vocabulary.' 'You are a teacher editing a (grade x)	F: Ensure feedback is specific and constructive.

Teaching task	Goal/use	Example prompt	Prompting tips (C-PROFIT in action)
Assessment and feedback			
Feedback generation (continued)		piece of writing. You are specifically assessing (x assessment criteria). Provide specific feedback for this piece of writing. The feedback should be actionable and provide specific examples based on patterns in the writing (copy and paste student writing in the same prompt).'	
Predicting student needs	Diagnose learning gaps.	'Based on this student's recent speaking/writing, suggest (x number) areas they need to improve.'	C: Provide sample text. F: Review for relevance.
Peer assessment templates	Create peer review instruments.	'Write a simple peer assessment form for (speaking activity), aimed at (x level) learners. Include short criteria with yes/no or scale questions.'	O: Request table format.
Classroom management			
Classroom management	Develop routines and expectations. You may transform this into a poster if needed to display in the classroom and virtual classroom.	'Suggest strategies for language teachers to develop effective classroom management for (12-year-old) (x level) learners. Include tips on setting clear expectations, establishing routines, using positive reinforcement and addressing behavioural issues.'	P: Include student age and level. O: Ask for bullet points.

Teaching task	Goal/use	Example prompt	Prompting tips (C-PROFIT in action)
Classroom management			
Giving instructions	Practice giving clear directions. You may transform this into a poster if needed to display in the classroom and virtual classroom.	'Give examples of step-by-step instructions for a group project for (intermediate) students.' 'Share strategies for language teachers to give instructions for (x level) students who are (x years old). Include tips on setting clear expectations and staging instructions, and questions to ask to ensure that students understand.'	C: Specify task and level.
Administrative tasks GenAI can speed administrative tasks so that teachers can focus on more relevant classroom issues.			
Drafting communications	Save time on paperwork. Draft welcoming and informative letters or emails for parents.	'Draft a friendly welcome email for parents of new students.'	O: Choose format (email, summary). T: Limit word count.
Summarising	Summarise long documents.	'Summarise this policy in 5 bullet points.' 'Here's some information I'd like to understand better: (copy/paste information from your source or pdf). Summarise this information and give me the key takeaways (in bullet points/in a short paragraph, etc.).'	

Teaching task	Goal/use	Example prompt	Prompting tips (C-PROFIT in action)
Administrative tasks GenAI can speed administrative tasks so that teachers can focus on more relevant classroom issues.			
Critical Awareness Tasks	Promote critical thinking and AI literacy.	'Generate 3 answers to this question with one deliberate error for students to identify.' 'Generate multiple responses to a question (which students may critique).'	F: Use errors for class analysis.

Prompting strategies for students

Students can use GenAI to augment their learning, research and creative processes. It's crucial for them to develop AI literacy, and within this, prompt literacy, to ensure they use these tools effectively and ethically. For this, students should take into account the C-PROFIT formula in all of their prompts. It is important to go over Chapter 7's guidelines of responsible use to check the different uses of AI and the AI code of conduct for each activity agreed with students so that they are aware of the scope of use of GenAI tools for each activity and its integration. In the case of primary students, we do not recommend autonomous use of GenAI, rather that they can use it as long as they don´t have to log in, and only for specific tasks supervised by teachers.

Below, we provide an adapted quick reference guide that students from both primary and secondary can resort to when prompting following the C-PROFIT formula.

Primary students quick reference prompting guide

We do not recommend having primary students directly prompting Gen AI, but the ideas in this guide can be facilitated by the teacher.

Table 10.3: Primary level prompting guide

Skill or area	Purpose	Example student prompt (copy & paste)	Quick tip (C-PROFIT)
Explanations and examples			
Clarify learning points	To better understand new words, grammar or ideas.	'Explain what a noun is for a 9-year-old and give 2 examples.'	C: Say your age and topic. P: Ask for clear and short examples.
Provide Examples	Request examples of words, phrases, or structures in use. to see how words or ideas are used in sentences.	'Show 3 sentences using the word "curious" for a (10-year-old).' 'What is (provide challenging word), and how does it relate to (x topic)? Explain it for a student (x age)(x level).'	O: Ask for short, simple sentences.
Content generation and ideas			
Summarise and/or simplify	To make hard texts easier to understand.	'Summarise this story for a (10-year-old): [paste story text].' 'Find and summarise, or simplify, (x document) for a student (x age) (x level).'	T: Ask for an easy version with simple words.
Brainstorm ideas	Request suggestions for essays, projects or other tasks.	'Give me 5 fun ideas for a story about (friendship).' 'Generate ideas or solutions to problems related to (x topic).'	F: Choose your favourite idea and improve it.
Produce drafts	Generate first drafts of titles or task outlines. In this way, students can generate the first idea of a topic, not the final product. This allows them to get started and avoid writer's block.	'Write a title/story outline for a short story about a lost puppy.'	I: You can edit and improve it later.

Skill or area	Purpose	Example student prompt (copy & paste)	Quick tip (C-PROFIT)
Content generation and ideas			
Study materials	Generate personalised study materials, summaries, quizzes, flashcards and visual aids to study better. Students can provide sources or links.	'Make 5 quiz questions about (planets) for a (10-year-old).'	O: Ask for quiz or flashcard format.
Writing enhancement			
Improve text quality	To improve the grammar, vocabulary and style of texts and compare before and after versions.	'Check my paragraph for (x level) mistakes and make it sound better: (paste text).'	F: Compare the original and corrected versions.
Modify genre and/or register	To see how tone or style changes in writing and explore how the same message can sound depending on the audience or purpose (genre awareness).	'Change this short story into a (funny) (poem) for kids.'	T: Ask for examples in fun or formal tones.
Get feedback and edit	To get comments and improve writing.	'Give feedback on my story: what is good and what could be better? (paste text)'	I: Read feedback and decide what to change.
Research assistance			
Suggest topics and/or sources	To find ideas for projects or reports.	'Give me 5 fun topics about (animals) for a school project.'	C: Always check facts with your teacher.
Inquiry-based learning	To turn a topic into a question to explore.	'Help me make a research question about (recycling) for school.'	F: Don't believe everything: think critically.

Skill or area	Purpose	Example student prompt (copy & paste)	Quick tip (C-PROFIT)
Speaking practice			
Conversational practice	To practice speaking or writing English.	'Ask me 5 easy questions about my favourite (food).'	R: Use GenAI as a speaking partner.
Role-play	To practice real-life situations in English.	'Pretend to be a (shopkeeper) and (I'll buy something). Suggest 5 functions I can use in my interaction.'	P: Try to speak naturally and politely.

Secondary students quick reference prompting guide

Table 10.4: Secondary level prompting guide

Skill or area	Purpose	Example student prompt (copy & paste)	Quick tip (C-PROFIT)
Explanations and examples			
Clarify learning points	Explain grammar, vocabulary or themes clearly with examples for a specific age.	'Explain the (past perfect tense) and give 2 simple examples for a (13-year-old) student.'	C: Specify age/level. O: Ask for examples. T: Keep it short.
Provide examples	Show words, phrases or structures used in context.	'What does ("resilient") mean? Give 3 short sentences about (resilience) for a (15-year-old).'	C: Include word and topic. O: Request number of examples.
Content generation and ideas			
Summarise/ simplify	Summarise or simplify a document so it is easier to understand.	'Summarise this article about (renewable energy) for a (14-year-old) in 5 bullet points. (Paste or attach article)'	P: Paste text or link. O: Ask for bullet points. T: Set a limit.

Skill or area	Purpose	Example student prompt (copy & paste)	Quick tip (C-PROFIT)
Content generation and ideas			
Brainstorm ideas	Generate ideas for essays, projects or creative tasks when stuck.	'Give me five creative ideas for a school project about (recycling), with a one-sentence description for each.'	C: Specify topic. O: Ask for a list. F: Pick and refine favourites.
Produce drafts	Create first drafts of titles, outlines or texts to start the writing process.	'Write a first draft introduction for my essay about (teamwork) of about 120 words.'	I: Revise the draft. F: Compare with your ideas. T: Set word count.
Study materials	Create personalised study aids like quizzes, summaries or visual prompts.	'Create a 10-question multiple-choice quiz about (the Industrial Revolution) for a (9th grader). Include the answer key.'	C: Specify level and topic. O: Quiz and key. T: Limit number of questions.
Writing enhancement			
Improve text quality	Improve grammar, vocabulary and style of a written text and compare before and after versions.	'Improve this paragraph to correct grammar and make it more (formal) for a (school report). (Paste paragraph)'	P: Paste text. F: Ask for explanations of changes. O: Request revised version and notes.
Modify genre and/or register	Change the genre or register to suit a different audience or purpose and explore how the same message can sound depending on the audience or purpose (genre awareness).	'Rewrite this paragraph as (an informal email to a friend). (Paste paragraph)'	R: State new audience/register. O: Ask for the rewritten version. T: Set word count.

Skill or area	Purpose	Example student prompt (copy & paste)	Quick tip (C-PROFIT)
Writing enhancement			
Get feedback and edit	Ask for strengths, areas to improve and edit suggestions.	'Point out two strengths and two areas to improve in this paragraph and suggest a revised sentence for each issue: (Paste paragraph)' 'Give feedback on this essay's coherence and vocabulary.' 'Suggest how I could make this introduction more engaging.'	O: Request strengths, improvements and sample edits. I: Apply and reflect.
Research assistance			
Suggest topics and/or sources	Get research topic ideas and starter sources (always crosscheck).	'Give me five research topics about (climate change) and 2 starter sources for each topic.'	C: Topic. O: List and sources. F: Verify sources independently.
Inquiry-based learning	Turn a topic into a research question and a simple method to investigate. Define research problems, conduct literature reviews, collect and process data, and create reports as researchers.	'Help me turn (plastic pollution) into one clear research question and suggest a simple method to investigate it.'	C: Provide topic. O: Question and method. F: Check feasibility.

Skill or area	Purpose	Example student prompt (copy & paste)	Quick tip (C-PROFIT)
Speaking practice			
Conversational practice	Practise speaking and fluency with agents, get corrections and suggestions.	'Let's have a 10-minute conversation about (my hobbies). Correct my grammar and suggest better phrases.'	R: Ask chatbot to correct and suggest. O: Set time/ duration.
Role-play	Simulate situations (e.g., ordering food) to practise language and receive feedback.	'Pretend to be (a waiter). I will (order food) in English. Correct my mistakes and give 3 phrases I can use next time.'	R: Assign role. O: Dialogue and feedback. I: Repeat and improve.

Teaching critical evaluation of GenAI output to students

It is important for teachers to make a point of critically evaluating every step of the way. As stated before, students should be reminded to be critical and to question outputs provided by GenAI tools. Different strategies to work on this with students are suggested below.

Identify flaws or bias: Students should be encouraged to criticise GenAI-generated text, identify potential errors or biases and question the GenAI's choices and inaccuracies.

Compare with human content: After GenAI produces content, students can be asked to compare it with human-created content on the same topic, identifying differences and similarities. This is an interesting task to spot certain recurring structures and vocabulary that GenAI tools rely on.

Assess veracity: Students can prompt an essay with GenAI and then reflect on their essay writing process using questions such as 'Was the essay generated by GenAI reliable? What kinds of references did GenAI use? What kinds of issues did GenAI highlight? What did the GenAI leave out?'

Figure 10.3: Critical evaluation of GenAI output

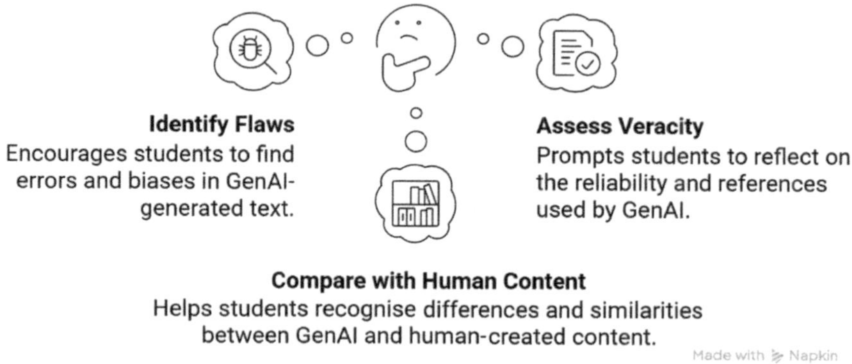

Creative co-creation

Brainstorm and refine: Collaborate with GenAI to brainstorm, generate and refine original ideas for creative projects such as stories, while considering ownership and attribution.

Iterative development: Students engage in iterative co-creation with GenAI to develop a concrete learning outcome, such as a short story, dialogue or presentation, linked to real-world contexts or classroom tasks. For example, a student might describe initial ideas for characters and themes to a GenAI tool, review the generated suggestions, and reflect on whether they suit the intended tone, context or audience before revising and refining the text.

Image generation: Students can design detailed prompts to generate images that express their perspectives on familiar themes such as daily life, family roles, professions, cultural traditions or communities. This allows learners to explore and challenge stereotypical representations by creating more diverse and inclusive images that reflect different identities, lifestyles and social contexts.

Figure 10.4: Creative co-creation

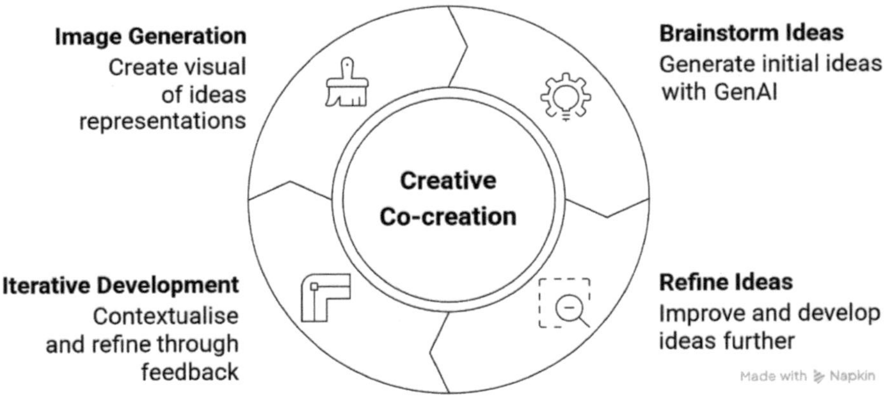

The role of human oversight and AI literacy

For both teachers and students, prompting should not be a one-time instruction but part of an ongoing human-GenAI collaboration. Humans must remain 'in the loop', reviewing, verifying and refining GenAI outputs, exercising critical thinking, ethical judgement and contextual understanding. This, however, has implications given the environmental impact of prompts. A balance should therefore be found by drafting the first prompt as specifically and carefully as possible to avoid unnecessary re-prompting. Over-reliance on GenAI, as we have repeated throughout the book, can lead to cognitive offloading, diminishing deep analytical thinking. Therefore, effective prompting is deeply intertwined with AI literacy, which includes understanding how GenAI works, its limitations, ethical implications and how to use it safely and effectively.

Reflective task 3

How can adjusting the *specificity* and *context* of your prompts (using the C-PROFIT formula) improve the quality and relevance of GenAI responses for your teaching or your students' learning?

The more specific and context-rich a prompt is, the more accurate, relevant and useful the GenAI response will be. Using the C-PROFIT formula helps teachers and students think critically before prompting; clarifying context, defining a clear purpose and requesting an appropriate output. By adding details such as grade level, learning goals and student needs, educators and learners transform GenAI from a generic answer generator into a personalised learning partner that supports creativity, reflection and deeper understanding.

Further reading

Boonstra, L. (2025, April). *Prompt Engineering* (Version 7.1) [PDF]. Innopreneur. https://www.innopreneur.io/wp-content/uploads/2025/04/22365_3_Prompt-Engineering_v7-1.pdf

Chapter 11:

AI-enhanced projects and activities

In Chapter 11, we show how the integration of AI can complement skills practice and revamp classroom activities and projects. We offer teachers practical frameworks for classroom use that include reflective tasks for learners.

Reflective task 1

Have you ever considered using AI in your teaching or encouraged students to engage with AI tools? What are your main concerns or hesitations?

Key considerations for integrating AI in the classroom

Integrating AI into the classroom requires thoughtful planning and careful consideration of your teaching objectives, the specific AI tools you choose, and the accessibility of these tools for your students. When done effectively, AI can enhance learning experiences and help students optimise their potential.

Bear in mind your learning objectives and context

The first and most important step in integrating AI into your teaching is to ensure that it aligns with your learning objectives and fits within the context of your curriculum. AI should not be used just because it is a trending technology; it should serve a clear purpose in supporting your educational goals.

Start with clear objectives before selecting any AI tool, reflect on the specific learning outcomes you want to achieve: are you aiming to help students improve their writing skills, foster creativity, develop their critical thinking or enhance their problem-solving skills? The AI tool you choose should be suitable for these goals.

Context matters

Consider the context of your classroom, whether it is a group of young learners, middle or high school students, or adult learners, and choose AI tools that are appropriate for their age, skill level and learning needs. How will AI complement your traditional teaching methods, and how will it enhance the students' understanding of the subject matter or help them co-create with AI?

Avoid overcomplicating

It is important not to overwhelm students or yourself with complex AI tools that may distract from the core learning objectives. Start small with AI tools that are easy to integrate, and gradually build up as you and your students become more comfortable and literate with the technology.

Get to know which AI can be integrated into your projects

With your learning objectives in mind, you need to identify which specific AI tools are best suited for your project or classroom activities. There are many types of AI tools available, each with different capabilities, so it is important to understand their strengths and limitations. Remember that smaller models, such as more specific AI tools specialised in a limited set of tasks, need a smaller database to run, can possibly run on your device offline, adding an extra layer of privacy, and therefore have a smaller environmental footprint. Summarising and classifying data are tasks performed really effectively by smaller models. Choose AI tools that actively support your project's goals and that complement your teaching style.

What are students going to craft?

When integrating AI into your classroom, think about what students will create using the technology. AI can empower students to produce a wide range of creative outputs, from written essays and interactive stories to music videos, digital art and more. The beauty of AI is that it can take over some of the more technical aspects, allowing students to focus on content creation and creativity. Consider how AI can enrich the projects your students are working on. For instance, can AI help students brainstorm ideas, offer suggestions for improvement or help them visualise concepts in new ways?

Trial and test

Before fully integrating an AI tool into your classroom, it is a good idea to test it out. Try the tool yourself and consider how user-friendly it is, how well it aligns with your project, and how intuitive it will be for your students to use. Testing ensures that the AI tool you choose will function smoothly and effectively within your lesson plan. The classroom is a big lab: keep a record of your experiments.

Consider accessibility for students

A crucial aspect of integrating AI into education is ensuring that it is accessible for all your students. Accessibility encompasses not only the physical availability of the technology (do your students have the necessary devices and internet access to use these tools?) but also how easy it is for students to use and engage with it meaningfully.

Ease of use

Consider how easy or difficult it will be for your students to learn and use the AI. Some AI tools require complex inputs or an advanced understanding of the technology, while others are more user-friendly and intuitive. Choose tools that are appropriate for your students' age and skill level. For younger students or those with less experience using digital tools, it's better to start with AI tools that have simple interfaces and clear instructions. A good rule of thumb is that a very complex tool to learn is not worth it if they are not going to use it again and again.

Support diverse learning styles

AI tools can be a great way to support different learning styles and abilities in the classroom. Some students may thrive with AI tools that offer visual representations, while others might benefit from text-based feedback or audio instructions. By offering various AI tools, you can create a more inclusive learning environment that caters to a broad range of student needs.

Figure 11.1: Integrating AI in education

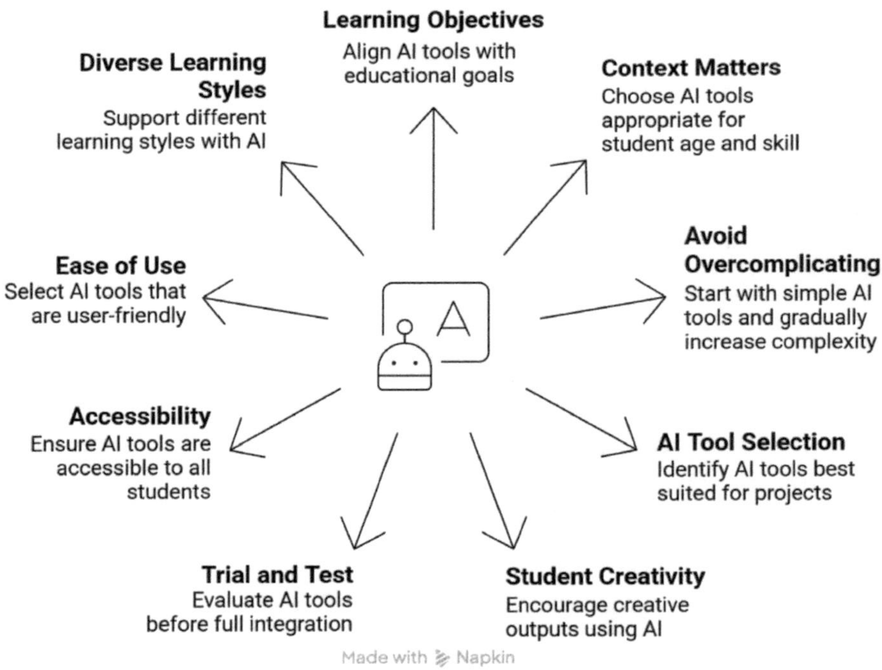

B.O.T.S.

A practical way for teachers to remember how to approach AI in the classroom can be summarised as B.O.T.S.

B – Balance AI with learning objectives.

O – Offer accessible and age-appropriate tools.

T – Test and experiment before full implementation.

S – Support creativity and critical thinking.

Figure 11.2: BOTS for AI integration

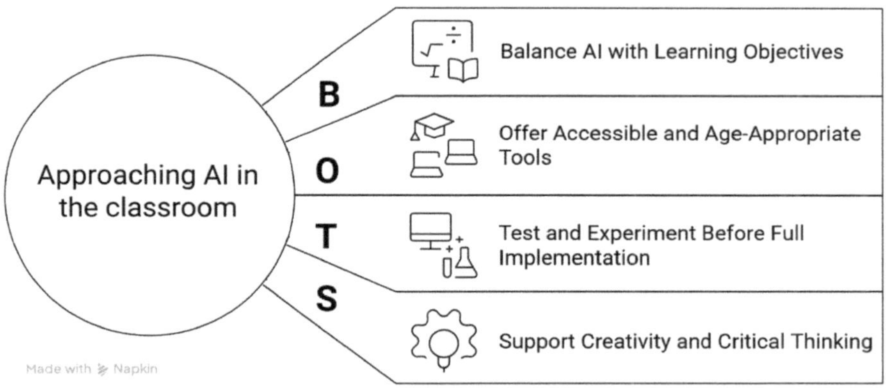

We can use AI to foster innovation, collaboration and problem solving, allowing students to co-create and explore new ideas. When integrating AI into your teaching, it is essential to align your choices with your objectives, choose the right tools for your projects, and ensure that these tools are accessible to all students. AI offers immense potential to enhance learning, but its success depends on thoughtful integration.

Reflective task 2

What are three key takeaways from this introduction that you find most helpful when approaching AI integration? Which principle of the B.O.T.S. framework (Balance, Offer, Test, Support) do you find most challenging to implement?

Here is a chart you can use to design or integrate GenAI tools into different projects or activities, and which you can use to consider the variables:

Table 11.1: GenAI tools integration guide

Category	Details
Title/level/duration	Write the name of the project or task. Indicate the student level or age group. Specify total time (e.g., 2 class periods, 1 week project).
Objective(s)	State what students will learn or demonstrate.
Tools/GenAI resources/sample prompts/GenAI integration role	List all GenAI tools or apps that could be used (e.g., ChatGPT, Canva, Copilot). Include example GenAI prompts for teachers or students. Summarise how GenAI supports the task (idea generation, feedback, etc.).
Plan/teacher role/ challenges	Write a step-by-step plan for implementing the project. Describe how the teacher facilitates, monitors or supports students.
Output/product	Explain what students will create, present or do.
Assessment criteria	Describe how students' work will be evaluated (rubric, checklist).
Reflection/follow-up	Add reflection or ethical discussion questions for students. (Check Chapter 8 worksheets.)

GenAI for speaking and listening skills

An interesting use of GenAI is for students to practise speaking skills. The advantages are that students may feel more relaxed and gain confidence in a stress-free environment where they can make mistakes and receive supportive feedback without peer exposure. It is useful if students have to sit for an exam and they can rehearse before facing a real examiner. This allows for a more personalised interaction between students and GenAI, though the prompting should be specific and detailed as to which aspects of speaking and interaction require improvement. Students should be guided as to how to approach this interaction, what to type in the prompt, and have a model of the interaction beforehand so that they can understand how it works and how they can solve possible problems. It also requires guidance from the teacher in the early stages. Students will need to keep track of these interactions with the GenAI and to reflect on them later, to record them if possible and jot down helpful feedback.

Below, you will find three possible ways to train students in the use of GenAI to enhance speaking. Interactions need monitoring and supervision by teachers. Teachers should project sample prompts on the board.

For speaking exams

Title: Speaking exams

Level: Primary and secondary students. Intermediate to advanced.

Duration: 20–30 minutes

Objective(s):

- To develop fluency, accuracy and interactional competence in exam-style speaking tasks.
- To use GenAI as a speaking coach to practise question-and-answer exchanges typical of international exams.
- To promote self-reflection and awareness of speaking performance through GenAI-generated feedback.

Tools/GenAI resources:

- Text or voice interaction mode
- Voice recorder (optional, for student self-review)
- Student's speaking journal or digital reflection log

Prompts students can use:

'I am (x age and level).You are my speaking examiner for the (x exam). Ask me five questions about (detail one of the possible speaking topics of the exam). After each answer, give me one piece of feedback about how to make my answer better.'

'I am a (x age and level) student sitting for the (x exam). Act as my speaking coach. Ask me about my daily routine. After I answer, give me one tip to improve my pronunciation in (x variety of English).'

'Simulate the (x exam) speaking part. Give me a topic card and let me speak for one minute. Then, tell me what I did well and what I should improve.'

Output/product:

- A recorded or written interaction log with GenAI.
- Student reflection notes including useful phrases, errors and GenAI feedback.
- A short oral report in the next class summarising what was learned.

Assessment criteria:

Criterion	Description	Focus area
Fluency and coherence	Smooth flow of ideas, use of connectors, minimal hesitation	Communication
Lexical range	Appropriate and varied vocabulary use	Vocabulary
Grammatical accuracy	Correct and varied use of structures	Grammar
Pronunciation	Clarity, stress, rhythm and intonation	Speaking delivery
Interaction	Ability to respond naturally and maintain conversation	Communication strategy
Reflection	Quality of insight and action plan after practice	Metacognition

Reflection/follow-up:
Students re-listen or re-read their conversation and note one strength and one area for improvement.

They complete a short reflection entry, e.g.:

Today I practised: ______________________________

I did well at: ______________________________

I want to improve: ______________________________

Feedback I received from the GenAI: ______________________________

Reflection and feedback:
Group follow-up session: Students share the prompts that worked best and discuss strategies to handle examiner questions. The group keeps track of the prompts, writes them down to use later. The teacher reviews reflection logs periodically to track progress.

For debates

Title: Debates

Level: Primary and secondary students. Intermediate to advanced.

Duration: 20–30 minutes

Objective(s):
- To develop fluency, accuracy and interactional competence in debate-style speaking tasks.
- To use GenAI as a debate partner or coach to rehearse structured arguments and rebuttals, to provide starters and functions tailored to the level.
- To promote self-reflection and awareness of speaking performance through GenAI-generated feedback.

Tools/GenAI resources:
- Text or voice interaction mode
- Voice recorder (optional, for student self-review)
- Student's speaking journal or digital reflection log

Prompts students can use:

'I am (x age and level). You are my debate coach. I am preparing for a classroom debate on the (x topic). Ask me to defend or oppose the statement. After I respond, give me feedback on my argument strength and clarity. Provide two possible arguments and two sentence starters.'

'I am (x age and level). Simulate a debate partner. Choose one side of the (x topic). Challenge my points and ask follow-up questions.'

'I am (x age and level). Act as my moderator in a debate on (x topic). Ask opening questions, allow me to respond and give feedback on my reasoning and delivery.'

Output/product:

- Recorded or written debate simulation with GenAI.
- Student reflection notes including key arguments, counterarguments and GenAI feedback.
- Short oral report in the next class summarising debate strategies learned.

Assessment criteria:

Criterion	Description	Focus area
Fluency and coherence	Logical flow of arguments, smooth delivery, minimal hesitation	Communication
Lexical range	Use of appropriate and varied debate-specific vocabulary	Vocabulary
Grammatical accuracy	Correct and varied use of complex structures	Grammar
Pronunciation	Clear articulation, intonation and emphasis on key ideas	Speaking delivery
Interaction	Ability to respond naturally to counterarguments and maintain turn-taking	Communication strategy
Critical thinking	Quality and strength of reasoning, evidence and rebuttals	Argumentation
Reflection	Depth of insight and self-evaluation after practice	Metacognition

Reflection/follow-up:
Students re-listen or re-read their debate and note one strength and one area for improvement. They complete a short reflection entry, e.g.:

Today I practised: ______________________________

My best argument was: ____________________________

I will use these sentence starters and functions in my future debates: ______________________________

Feedback I received from the GenAI: ____________________

Reflection and feedback:
Group follow-up session: Students share the prompts that worked best and discuss strategies to handle arguments and counterarguments. The group keeps track of effective prompts, writes them down to refine and reuse, and monitors improvement over time. The teacher reviews reflection logs periodically to track individual and group progress.

For dictation practice

Title: Dictation practice

Level: Primary and secondary students. Intermediate.

Duration: 15–25 minutes

Objective(s):

- To improve listening accuracy, spelling and punctuation through GenAI-delivered dictations.
- To use GenAI in voice interaction mode for realistic dictation input and immediate repetition.
- To develop self-correction strategies and enhance awareness of English rhythm, stress and intonation.

Tools/GenAI resources:

- GenAI with voice interaction mode
- Notebook or Google Docs for transcription
- Headphones for focused listening
- Voice recorder (optional, for replaying and checking)
- Student's dictation log for error analysis and reflection

Implementation steps:

Preparation

The teacher selects short texts (50–120 words) that are appropriate for the students' level,
such as descriptive paragraphs, dialogues, short news reports or exam-related topics. The short text can even be GenAI created if you want it to include certain words, vocabulary or grammar structures.

Possible prompt for text generation:

'Create a (x-word) paragraph for dictation for (x level and age of students) that contains the following: (x words, vocabulary, tense or target structures or functions).'

The teacher models a GenAI prompt and shows how to use 'pause', 'repeat' and 'check' commands.

Prompts students can use:

'You are my English teacher. Please dictate a short paragraph (copy/paste text) suitable for (x level). Read slowly and clearly, with short pauses between phrases. After finishing, ask me if I want you to repeat any part.'

'You are my dictation coach. Dictate five sentences at (x level) about daily routines. Speak slowly and repeat each sentence once.'

'Dictate a paragraph about healthy eating at (x level). After I finish writing, show me the correct version and tell me how many words I missed.'

'Read a short news article for (x level). Pause after each sentence, then ask if I'm ready for the next one.'

Student practice
Students listen to the GenAI dictation and write down exactly what they hear. They can say commands like:

- 'Please repeat the last sentence.'
- 'Can you spell that word?'
- 'Could you read the paragraph again at normal speed?'

Checking and feedback
Students ask the GenAI to display or read the correct version: 'Now show me the original text so I can check my dictation.'

They compare and highlight their spelling and punctuation errors.

GenAI provides targeted feedback if prompted: 'Tell me which words I misspelled and how I can improve my listening.'

Reflection
Students complete a dictation log after each practice:

Date	Topic	Type of errors and correction

Output/product:
- A written dictation text produced by the student.
- A corrected version with errors marked and annotated.
- A reflection log noting common listening and spelling issues.

Criterion	Description	Focus area
Listening accuracy	Correct transcription of spoken text	Listening
Spelling	Accurate word spelling	Writing mechanics
Punctuation	Correct use of punctuation marks	Grammar
Attention to detail	Ability to notice and self-correct	Concentration
Pronunciation awareness	Understanding of rhythm, stress and intonation	Phonological awareness
Reflection	Quality of self-assessment and improvement planning	Metacognition

Reflection and feedback:
Group follow-up: Students share common mistakes and effective prompts (e.g., 'Repeat more slowly', or, 'Spell unknown words').

The teacher monitors reflection logs weekly to identify patterns in listening difficulties and supervises interactions during dictations.

Students build a personalised word bank of frequently misspelled words for revision.

Reflective task 3

How did practising with GenAI help you become more aware of your speaking strengths and weaknesses? What strategies or GenAI prompts did you find most effective for improving your student's speaking confidence?

GenAI for reading and writing skills

GenAI can play a valuable role in supporting the development of reading and writing skills.One of the main advantages is that students can work at their own pace in a low-pressure environment, where they can draft, revise and experiment with language while receiving immediate, supportive feedback. This is particularly useful when students are preparing for written exams or extended writing tasks, as they can practise planning, organising ideas and refining language before submitting work for teacher feedback.

GenAI also allows for more personalised support, as prompts can be tailored to target specific aspects of reading comprehension or writing development, such as text organisation, vocabulary choice, cohesion or register. However, students need clear guidance by their teachers on how to interact with GenAI, what to include in their prompts following the C-PROFIT framework, and how to evaluate and use the feedback provided. Teachers should model sample prompts, monitor early interactions and encourage students to keep a record of drafts, feedback and revisions. Reflection is essential: students should review how their texts evolve and note which strategies and suggestions are most helpful.

Below, you will find several classroom-ready ways to train students in the effective use of GenAI to enhance reading and writing. All activities require teacher guidance, monitoring and the projection of sample prompts to ensure purposeful and responsible use.

For writing scripts for TED-Ed talk presentations

Title: TED-Ed talk presentations

Level: Primary and secondary students. Intermediate to advanced.

Duration: 2–3 lessons (60–90 minutes each)

Objective(s):

- To guide students in developing and structuring their own TED-Ed style talk using GenAI as a brainstorming and drafting assistant.
- To enhance students' idea development, organisation and vocabulary range following the Ted Ed Journal and with the teacher's supervision.
- To integrate GenAI for script writing, refining ideas and coaching for oral delivery (intonation, emphasis and body language).
- To promote reflection, fact-checking and ethical GenAI use in the creative process.

Tools/GenAI resources:

- GenAI text generation (e.g., ChatGPT, Gemini, Claude)
- Research tools and online references (students must verify all information used)
- Word processor or note-taking app
- Optional: Voice interaction mode or text-to-speech tool for pronunciation rehearsal
- Recording device for final presentation practice

Prompts students can use:

For brainstorming ideas:
'I am preparing a TED-Ed talk for my school club. Suggest five creative topics connected to (x area of interest). For each, give me a short description and why it could inspire the audience.'

For structuring the script:
'Act as a TED-Ed coach. Help me write a three-minute talk about (x topic). Include an engaging hook as an intro that could be a rhetorical question, an impactful statistic or image, a joke, a stanza from a poem, a clear message, and a closing idea that inspires reflection.'

For vocabulary building:
'Suggest more advanced or expressive words I can use instead of (x common word). Show me examples of how to use them in my TED talk.'

For delivery coaching:
'Give me tips on how to use body language, pauses and voice tone when presenting this part of my script.'

For reflection and self-improvement:
'After reading my script, give me one suggestion to make my story more personal or emotionally engaging and how I can enhance the talk with a personal experience.'

Output/product:

- A well-structured TED-Ed talk script written with GenAI guidance using verified sources with the teacher's guidance and suggestions.
- A short, recorded rehearsal or live presentation.
- A reflection journal including GenAI feedback and teacher's feedback, vocabulary improvements and delivery notes.

Assessment criteria:

Criterion	Description	Focus area
Idea development	Clarity, originality and coherence of main message	Content
Structure and organisation	Logical flow: introduction, development and conclusion	Writing
Language and vocabulary	Range, accuracy and appropriacy of vocabulary	Lexical/grammar
Engagement and delivery	Storytelling, tone and use of non-verbal communication (body language)	Speaking/ performance
GenAI integration and reflection	Ethical use of GenAI, quality of reflection and independence	Metacognitive skills

Reflection/follow-up:
Students' reflection: What did GenAI help you improve most: your ideas, language or delivery? Which part of the AI-generated feedback did you find most useful or surprising?

How will you and your teacher continue refining your talk to make it more authentic and powerful before your final presentation?

For creative writing projects

Title: The Road Not Taken: Creative digital storytelling with Twine

Level: Upper primary to lower secondary.

Duration: 3–4 sessions (60–90 minutes each)

Objective(s):

- To engage students in interactive storytelling using the digital tool Twine and GenAI to enhance creativity and narrative design.
- To develop writing, decision-making and digital literacy skills through the creation of nonlinear stories in the fashion of a 'choose your own adventure'.
- To use AI-powered tools for generating adaptive dialogues, enriching plotlines and expanding vocabulary.
- To foster collaboration, peer feedback and reflective learning as students design, share and refine their stories.

- To encourage teachers to revamp traditional projects by integrating GenAI in meaningful, ethical and creative ways.

Tools/GenAI resources:
- Twine (open-source tool for nonlinear, interactive digital stories)
- GenAI text generators (for adaptive dialogue creation, plot development and vocabulary enhancement)
- GenAI-based feedback systems (for self-assessment and narrative improvement)
- Optional: Audio narration tools or text-to-speech for immersive story presentations

Prompts students can use:
For brainstorming story ideas:
'I'm a (x age and level) student writing a choose-your-own-adventure story for my classmates. Suggest three possible plots inspired by the (x theme).'

For story development:
'Act as a creative writing coach. Help me design branching story paths with three possible endings where the reader's choices affect the outcome.'

For enriching the narrative:
'Suggest more vivid vocabulary or expressions to make my story more immersive and emotionally engaging.'

For GenAI integration:
'Help me create intelligent dialogue between characters that changes based on the reader's choices.'

For reflection:
'Give me feedback on how my story promotes creativity and what I could do to make the interactive experience stronger.'

Output/product:
- A complete Twine-based interactive story integrating AI-generated enhancements with teacher's supervision and suggestions where other students become active readers in the story.

- A presentation or short demo where students showcase how GenAI influenced their creative process.
- A reflection journal documenting GenAI prompts, feedback received and lessons learned.

Assessment criteria:

Criterion	Description	Focus area
Creativity and originality	Quality, uniqueness and imagination in story concept	Content/idea Development
Narrative structure	Logical flow, clarity and effectiveness of branching story paths	Writing organisation
Language and vocabulary	Range, richness and accuracy of vocabulary and expressions	Lexical/grammar
GenAI integration	Effective and ethical use of GenAI to enhance storytelling	Digital literacy/ creativity
Collaboration and reflection	Quality of peer feedback, depth of reflection on GenAI use	Metacognition/ teamwork

Reflection/follow-up:
Students' reflection: How did GenAI help you make your story more creative, interactive or engaging for readers? What challenges did you face when using GenAI tools, and how did you solve them?

For creative image generation projects

Title: 'The Gruffalo Animal Fusion'

Level: Lower primary

Duration: 50 minutes

Objective(s):

- To develop creativity and descriptive language through imaginative storytelling and visual expression.
- To introduce students to GenAI as a tool for visualising ideas and comparing human and AI interpretations.
- To build speaking confidence through presentation and reflection on the creative process.

Tools/GenAI resources:
- OpenArt – Image Blender
- Canva AI Image Generator
- Drawing materials (paper, coloured pencils, markers)
- Projector or shared screen for class comparison

Sample prompts/GenAI integration role:
- Students brainstorm and draw a new creature that combines two animals from *The Gruffalo* (e.g., fox + owl, mouse + snake).
- After describing their creatures, students use GenAI to generate a digital version of the same animal fusion.
- GenAI's role: to visualise the students' imagined fusion and provide a digital comparison for creative reflection.

Prompt students can use:
'Create an image of a creature that combines (a fox and an owl). It should have the (wings of an owl), the (tail of a fox) and (sharp claws). The creature should look (friendly but wild).'

Students may also describe their ideas orally before generating the image.

Output/product:
- A hand-drawn 'fusion creature' accompanied by a written and spoken description using target vocabulary (e.g., tusks, claws, prickles).
- A GenAI-generated image representing the same concept.
- A short comparison between the student's version and the GenAI's version (oral or written).

Assessment criteria:

Criteria	Description
Creativity and imagination	Originality of the fused creature and idea generation
Vocabulary use	Correct and varied use of descriptive terms (e.g., claws, fangs, wings)
Language production	Clarity and fluency in describing the creature

Criteria	Description
Engagement with AI	Ability to interpret and compare AI output thoughtfully
Reflection	Depth of insight when analysing differences between human and GenAI-created versions

Reflection/follow-up:
Students' reflection: Students discuss:

- 'What do you see in the GenAI picture? How did it mix the two animals?'
- 'Did the GenAI make anything that surprised you or looked funny?'
- 'Would you change your drawing after seeing GenAI's creature? What would you add or keep the same?'

Teachers can extend the activity by having students write a short story featuring their hybrid creature, applying the new vocabulary in context.

Reflection and feedback (for teachers): This activity effectively merges creativity, vocabulary learning and digital literacy. Students are encouraged to express their imagination first, then see how GenAI visualises their ideas, prompting critical comparison and reflective thinking. Teachers can use this structure to foster higher-order skills: students not only produce content but analyse *how* both human and GenAI creativity intersect. This makes GenAI a genuine learning partner rather than a content producer.

Reflective task 4

Think of a project you have previously worked on with students in previous years that you feel proud of and are comfortable with. How can insights from the TED-Ed Talk and Twine projects motivate you to integrate GenAI not just as a tool for speed or polish, but as a true partner in the creative and reflective process? How is your role as a teacher redefined?

Integrating GenAI into the classroom represents a transformative step in how teachers design, deliver and evaluate learning. When guided by clear objectives and ethical principles, GenAI becomes far more than a digital assistant, it becomes a co-creator that enhances creativity, reflection and engagement. One of the keys is its intentional integration, where teachers balance innovation with pedagogy. As the B.O.T.S. framework reminds us (Balance, Offer, Test, and Support), successful AI-enhanced learning environments require thoughtful planning, accessible tools, continuous experimentation and teacher supervision so they can facilitate the dynamics. Teachers cultivate a classroom culture of exploration, agency and critical thinking when they make their students reflect and share what has worked in the experimentation process.

In this last chapter, each reflective task highlights a dimension of how GenAI can enrich teaching and learning. They encourage educators to reconsider their role as facilitators of responsible GenAI use, ensuring that integration supports (not replaces) human creativity and judgement; they demonstrate how GenAI can act as a speaking coach and listener, helping students rehearse, self-correct and build confidence in a low-stakes environment; they explore GenAI's potential to expand reading and writing skills, transforming traditional projects like TED-Ed Talks and Twine stories into spaces for adaptive storytelling, emotional engagement and the expression of authentic voices. Finally, they invite teachers to reimagine past projects, positioning GenAI not merely as a productivity tool, but as a creative and reflective partner that empowers both teachers and learners.

Ultimately, integrating GenAI calls for a pedagogical shift, from teacher as 'knowledge provider' to teacher as 'designer of intelligent learning experiences'. By blending human insight with machine capabilities, educators can foster personalised, interactive and deeply meaningful learning journeys on which students don't just consume information: they create, collaborate and think critically with AI.

Conclusion

Throughout the book, we have tried to provide an in-depth analysis of AI issues that are sometimes overlooked, and provide strategies for responsible use.

We have mostly focused on general, multitask GenAI models and tried to avoid naming or reviewing tools as these evolve quite rapidly. We have not covered teacher-specific tools as these are quite straightforward to use. Many of these allow you to create texts, summarise them, simplify them, create reading comprehension questions, true or false, quizzes and vocabulary lists, help with writing emails and creating report card comments, for example.

We haven't covered these other uses but we have seen interesting examples of:

Tailor-made AI agents: We have noticed a growth in the creation of custom GPTs and Gems for specific uses. Kateryna Protsenko, a teacher trainer from the UK, has been using custom GPTs and Gems for a while for writing emails, for formatting feedback she gives to teachers, for identifying someone's English level and for creating lesson materials.

AI for teacher development: Sam Gravell, an Ed Tech consultant in Germany, has created a custom GPT that lets you interact with the Dogme ELT discussion group, originally hosted in Yahoo Groups, and extend the ideas further into lessons, workshops, and more. You can search by keyword, theme, or contributor; contrast perspectives from the forum contributors, generate a chronological history of how the movement evolved, etc.. You can access it here: https://chatgpt.com/g/g-694642c266408191a9c35ded1a926b57-dogme-forum-archivist

AI as a mentor: Shaun Wilden, a teacher and trainer from the UK, has written a series of posts in his Substack about an experiment with ChatGPT where he asks it to become his self-observation mentor. His posts raise some really engaging points, such as the realisation that it cannot act as a human, but it can act as a mirror and let you see things you may have failed to notice, and it can recognise patterns of practice. And this can be conducive to further self-reflection. You can access it here: https://wildeshaun.substack.com/archive

AI for planning lessons: We have seen interesting examples of refining prompts to create more effective lessons that align with a teacher's beliefs and context. Adding the methodology or approach for the lesson: project-based learning, task based learning, dogme, etc., is particularly successful. Paola Danesi, a teacher and trainer from Buenos Aires, Argentina, has been experimenting with including Bloom's taxonomy in the prompt, with very interesting results that divide the lesson into Bloom's six stages. Sam Gravell has also created other custom GPTs to aid with lesson planning. There's one that generates task sequences with a variety of TBLT types based on group/learner info and context. You can access it here: https://chatgpt.com/g/g-o91tvyYHu-task-generator

Conversational AI: We have also seen creative uses of conversational AI, where a GenAI chatbot acts as a 'sparring partner' rather than a tool that simply gives you answers. Joe Dale, a teacher trainer from the UK, has been using this approach for building his own Chrome extension, and has also seen the same pattern working for teachers and learners.

In his own words, he "used AI to build something for him over several weeks of constant back and forth. He would describe what he wanted, see what it produced, realise what he did not like or what was missing, push back, and then refine the idea. Quite often the most useful moments were when the AI got something wrong or confidently said it had fixed an issue when it clearly had not. That forced [him] to think more carefully about what [he] actually wanted and how to explain it better. The value was not in the output itself, but in the dialogue. Each exchange helped [him] sharpen [his] thinking, make better decisions, and stay in control of the final outcome.

He also thinks students can use conversational AI to rehearse ideas, explanations, or spoken responses, pushing and reshaping their thinking through dialogue. Teachers can use it in the same way for lesson reflection, planning, or problem-solving, using the AI to create productive friction rather than to replace professional judgement.This helps shift the conversation away from AI as an answer machine and towards AI as something you think with.

We believe the future holds a paradigm shift from a purely technocentric focus toward human-AI co-thinking, where AI systems can serve as intellectual partners rather than just automation tools. We believe humans should remain firmly in control, but their effort can be multiplied by a supportive technological enhancement. While AI will not replace human teachers, it will augment their roles, transforming them into facilitators of cognitive interactions who prioritise empathy and high-value human relationships.

For students, AI literacy (around operational, contextual, critical, and creative domains) will become a fundamental competency as essential as traditional reading or writing. We remain hopeful that personalised learning will become reliable, providing 24/7 tutoring and non-judgmental practice environments that significantly reduce language-learning anxiety.

However, the field must navigate the critical risks we have enumerated and discussed in detail, such as linguistic bias and the standardisation of language, which threaten to marginalise diverse dialects and world Englishes, data management and copyright issues, and technological developments to minimise the environmental impact. Consequently, assessments will evolve from judging static outputs to valuing the collaborative process between humans and AI. And to ensure an equitable future, we must take action to bridge the digital divide, ensuring these powerful capabilities empower all learners regardless of their socioeconomic status.

Glossary

AI literacy is the foundational knowledge, understanding, and skills that empower individuals to effectively, ethically, and critically use, evaluate, and understand artificial intelligence (AI) systems and technologies.

Algorithmic colonisation is the control and domination of societies through algorithms and data, driven by corporate interests seeking profit and market influence.

Algorithms are a set of instructions to be followed in calculations or other operations.

Annotation is the process of labelling raw data (like text, prompts, or model responses) with meaningful tags, ratings, or descriptions by human experts or automated tools to create a structured dataset.

Artificial intelligence (AI) is the application of computer systems able to perform tasks or produce output normally requiring human intelligence, especially by applying machine learning techniques to large collections of data.

Artificial neural networks are a type of machine learning algorithm, inspired by the structure and function of the human brain, that uses a network of interconnected nodes (or artificial neurons) to process data and learn from it.

Bias is the mismatch of ideal and actual distributions of labels and user attributes in training and application of a system.

Central Processing Units (CPU) are the hardware component that functions as the "brain" or "control centre" of a computer system, responsible for executing instructions and performing the necessary calculations to run the operating system and applications.

Cognitive debt is the diminished thinking and critical engagement that results from outsourcing cognitive tasks to AI or other external systems, leading to a decline in critical thinking, memory, and creativity.

Cognitive laziness is the tendency for people to avoid deep or complex thinking by using mental shortcuts called heuristics, settling for superficial information, or accepting initial impressions without thorough evaluation.

Cognitive offloading is the act of delegating mental tasks to AI tools, such as generating content, summarising information, or performing calculations, to reduce the cognitive load on the user's brain.

Data centres are a physical facility housing an organisation's critical IT infrastructure, such as servers, storage, and networking equipment, for storing, processing, and distributing data.

Deep Learning (DL) is a type of machine learning based on artificial neural networks in which multiple layers of processing are used to extract progressively higher-level features from data.

Deepfakes are videos, images, etc. in which a person's face, body, or voice has been digitally altered so that they appear to be someone else, typically used maliciously or to spread false information.

Distributional semantic models are computational frameworks that represent word meanings based on their usage patterns in large text corpora, following the distributional hypothesis that words with similar contexts have similar meanings.

Echo chambers are an environment in which a person encounters only beliefs or opinions that coincide with their own, so that their existing views are reinforced and alternative ideas are not considered.

Environmental equity is the state where all people and communities have fair and just access to environmental benefits, such as clean air and water, and are equally protected from environmental hazards and pollution, regardless of their social position.

GenAI agents are software systems that use AI to pursue goals and complete tasks on behalf of users. They show reasoning, planning, and memory and have a level of autonomy to make decisions, learn, and adapt.

Generative artificial intelligence (Generative AI, GenAI) is a subfield of artificial intelligence that uses generative models to produce text, images, videos, or other forms of data.

Generative models are advanced neural networks that mimic the structure of the human brain and apply complex machine learning algorithms to process training data and manufacture novel outputs.

Geographical load balancing distributes internet and application traffic across servers in different geographic locations to improve performance, increase reliability, and ensure high availability.

Graphic Processing Units (GPU) are a specialised electronic circuit or chip designed to rapidly perform mathematical calculations to accelerate graphics rendering and process large datasets, working in parallel to offload tasks from the main CPU.

Hallucinations are a phenomenon where AI generates information not based on its training data that can be misleading or incorrect.

High resource languages are languages with an abundance of digital and physical data, like texts, articles, and grammar databases, that are used to train AI models and build natural language technologies.

Human-in-the-loop (HITL) is a system where humans actively collaborate with AI/machine learning models, providing essential feedback, judgment, and oversight during training, testing, and operation to improve accuracy, handle complex edge cases, and ensure ethical, reliable outcomes, blending human nuance with machine efficiency for better decisions.

Inference phase is the process of using the already-trained model to generate human-like text outputs from new, unseen inputs (prompts).

Labels are a specific piece of metadata or a predefined category assigned to a piece of data, such as text or images, to serve as a correct or target output for a machine learning task.

Low resource languages are languages with a scarcity of digital text and audio data, leading to a lack of tools, research, and infrastructure for tasks like speech recognition, translation, and natural language processing (NLP).

Machine Learning (ML) is the use and development of computer systems that are able to learn and adapt without following explicit instructions, by using algorithms and statistical models to analyse and draw inferences from patterns in data.

Machine translation is the automatic, human-free process of converting text or speech from a source language into a target language using computational algorithms and models.

Model collapse is the process where a generative AI model's performance degrades over time as it's trained on data generated by previous versions of itself.

Morphologically complex languages are languages where words are built from multiple morphemes, the smallest units of meaning.

Multilingual large language models (MLLM) are LLMs capable of handling and producing content in various languages simultaneously

Neural word embedding models are models that convert words into dense numerical vectors (embeddings) by training a neural network on a large corpus of text, capturing semantic meaning and relationships between words.

N-grams are a contiguous sequence of n words that helps the model understand word order and context by analysing how words appear together in text.

Prompt engineering is the practice of carefully designing, testing, and refining text-based instructions, or "prompts," to guide generative AI models toward producing specific, desired outputs.

Reasoning models are large language models (LLM) that have been fine-tuned to break complex problems into smaller steps, often called "reasoning traces," prior to generating a final output.

Retrieval Augmented Generation (RAG) is an AI framework that enhances large language models (LLMs) by connecting them with external knowledge bases, such as databases or specific documents, before they generate a response.

Sentiment analysis is the process of computationally identifying and categorising opinions expressed in a piece of text, especially in order to determine whether the writer's attitude towards a particular topic, product, etc. is positive, negative, or neutral.

Spurious correlations are a statistically significant relationship between two variables that is misleading and not a genuine cause-and-effect connection, often resulting from coincidence or a shared, unseen "third variable" or confounding factor.

Standard language ideology is the widely held belief that one particular version of a language is inherently correct, superior, and should be the standard for all speakers, while other varieties are considered inferior or incorrect.

Text and data mining (TDM) is the process of deriving information from machine-read material. It works by copying large quantities of material, extracting the data, and recombining it to identify patterns.

Tokens are words, character sets, or combinations of words and punctuation that are generated by large language models (LLMs) when they decompose text.

Training phase is a multi-stage process that teaches the model to understand and generate human-like text by learning from massive datasets.

Types of languages is the grouping of languages into categories based on shared structural features, such as word order or morphological complexity, rather than by their historical or genetic relationships.

Vector space representation is a technique that converts words, sentences, or entire documents into high-dimensional numerical vectors, called embeddings.

Web crawling is the process of systematically browsing public internet sites and collecting information from each available web page using specific software.

WEIRD is an acronym used to describe the specific demographic: western, educated, industrialised, rich and democratic.

Word embeddings are numerical representations of words or pieces of text (tokens) as high-dimensional vectors, which capture their semantic meaning, context, and relationships with other words.

References

AI for Education. (2023). *AI's Impact on the Environment.* www.aiforeducation.io/ai-resources/ais-impact-on-the-environment

Allen, M. (2022, December 26). Professor warns about chatbot cheating: "Expect a flood". Axios, www.axios.com/2022/12/26/chatbot-cheating-university-warning-chatgpt

Amazon (2025). 2024 Sustainability Report. Amazon. https://sustainability.aboutamazon.com/reports?sort=latest

Appel, G., Neelbauer, J., & Schweidel, D. A. (2023). *Generative AI Has an Intellectual Property Problem* (Vol. 19, p. 58). Retrieved from https://hbr.org/2023/04/generative-ai-has-an-intellectual-property-problem

Atari, M., Xue, Mona, J., Park, P. S., Blasi, D. E., & Henrich, J. (2023). Which Humans? *PsyArXiv Preprint*, 1–23.

Barker, C. (2025, May 2). *Artificial intelligence and the environment: Putting the numbers into perspective.* JISC National Centre for AI. https://nationalcentreforai.jiscinvolve.org/wp/2025/05/02/artificial-intelligence-and-the-environment-putting-the-numbers-into-perspective/

Baskara, R., & Mukarto, M. (2023). Exploring the implications of ChatGPT for language learning in Higher Education. *IJELTAL (Indonesian Journal of English Language Teaching and Applied Linguistics)*, *7*(2), 343. https://doi.org/10.21093/ijeltal.v7i2.1387

Bender, E. M. (2011). On achieving and evaluating language-independence in NLP. *Linguistic Issues in Language Technology, 6*. https://doi.org/10.33011/lilt.v6i.1239

Bergstrom, C. T., & Brandon Ogbunu, C. (2023). *Opinion: ChatGPT isn't 'hallucinating.' It's bullshitting*. Undark. https://undark.org/2023/04/06/chatgpt-isnt-hallucinating-its-bullshitting/

Bhuiyan, J. (2025). *ChatGPT encouraged Adam Raine's suicidal thoughts. His family's lawyer says OpenAI knew it was broken.* The Guardian. https://www.theguardian.com/us-news/2025/aug/29/chatgpt-suicide-openai-sam-altman-adam-raine?fbclid=IwZXh0bgNhZW0CMTAAYnJpZBExMnF4TVdPejNSU3d6ZEJiSAEe8AksTR1DZxIQPSTaIAaOaxqstLU-XA8cuFcfvTT7Ix8x2lYqaKq-5gJZVVk_aem_m64fgnCMm2TVEl_gpSYJ_w

Black, N. B., & Brooks-Young, S. (2024). *Hands-On AI Projects for the Classroom: A guide on ethics and AI.* International Society for Technology in Education.

Black, N. B., & Brooks-Young, S. (2024). *Hands-On AI Projects for the Classroom: A guide for secondary teachers.* International Society for Technology in Education.

Blasi, D., Anastasopoulos, A., & Neubig, G. (2022). Systematic inequalities in language technology performance across the world's languages. In *Proceedings of the Annual Meeting of the Association for Computational Linguistics* (Vol. 1, pp. 5486–5505). Association for Computational Linguistics (ACL). https://doi.org/10.18653/v1/2022.acl-long.376

Bock, T (2025). *What is Spurious Correlation?* Displayr.com www.displayr.com/learn-what-is-spurious-correlation/#: ~ :text = A%20spurious%20correlation%20occurs%20when,to%20an%20unseen%2C%20third%20factor.

Bolukbasi, T., Chang, K. W., Zou, J., Saligrama, V., & Kalai, A. (2016). Man is to computer programmer as woman is to homemaker? Debiasing word embeddings. In: *Advances in Neural Information Processing Systems* (pp. 4356–4364). Neural information processing systems foundation.

Boonstra, L. (2025, April). *Prompt engineering* (Version 7.1) [PDF]. Innopreneur. www.innopreneur.io/wp-content/uploads/2025/04/22365_3_Prompt-Engineering_v7-1.pdf

Brookfield, S. D. (2012). *Teaching for Critical Thinking: Tools and techniques to help students question their assumptions*. Jossey Bass.

Brookfield, S. D., Rudolph, J., & Yeo, E. (2019). The power of critical thinking in learning and teaching. An interview with Professor Stephen D. Brookfield. *Journal of Applied Learning and Teaching*, 2(2), 76-90. https://doi.org/10.37074/jalt.2019.2.2.11

Brundtland, G.H. (1987). Our Common Future: Report of the World Commission on Environment and Development. Geneva, UN-Document A/42/427. www.un-documents.net/ocf-ov.htm

Burgess, M. (2023). *ChatGPT Has a Big Privacy Problem*, Wired. www.wired.com/story/italy-ban-chatgpt-privacy-gdpr/

Calvert, B. (2024). *AI already uses as much energy as a small country. It's only the beginning.* Vox. www.vox.com/climate/2024/3/28/24111721/climate-ai-tech-energy-demand-rising

Capgemini Research Institute (2024). *Organizations are increasingly aware of the environmental footprint of Gen AI, but most aren't able to address it alone*. Capgemini. www.capgemini.com/news/press-releases/organizations-are-increasingly-aware-of-the-environmental-footprint-of-gen-ai-but-most-arent-able-to-address-it-alone/

Carlini, N. (2020). *Privacy Considerations in Large Language Models*. Google Research Blog https://ai.googleblog.com/2020/12/privacy-considerations-in-large.html.

Carr, N., & Reichard, J. D. (2022). The shallows: What the internet is doing to our brains. *Journal of Interdisciplinary Studies*, *34*(1), 197–199. https://doi.org/10.5840/jis2022341/212

Cassidy, C. (2023). *Australian universities to return to 'pen and paper' exams after students caught using AI to write essays*. The Guardian, www.theguardian.com/australia-news/2023/jan/10/universities-to-return-to-pen-and-paper-exams-after-students-caught-using-ai-to-write-essays

Chang, K. K., Cramer, M., Soni, S., & Bamman, D. (2023). Speak, Memory: An archaeology of books known to ChatGPT/GPT-4. In: *EMNLP 2023 - 2023 Conference on Empirical Methods in Natural Language Processing, Proceedings* (pp. 7312–7327). Association for Computational Linguistics (ACL). https://doi.org/10.18653/v1/2023.emnlp-main.453

Claburn, T. (2025). *AI agents get office tasks wrong around 70% of the time, and a lot of them aren't AI at all*. The Register. www.theregister.com/2025/06/29/ai_agents_fail_a_lot/

Code.org, CoSN, Digital Promise, European EdTech Alliance, Larimore, J., & Policy Analysis for California Education (PACE) (2023). *AI Guidance for Schools Toolkit*. teachai.org. Retrieved from https://teachai.org/toolkit

Code.org, CoSN, Digital Promise, European EdTech Alliance, Larimore, J., & Policy Analysis for California Education (PACE) (2023). *AI guidance for schools toolkit*. TeachAI. https://teachai.org/toolkit

Conneau, A., Khandelwal, K., Goyal, N., Chaudhary, V., Wenzek, G., Guzmán, F., & Stoyanov, V. (2020). Unsupervised cross-lingual representation learning at scale. In: *Proceedings of the Annual Meeting of the Association for Computational Linguistics* (pp. 8440–8451). Association for Computational Linguistics (ACL). https://doi.org/10.18653/v1/2020.acl-main.747

Couldry, N., & Mejias, UA (2019). Data colonialism: rethinking big data's relation to the contemporary subject. *Television & New Media*, 20 (4), 336–349.

Crompton, H., Edmett, A., and Ichaporia, N. (2023). *Artificial intelligence and English language teaching: A systematic literature review*. British Council.

Crompton, H., Edmett, A., Ichaporia, N., & Burke, D. (2024). AI and English language teaching: Affordances and challenges. *British Journal of Educational Technology*. 55. 2503-2529. 10.1111/bjet.13460. https://bera-journals.onlinelibrary.wiley.com/doi/epdf/10.1111/bjet.13460

Crothers, E. N., Japkowicz, N., & Viktor, H. L. (2023). Machine-Generated Text: A Comprehensive Survey of Threat Models and Detection Methods. *IEEE Access*, *11*, 70977–71002. https://doi.org/10.1109/ACCESS.2023.3294090

Data Science (2019). *High/low resources language: what does it mean?* https://datascience.stackexchange.com/questions/62868/high-low-resources-language-what-does-it-mean#:~:text=High%20resource%20languages%20are%20languages,%2C%20named%20entities%2C%20etc

Dauner, M., & Socher, G. (2025) *Energy costs of communicating with AI*. Frontiers. www.frontiersin.org/journals/communication/articles/10.3389/fcomm.2025.1572947/full

Dave, A. (2025). The ethical implications of AI in education. *Research Review Journal of Social Science*. June 2025

de Vries, W., Wieling, M., & Nissim, M. (2022). Make the Best of Cross-lingual Transfer: Evidence from POS Tagging with over 100 Languages. In: *Proceedings of the Annual Meeting of the Association for Computational Linguistics* (Vol. 1, pp. 7676–7685). Association for Computational Linguistics (ACL). https://doi.org/10.18653/v1/2022.acl-long.529

Dhanani, R. (2024). *Environmental Impact of Generative AI: 20 stats and facts*. Akepa. https://thesustainableagency.com/blog/environmental-impact-of-generative-ai/

Digital Promise (2024). *AI literacy*. https://digitalpromise.org/initiative/artificial-intelligence-in-education/ai-literacy/

Dinçer, S. (2024). The use and ethical implications of artificial intelligence in scientific research and academic writing. *Educational Research & Implementation*, 1(2), 139-144. https://doi.org/10.14527/edure.2024.10

Dixon, L., Li, J., Sorensen, J., Thain, N., & Vasserman, L. (2018). Measuring and Mitigating Unintended Bias in Text Classification. In: *AIES 2018 - Proceedings of the 2018 AAAI/ACM Conference on AI, Ethics, and Society* (pp. 67–73). Association for Computing Machinery, Inc. https://doi.org/10.1145/3278721.3278729

Donatus, U., Obinna, V., Samuel, U., Odera, C., & Nkechi, F. (2024). The ethical implications of artificial intelligence in education. *AMAMIHE: Journal of Applied Philosophy*, 22(2).

Eadicicco, L. (2025). After a wave of lawsuits, Character.AI will no longer let teens chat with its chatbots. CNN. https://edition.cnn.com/2025/10/29/tech/character-ai-teens-under-18-app-changes

Edgar, M. (2025). *Generative AI vs Traditional search: Technical differences*. www.matthewedgar.net/generative-ai-vs-traditional-search-technical-differences/

Educational Technology and Mobile Learning. (2010). *SAMR model: Substitution, augmentation, modification, and redefinition.* https://educationaltechnology.net/samr-model-substitution-augmentation-modification-and-redefinition/

Efe, A. (2022). The Impact of Artificial Intelligence on Social Problems and Solutions: An analysis on the context of digital divide and exploitation. *Yeni Medya Dergisi.* https://doi.org/10.55609/yenimedya.1146586

El Mestari, S. Z., Lenzini, G., & Demirci, H. (2024). Preserving data privacy in machine learning systems. *Computers and Security,* 137. https://doi.org/10.1016/j.cose.2023.103605

Esther, T., Ahmed, A., Edward, T., Kolade, M., & Mayowa, A. (2023). A review of the ethics of artificial intelligence and its applications in the United States. *International Journal on Cybernetics & Informatics,* 12(6), 122–137. https://doi.org/10.5121/ijci.2023.120610

EU (2024). *The EU Artificial Intelligence Act.* https://artificialintelligenceact.eu/

European Commission (2022). *Ethical guidelines on the use of artificial intelligence.*

European Commission and the Organization for Economic Cooperation and Development (OECD) (2025). Empowering Learners for the Age of AI: An AI Literacy Framework for Primary and Secondary Education.

Everypixel Journal (2025) *How to Spot AI Generated Images.* https://journal.everypixel.com/how-to-spot-ai-generated-images

Fleisig, E., Smith, G., Bossi, M., Rustagi, I., Yin, X., & Klein, D. (2024). Linguistic Bias in ChatGPT: Language models reinforce dialect discrimination. In: *EMNLP 2024 - 2024 Conference on Empirical Methods in Natural Language Processing, Proceedings of the Conference* (pp. 13541–13564). Association for Computational Linguistics (ACL). https://doi.org/10.18653/v1/2024.emnlp-main.750

Flodén, J. (2025). Grading exams using large language models: A comparison between human and AI grading of exams in higher education using ChatGPT. *British Educational Research Journal,* 51(1), 201–224. https://doi.org/10.1002/berj.4069

Franklin, N. (2024). *Generative AI will lead to a threefold increase in greenhouse gases from data centres.* Insight. https://workplaceinsight.net/generative-ai-will-lead-to-a-threefold-increase-in-greenhouse-gases-from-data-centres/

Fu, Y., & Weng, Z. (2024). Navigating the Ethical Terrain of AI in Education: A systematic review on framing responsible human-centered AI practices. *Computers and Education: Artificial Intelligence.* 7. 100306. 10.1016/j.caeai.2024.100306.

Garimella, A., Banea, C., Hovy, D., & Mihalcea, R. (2020). Women's syntactic resilience and men's grammatical luck: Gender-bias in part-of-speech tagging and dependency parsing. In *ACL 2019 - 57th Annual Meeting of the Association for Computational Linguistics, Proceedings of the Conference* (pp. 3493–3498). Association for Computational Linguistics (ACL). https://doi.org/10.18653/v1/p19-1339

Gerlich, M. (2025). AI Tools in Society: Impacts on Cognitive Offloading and the Future of Critical Thinking. *Societies,* 15(1). https://doi.org/10.3390/soc15010006

Gibbons, E. D. (2021). Toward a More Equal World: The Human Rights Approach to Extending the Benefits of Artificial Intelligence. *IEEE Technology and Society Magazine,* 40(1), 25–30. https://doi.org/10.1109/MTS.2021.3056295

Gupta, M., Akiri, C., Aryal, K., Parker, E., & Praharaj, L. (2023). From ChatGPT to ThreatGPT: Impact of Generative AI in Cybersecurity and Privacy. *IEEE Access.* Institute of Electrical and Electronics Engineers Inc. https://doi.org/10.1109/ACCESS.2023.3300381

Gwagwa, A., Kraemer-Mbula, E., Rizk, N., Rutenberg, I., & De Beer, J. (2020). Artificial intelligence (AI) deployments in Africa: Benefits, challenges and policy dimensions. *The African Journal of Information and Communication* (26). https://doi.org/10.23962/10539/30361

Havaldar, S., Rai, S., Singhal, B., Liu, L., Guntuku, S. C., & Ungar, L. (2023). Multilingual Language Models are not Multicultural: A case study in emotion. In: *Proceedings of the Annual Meeting of the Association for Computational Linguistics* (pp. 202–214). Association for Computational Linguistics (ACL). https://doi.org/10.18653/v1/2023.wassa-1.19

Heikkilä, M. (2022). How to spot AI-generated text | MIT Technology Review. www.technologyreview.com/2022/12/19/1065596/how-to-spot-ai-generated-text/

Henrich, J., Heine, S. J., & Norenzayan, A. (2010). The weirdest people in the world? *Behavioral and Brain Sciences*. Cambridge University Press. https://doi.org/10.1017/S0140525X0999152X

Hooks, B. (2010). *Teaching Critical Thinking.* Routledge.

Horwitz, J. (2025) Meta's AI rules have let bots hold 'sensual' chats with kids, offer false medical info. Reuters. www.reuters.com/investigates/special-report/meta-ai-chatbot-guidelines/

Hosseini, M., Gao, P., & Vivas-Valencia, C. (2025). A social-environmental impact perspective of generative artificial intelligence. *Environmental Science and Ecotechnology*. Elsevier B.V. https://doi.org/10.1016/j.ese.2024.100520

Hovy, D., & Prabhumoye, S. (2021). Five sources of bias in natural language processing. *Language and Linguistics Compass*, 15(8). https://doi.org/10.1111/lnc3.12432

Hovy, D., Bianchi, F., & Fornaciari, T. (2020). 'You sound just like your father': Commercial machine translation systems include stylistic biases. In: *Proceedings of the Annual Meeting of the Association for Computational Linguistics* (pp. 1686–1690). Association for Computational Linguistics (ACL). https://doi.org/10.18653/v1/2020.acl-main.154

International Energy Agency (2025). *Energy and AI.* https://iea.blob.core.windows.net/assets/601eaec9-ba91-4623-819b-4ded331ec9e8/EnergyandAI.pdf

Ism, I. (2025). *Does ChatGPT Save Your Data? 2025 Privacy Guide.* Chatbase

Jawahar, G., Abdul-Mageed, M., & Lakshmanan, L. V. S. (2020). Automatic detection of machine generated text: A critical survey. In: *COLING 2020 - 28th International Conference on Computational Linguistics, Proceedings of the Conference* (pp. 2296–2309). Association for Computational Linguistics (ACL). https://doi.org/10.18653/v1/2020.coling-main.208

Jiang, S., McClure, J., Tatar, C., Bickel, F., Rosé, C. P., & Chao, J. (2024). Towards inclusivity in AI: A comparative study of cognitive engagement between marginalized female students and peers. *British Journal of Educational Technology*, 55, 2557–2573. https://doi.org/10.1111/bjet.13467

Jones, B. (2024). *What Is AI Literacy?* Data literacy. https://dataliteracy.com/what-is-ai-literacy/

Joseph, K., Friedland, L., Hobbs, W., Lazer, D., & Tsur, O. (2017). Constance: Modeling annotation contexts to improve stance classification. In *EMNLP 2017 - Conference on Empirical Methods in Natural Language Processing, Proceedings* (pp. 1115–1124). Association for Computational Linguistics (ACL). https://doi.org/10.18653/v1/d17-1116

Joshi, P., Santy, S., Budhiraja, A., Bali, K., & Choudhury, M. (2020). The state and fate of linguistic diversity and inclusion in the NLP world. In: *Proceedings of the Annual Meeting of the Association for Computational Linguistics* (pp. 6282–6293). Association for Computational Linguistics (ACL). https://doi.org/10.18653/v1/2020.acl-main.560

Kemene, E., Valkhof, B., and Tladi, T. (2024, July 22). *AI and Energy: Will AI help reduce emissions or increase demand? Here's what to know.* World Economic Forum. www.weforum.org/stories/2024/07/generative-ai-energy-emissions/

Kerner, S. M. (2025). *ChatGPT Search vs. Google: How do they differ?* TechTarget. www.techtarget.com/whatis/feature/ChatGPT-search-vs-Google-How-do-they-differ

Kerr, D. (2024). *AI brings soaring emissions for Google and Microsoft, a major contributor to climate change.* NPR. www.npr.org/2024/07/12/g-s1-9545/ai-brings-soaring-emissions-for-google-and-microsoft-a-major-contributor-to-climate-change

Kiritchenko, S., & Mohammad, S. M. (2018). Examining gender and race bias in two hundred sentiment analysis systems. In: *NAACL HLT 2018 - Lexical and Computational Semantics, SEM 2018, Proceedings of the 7th Conference* (pp. 43–53). Association for Computational Linguistics (ACL). https://doi.org/10.18653/v1/s18-2005

Kofinas, A. K., Tsay, C. H. H., & Pike, D. (2025). The impact of generative AI on academic integrity of authentic assessments within a higher education context. *British Journal of Educational Technology*. https://doi.org/10.1111/bjet.13585

Koidan, K. (2023) When AI Image Generators Fail. Kiki and Mozart. https://kikiandmozart.beehiiv.com/p/when-ai-image-generators-fail

Kosmyna, N., Hauptmann, E., Yuan, Y. T., Situ, J., Liao, X.-H., Beresnitzky, A. V., Braunstein, I., & Maes, P. (2025). *Your Brain on ChatGPT: Accumulation of cognitive debt when using an AI assistant for essay writing task*. http://arxiv.org/abs/2506.08872

Krishna, K., Song, Y., Karpinska, M., Wieting, J. & Iyyer, M. (2023). *Paraphrasing evades detectors of ai-generated text, but retrieval is an effective defense*. arXiv preprint arXiv:2303.13408

Lavi, H. (2023). *Measuring greenhouse gas emissions in data centres: the environmental impact of cloud computing*. Climatiq. www.climatiq.io/blog/measure-greenhouse-gas-emissions-carbon-data-centres-cloud-computing

Lee, S. (2023). AI Toolkit for Educators. *EIT InnoEnergy Master School Teachers Conference 2023*. www.paradoxlearning.com

Lefkeli, D., Karataş, M., & Gürhan-Canli, Z. (2024). Sharing information with AI (versus a human) impairs brand trust: The role of audience size inferences and sense of exploitation. *International Journal of Research in Marketing*, 41(1), 138–155. https://doi.org/10.1016/j.ijresmar.2023.08.011

Liang, W., Yuksekgonul, M., Mao, Y., Wu, E., & Zou, J. (2023). GPT detectors are biased against non-native English writers. *Patterns*. Cell Press. https://doi.org/10.1016/j.patter.2023.100779

Ligozat, A., & De Vries, A. (2024). *Generative AI: Energy consumption soars*. Polytechnique Insights. https://www.polytechnique-insights.com/en/columns/energy/generative-ai-energy-consumption-soars/

Lim, V. F. (2022). *ChatGPT raises uncomfortable questions about teaching and classroom learning*. The Straits Times. www.straitstimes.com/opinion/need-to-review-literacy-assessment-in-the-age-of-chatgpt

Lippi-Green, R. (1994). Accent, standard language ideology, and discriminatory pretext in the courts. *Language in Society*, 23(2), 163–198. https://doi.org/10.1017/S0047404500017826

Lo, P. (2025) *What's the real cognitive cost of AI convenience? MIT's Brain Research Has Answers*. https://www.linkedin.com/pulse/whats-real-cognitive-cost-ai-convenience-mits-brain-research-peter-lo-lbqic/

Loga, R. (2025) *AI's Cognitive Implications: The decline of our thinking skills?* IE Universitywww.ie.edu/center-for-health-and-well-being/blog/ais-cognitive-implications-the-decline-of-our-thinking-skills/

Luccioni, S., Jernite, Y., & Strubell, E. (2024). Power Hungry Processing: Watts driving the cost of AI deployment? In: *2024 ACM Conference on Fairness, Accountability, and Transparency, FAccT 2024* (pp. 85–99). Association for Computing Machinery, Inc. https://doi.org/10.1145/3630106.3658542

Ma, W., Adesope, O. O., Nesbit, J. C., & Liu, Q. (2014). Intelligent tutoring systems and learning outcomes: A meta-analysis. *Journal of Educational Psychology*, 106(4), 901–918. https://doi.org/10.1037/a0037123

Manzini, T., Lim, Y. C., Tsvetkov, Y., & Black, A. W. (2019). Black is to criminal as Caucasian is to police: Detecting and removing multiclass bias in word embeddings. In: *NAACL HLT*

2019 - 2019 Conference of the North American Chapter of the Association for Computational Linguistics: Human Language Technologies - Proceedings of the Conference (Vol. 1, pp. 615–621). Association for Computational Linguistics (ACL). https://doi.org/10.18653/v1/n19-1062

Marcus, G. (2024). *One GenAI image; Ten Errors.* Marcus on AI. https://garymarcus.substack.com/p/one-genai-image-ten-errors

Marin, L. M., & Halpern, D. F. (2011). Pedagogy for developing critical thinking in adolescents: Explicit instruction produces greatest gains. *Thinking Skills and Creativity*, 6(1), 1–13. https://doi.org/10.1016/j.tsc.2010.08.002

Masley, A. (2025). *Using ChatGPT is not bad for the environment.* The Weird Turn Pro. https://andymasley.substack.com/p/individual-ai-use-is-not-bad-for

McLean, S. (2023). *The Environmental Impact of ChatGPT: A call for sustainable practices in AI development.* Earth.org. https://earth.org/environmental-impact-chatgpt/

McMurtrie, B. (2022). AI and the future of undergraduate writing. *The Chronicle of Higher Education.* www.chronicle.com/article/ai-and-the-future-of-undergraduate-writing

Miao, F., & Holmes, W. (2023). *Guidance for generative AI in education and research.* UNESCO. https://doi.org/10.54675/EWZM9535.

Mihai Leta, F., & Vancea, D. P. C. (2023). Ethics in Education: Exploring the ethical implications of artificial intelligence implementation. *Ovidius University Annals. Economic Sciences Series*, 23(1), 413–421. https://doi.org/10.61801/ouaess.2023.1.54

Mills, A. (2023a). *How do we prevent learning loss due to AI text generators?.* Blog post.

Mills, A. (2023b). *AI text generators: Sources to stimulate discussion among teachers.*

MLML. (2023). *AI Code of Conduct.* https://aicodeofconduct.mlml.io/

Model Evaluation & Threat Research (2025). *Measuring the Impact of Early-2025 AI on Experienced Open-Source Developer Productivity.* https://metr.org/blog/2025-07-10-early-2025-ai-experienced-os-dev-study/#:%7E:text=Core%20Result,evidence%20for%20in%20Table%202.

Myers-West, S., Whittaker, M., & Crawford, K. (2019). *Discriminating Systems.* AI Now Institute (p. 33). https://ainowinstitute.org/discriminatingsystems.pdf

Net Zero Business. (2024). *AI's Carbon Footprint: How does the popularity of artificial intelligence affect the climate?* Plan Be Eco. https://planbe.eco/en/blog/ais-carbon-footprint-how-does-the-popularity-of-artificial-intelligence-affect-the-climate/

Newman, M., & Cantrill, A. (2023). *The Future of AI Relies on a High School Teacher's Free Database.* Bloomberg. www.bloomberg.com/news/features/2023-04-24/a-high-school-teacher-s-free-image-database-powers-ai-unicorns#xj4y7vzkg.

Nezhad, S. B., & Agrawal, A. (2024). What Drives Performance in Multilingual Language Models? In *VarDial 2024 - 11th Workshop on NLP for Similar Languages, Varieties and Dialects, Proceedings of the Workshop* (pp. 16–27). Association for Computational Linguistics (ACL). https://doi.org/10.18653/v1/2024.vardial-1.2

Nightfall AI (2025) *Hallucination, Inconsistency, and Bias.* www.nightfall.ai/ai-security-101/hallucination-inconsistency-and-bias

Nowik, C. (2022). The robots are coming! The robots are coming! Nah, the robots are here. Substack. https://christinenowik.substack.com/p/the-robots-are-coming-the-robots#details

Nuñez, M. (2025a). *Anthropic Takes on OpenAI and Google with New Claude AI Features Designed for Students and Developers.* Venture Beat. https://venturebeat.com/ai/anthropic-takes-on-openai-and-google-with-new-claude-ai-features-designed-for-students-and-developers?ref=aisecret.us

Nuñez, M. (2025b) *That 'Cheap' Open-source AI Model is Actually Burning Through Your Compute Budget.* Venture Beat. https://venturebeat.com/ai/that-cheap-open-source-ai-model-is-actually-burning-through-your-compute-budget/?ref = aisecret.us

Nyachiro (2024). *Ethical Considerations in the Development and Deployment of AI-Powered Systems. International Journal of Computer Applications Technology and Research Volume* 13(08). DOI:10.7753/IJCATR1308.1001

O'Brien, I. (2024. *Data center emissions probably 662% higher than big tech claims. Can it keep up the ruse?* The Guardian. https://www.theguardian.com/technology/2024/sep/15/data-center-gas-emissions-tech

O'Brien, M., & Fingerhut, H. (2023). *Artificial intelligence technology behind ChatGPT was built in Iowa — with a lot of water.* AP News, 4–9. https://apnews.com/article/chatgpt-gpt4-iowa-ai-water-consumption-microsoft-f551fde98083d17a7e8d904f8be822c4

OpenAI (2025). *OpenAI o3 and o4-mini System Card.* https://cdn.openai.com/pdf/2221c875-02dc-4789-800b-e7758f3722c1/o3-and-o4-mini-system-card.pdf

OpenAI, Achiam, J., Adler, S., Agarwal, S., Ahmad, L., Akkaya, I., & Zoph, B. (2024). *GPT-4 Technical Report.* http://arxiv.org/abs/2303.08774

OpenAI. (2021). *Lessons learned on language model safety and misuse.* https://openai.com/index/language-model-safety-and-misuse/

OpenAI. (2021). *OpenAI Data Usage Policy.* https://openai.com/security-and-privacy/

OpenAI. (2024) *GPT-4 Technical Report.*

OpenAI. (2025) *Trust portal.* https://trust.openai.com/

Paradox Learning (2024). *AI Literacy Competency Framework for Educators.*

Pearson, J. (2024) *Why "Hallucination"? Examining the history, and stakes, of how we label AI's undesirable output.* Los Angeles Review of Books https://lareviewofbooks.org/article/why-hallucination-examining-the-history-and-stakes-of-how-we-label-ais-undesirable-output/

Pegrum, M. (2025) From revolution to evolution: What generative AI really means for language learning. *Language Teaching.* 1-17. doi:10.1017/S0261444825000151

Périssère, C. (2025). *The Environmental Impact of AI: how can we balance innovation and sustainability?* Atlantic Vantage Point. https://avpcap.com/the-environmental-impact-of-ai-how-can-we-balance-innovation-and-sustainability/

Perkins, M., Furze, L., Roe, J., & MacVaugh, J. (2024). The Artificial Intelligence Assessment Scale (AIAS): A framework for ethical integration of Generative AI in educational assessment. *Journal of University Teaching & Learning Practice*, 21(06). https://doi.org/10.53761/q3azde36

Philippy, F., Guo, S., & Haddadan, S. (2023). Towards a Common Understanding of Contributing Factors for Cross-Lingual Transfer in Multilingual Language Models: A Review. In: *Proceedings of the Annual Meeting of the Association for Computational Linguistics* (Vol. 1, pp. 5877–5891). Association for Computational Linguistics (ACL). https://doi.org/10.18653/v1/2023.acl-long.323

Pires, T., Schlinger, E., & Garrette, D. (2020). How multilingual is multilingual BERT? In *ACL 2019 - 57th Annual Meeting of the Association for Computational Linguistics, Proceedings of the Conference* (pp. 4996–5001). Association for Computational Linguistics (ACL). https://doi.org/10.18653/v1/p19-1493

Plank, B., Hovy, D., & Søgaard, A. (2014). Linguistically debatable or just plain wrong? In: *52nd Annual Meeting of the Association for Computational Linguistics, ACL 2014 - Proceedings of the Conference* (Vol. 2, pp. 507–511). Association for Computational Linguistics (ACL). https://doi.org/10.3115/v1/p14-2083

Qin, L., Chen, Q., Zhou, Y., Chen, Z., Li, Y., Liao, L., & Yu, P. S. (2025). A survey of multilingual large language models. *Patterns*. Cell Press. https://doi.org/10.1016/j.patter.2024.101118

Ramachandran, K., Stewart, D., Hardin, K., & Crossan, G. (2024). *As generative AI asks for more power, data centers seek more reliable, cleaner energy solutions.* Deloitte Center for Technology Media and Telecommunications. www2.deloitte.com/us/en/insights/industry/technology/technology-media-and-telecom-predictions/2025/genai-power-consumption-creates-need-for-more-sustainable-data-centers.html

Ramnani, S. (2024). Exploring ethical considerations of artificial intelligence in educational settings: An examination of bias, privacy, and accountability. *International Journal Of Novel Research And Development*, 9(2), b173-b191. http://doi.one/10.1729/Journal.37869

Ranathunga, S., & de Silva, N. (2024). Some Languages are More Equal than Others: Probing deeper into the linguistic disparity in the NLP world (pp. 823–848). Association for Computational Linguistics (ACL). https://doi.org/10.18653/v1/2022.aacl-main.62

Rejeb, A., Rejeb, K., Appolloni, A., Treiblmaier, H., & Iranmanesh, M. (2024). Exploring the impact of ChatGPT on education: A web mining and machine learning approach. *International Journal of Management Education*, 22(1). https://doi.org/10.1016/j.ijme.2024.100932

Ren, S. (2023, November 30). *How Much Water Does AI Consume? The public deserves to know*. OECD. AI Policy Observatory. https://oecd.ai/en/wonk/how-much-water-does-ai-consume

Ren, S. (2024, October 28). *Generative AI expansion could create up to five million tonnes of e-waste*. Science Media Centre Spain. https://sciencemediacentre.es/en/generative-ai-expansion-could-create-five-million-tonnes-e-waste

Ren, S., & Wierman, A. (2024). The Uneven Distribution of AI's Environmental Impacts. *Harvard Business Review*, 1–8. Retrieved from https://hbr.org/2024/07/the-uneven-distribution-of-ais-environmental-impacts

Risko. E.F., & Gilbert, S.J. (2016). Cognitive Offloading. *Trends Cogn Sci*. 2016 Sep; 20(9):676-688. doi: 10.1016/j.tics.2016.07.002. Epub 2016 Aug 16. PMID: 27542527.

Rogoway, M. (2023). *Google's Water Use is Soaring in The Dalles, Records Show, with Two More Data Centers to Come*. The Oregonian/Oregon Live. https://www.oregonlive.com/silicon-forest/2022/12/googles-water-use-is-soaring-in-the-dalles-records-show-with-two-more-data-centers-to-come.html

Rosati, E. (2025). Infringing AI: Liability for AI-generated outputs under international, EU, and UK copyright law (August 31, 2024). 16 (2) *European Journal of Risk Regulation 603.*

Rosenblatt, K. (2023). ChatGPT Banned From New York City Public Schools' Devices and Networks. NBC News.

Rudolph, J., & Tan, S. (2022). The war in Ukraine as an opportunity to teach critical thinking. *Journal of Applied Learning and Teaching*, 5(1), 165-173. https://doi.org/10.37074/jalt.2022.5.1.24

Rudolph, J., & Tan, S. (2023) ChatGPT: Bullshit spewer or the end of traditional assessments in higher education? *Journal of Applied Learning and Teaching* 6(1): 342–363.

Rungta, M., Singh, J., Mohammad, S. M., & Yang, D. (2022). Geographic Citation Gaps in NLP Research. In: *Proceedings of the 2022 Conference on Empirical Methods in Natural Language Processing, EMNLP 2022* (pp. 1371–1383). Association for Computational Linguistics (ACL). https://doi.org/10.18653/v1/2022.emnlp-main.89

Sadasivan, V. S., Kumar, A., Balasubramanian, S., Wang, W. & Feizi, S. (2023). *Can ai-generated text be reliably detected?* arXiv preprint arXiv:2303.11156

Saenko, K., & The Conversation USA. (2023). *Computer Scientist Breaks Down Generative AI's Hefty Carbon Footprint*. Scientific American. www.scientificamerican.com/article/a-computer-scientist-breaks-down-generative-ais-hefty-carbon-footprint/

Sain, Z., Aziz, A., & Lawal, U.S. (2024). Ethics of AI integration in higher education: Exploring moral dimensions. *Journal of Asian Islamic Educational Management (JAIEM)*. 2. 1-10. 10.53889/jaiem.v2i1.431.

Samuelson, P. (2023). Generative AI meets copyright. *Science*, 381(6654), 158–161. https://doi.org/10.1126/science.adi0656

Sap, M., Card, D., Gabriel, S., Choi, Y., & Smith, N. A. (2020). The risk of racial bias in hate speech detection. In *ACL 2019 - 57th Annual Meeting of the Association for Computational Linguistics, Proceedings of the Conference* (pp.1668–1678). Association for Computational Linguistics (ACL). https://doi.org/10.18653/v1/p19-1163

Sap, M., Gabriel, S., Qin, L., Jurafsky, D., Smith, N. A., & Choi, Y. (2020). Social Bias Frames. *Proceedings of the 58th Annual Meeting of the Association for Computational Linguistics*, 5477–5490.

Sebastian, G. (2023). Privacy and data protection in ChatGPT and other AI chatbots. *International Journal of Security and Privacy in Pervasive Computing*, 15(1), 1–14. https://doi.org/10.4018/ijsppc.325475

Shah, D., Schwartz, H. A., & Hovy, D. (2020). Predictive biases in natural language processing models: A conceptual framework and overview. In: *Proceedings of the Annual Meeting of the Association for Computational Linguistics* (pp. 5248–5264). Association for Computational Linguistics (ACL). https://doi.org/10.18653/v1/2020.acl-main.468

Shepherd (2025). *Navigating the Terms and Conditions of Generative AI*. Jisc. https://nationalcentreforai.jiscinvolve.org/wp/2025/08/28/navigating-the-terms-and-conditions-of-generative-ai/

Shumba, N., Tshekiso, O., Li, P., Fanti, G., & Ren, S. (2025). A water efficiency dataset for African data centers. In: *Proceedings of the 2025 ACM SIGCAS/SIGCHI Conference on Computing and Sustainable Societies (COMPASS '25)*. Association for Computing Machinery, New York, NY, USA, 453–460. https://doi.org/10.1145/3715335.3735483

Silva, A., & Amarathunga, C. (2019). On learning word embeddings from linguistically augmented text corpora. In: *IWCS 2019 - Proceedings of the 13th International Conference on Computational Semantics - Short Papers* (pp. 52–58). Association for Computational Linguistics (ACL). https://doi.org/10.18653/v1/w19-0508

Smith, G., Fleisig, E., Bossi, M., Rustagi, I., & Yin, X. (2024). Standard Language Ideology in AI-Generated Language. http://arxiv.org/abs/2406.08726

Sparrow, B., Liu, J., & Wegner, D. M. (2011). Google effects on memory: Cognitive consequences of having information at our fingertips. *Science*, 333(6043), 776–778. https://doi.org/10.1126/science.1207745

Statista (2025). *Languages Most Frequently Used for Web Content as of February 2025, By Share of Websites*. www.statista.com/statistics/262946/most-common-languages-on-the-internet/

Stevens, D. S. (2019). *Write more, publish more, stress less!* Stylus.

Stodd, J., Schatz, S., & Stead, G. (2023). *Engines of Engagement: A curious book about generative AI*. Bournemouth, UK: Sea Salt Publishing. https://seasaltlearning.com/engines-of-engagement-generative-ai-book/

Swinton, S. S. (1981). Predictive bias in graduate admissions tests. *ETS Research Report Series*, 1981(1). https://doi.org/10.1002/j.2333-8504.1981.tb01259.x

Ta, R., & Turner Lee, N. (2023). *How Language Gaps Constrain Generative AI Development*. Brookings.

The Green Grid (2011) *Water Usage Effectiveness (WUE): A green grid data center sustainability metric*.

The Human Line Project www.thehumanlineproject.org/about-us?utm_source = substack&utm_medium = email

Topics European Parliament (2023) *EU AI Act: First regulation on artificial intelligence.* www.europarl.europa.eu/topics/en/article/20230601STO93804/eu-ai-act-first-regulation-on-artificial-intelligence

Tour, E., Pegrum, M., & Macdonald, S. (2025) Engaging English language learners in AI literacy practices: A conceptual framework and practical strategies for educators. *English Australia Journal*, 41(1) (pp. 27-46). https://files.eric.ed.gov/fulltext/EJ1474972.pdf

Touvron, H., Lavril, T., Izacard, G., Martinet, X., Lachaux, M.-A., Lacroix, T., & Lample, G. (2023). LLaMA: Open and Efficient Foundation Language Models. http://arxiv.org/abs/2302.13971

U.S. Congressional Research Service. (2023). *Generative Artificial Intelligence and Data Privacy: A primer.* www.congress.gov/crs-product/R47569

U.S. Congressional Research Service. (2023). *Generative Artificial Intelligence and Copyright Law.* www.congress.gov/crs-product/LSB10922

U.S. Copyright Office (2023) *Copyright Registration Guidance: Works containing material generated by artificial intelligence.* www.govinfo.gov/content/pkg/FR-2023-03-16/pdf/2023-05321.pdf

U.S. Copyright Office (2024). *Copyright and Artificial Intelligence. Part 1: Digital replicas.* www.copyright.gov/ai/Copyright-and-Artificial-Intelligence-Part-1-Digital-Replicas-Report.pdf

U.S. Copyright Office (2025). *Copyright and Artificial Intelligence. Part 2: Copyrightability.* www.copyright.gov/ai/Copyright-and-Artificial-Intelligence-Part-2-Copyrightability-Report.pdf

U.S. Copyright Office (2025). *Copyright and Artificial Intelligence. Part 3: Generative AI Training.* www.copyright.gov/ai/Copyright-and-Artificial-Intelligence-Part-3-Generative-AI-Training-Report-Pre-Publication-Version.pdf

United Nations (2024). *Mind the AI Divide: Shaping a global perspective on the future of work.*

United Nations Environment Programme (2024). *AI Has an Environmental Problem: Here's what the world can do about that.* www.unep.org/news-and-stories/story/ai-has-environmental-problem-heres-what-world-can-do-about

Walsh, D. (2023). *The Legal Issues Presented by Generative AI.* MIT Sloan School of Management. https://mitsloan.mit.edu/ideas-made-to-matter/legal-issues-presented-generative-ai

Wang, P., Zhang, LY., Tzachor, A. *et al.* (2024). E-waste challenges of generative artificial intelligence. *Nat Comput Sci* 4, 818–823. https://doi.org/10.1038/s43588-024-00712-6

Weng, X., & Chiu, T. K. F. (2023). Instructional design and learning outcomes of intelligent computer assisted language learning: Systematic review in the field. *Computers and Education: Artificial Intelligence*. Elsevier B.V. https://doi.org/10.1016/j.caeai.2022.100117

WIPO (1996). *WIPO Copyright Treaty, Agreed Statements concerning Article 1(4).* www.wipo.int/wipolex/en/text/295456

WIPO (1996). *WIPO Performances and Phonograms Treaty, Agreed statement concerning Articles 7, 11 and 16.* www.wipo.int/wipolex/en/text/295578

Xu, Y., Hu, L., Zhao, J., Qiu, Z., Xu, K., Ye, Y., & Gu, H. (2025). A survey on multilingual large language models: corpora, alignment, and bias. *Frontiers of Computer Science*. Higher Education Press Limited Company. https://doi.org/10.1007/s11704-024-40579-4

Xue, L., Constant, N., Roberts, A., Kale, M., Al-Rfou, R., Siddhant, A., ... Raffel, C. (2021). mT5: A massively multilingual pre-trained text-to-text transformer. In: *NAACL-HLT 2021 - 2021 Conference of the North American Chapter of the Association for Computational Linguistics: Human Language Technologies, Proceedings of the Conference* (pp. 483–498). Association for Computational Linguistics (ACL). https://doi.org/10.18653/v1/2021.naacl-main.41

Yan, L., Pammer-Schindler, V., Mills, C., Nguyen, A. & Gašević, D. (2025). Beyond efficiency: Empirical insights on generative AI's impact on cognition, metacognition and epistemic agency in learning. *Br J Educ Technol,* 56 1675-1685. https://doi.org/10.1111/bjet.70000

Yatskar, M., Zettlemoyer, L., & Farhadi, A. (2016). Situation recognition: Visual semantic role labeling for image understanding. In: *Proceedings of the IEEE Computer Society Conference on Computer Vision and Pattern Recognition* (Vol. 2016-December, pp. 5534–5542). IEEE Computer Society. https://doi.org/10.1109/CVPR.2016.597

Yigitcanlar, T., Mehmood, R., & Corchado, J.M. (2021). Green artificial intelligence: towards an efficient, sustainable and equitable technology for smart cities and futures. *Sustainability* (Switzerland), 13(16). https://doi.org/10.3390/su13168952

Zhang, X., Li, S., Hauer, B., Shi, N., & Kondrak, G. (2023). Don't trust ChatGPT when your question is not in English: A study of multilingual abilities and types of LLMs. In: *EMNLP 2023 - 2023 Conference on Empirical Methods in Natural Language Processing, Proceedings* (pp. 7915–7927). Association for Computational Linguistics (ACL). https://doi.org/10.18653/v1/2023.emnlp-main.491

Zhao, J., Wang, T., Yatskar, M., Ordonez, V., & Chang, K. W. (2017). Men also like shopping: Reducing gender bias amplification using corpus-level constraints. In: *EMNLP 2017 - Conference on Empirical Methods in Natural Language Processing, Proceedings* (pp. 2979–2989). Association for Computational Linguistics (ACL). https://doi.org/10.18653/v1/d17-1323